■

The Victim of Rape:
Institutional Reactions

The Victim of Rape

■

Institutional Reactions

LYNDA LYTLE HOLMSTROM, Ph. D.
ANN WOLBERT BURGESS, R.N., D.N.Sc.

A WILEY-INTERSCIENCE PUBLICATION

JOHN WILEY & SONS,   New York   Chichester   Brisbane   Toronto

Library of Congress Cataloging in Publication Data:

Holmstrom, Lynda Lytle.
    The victim of rape.

    "A Wiley-Interscience publication."
    Includes bibliographical references and index.
    1. Rape—Massachusetts—Boston—Case studies.
2. Rape victim services—Massachusetts—Boston.
I. Burgess, Ann Wolbert, joint author. II. Title.

HV6568.B7H64   364.1'53   77-27074
ISBN 0-471-40785-2

Printed in the United States of America

10 9 8 7 6 5 4 3

To

Everett C. Hughes and Rose A. Godbout
mentors

Preface

This book looks at how three major institutions—police, hospital, and court—respond to the rape victim and what impact this response has on victims. In our research, we followed a group of victims from the time they arrived at the emergency ward until the end of the legal process. Our data clearly show that rape does not end with the departure of the assailant. Instead, the institutional processing that occurs can be equally devastating. Those institutions that are to help victims can at the same time also further victimize them. Finding out what aspects cause further harm is essential. It is only by knowing what features are upsetting that we are in a position to provide support to victims and to recommend constructive change.

Research projects are guided by various assumptions and ours is no exception. Perhaps some of these should be made explicit here. First, we have a strong preference for seeing things firsthand. We thought it important to be where the action was. This led us to use participant observation as one of our main sources of information. We went to the emergency ward when victims were brought in, often in the middle of the night. We went to the courthouse and spent countless hours waiting and observing before the cases were called. We sat through the hearings and trials to hear the testimony word for word and watch the drama of the courtroom unfold. We also believe it is important to know what the situation means to the participants involved, to listen to what they have to say about their subjective experiences. Hence, our observations were complemented by many in-depth interviews, especially with victims.

Second, we believe in the value of interdisciplinary work. Our colleagueship began through a chance introduction that led to interdisciplinary teaching on the organization of health care. Later, when one of us (Holmstrom, a sociologist) became interested in rape, she approached the other (Burgess, a psychiatric nurse) for an exchange of ideas on how to study the problem. Burgess said that if a counseling component could be added to the research, she would be interested in being involved in the project. Thus, our research partnership came into being. Instructing each other in the relevant aspects of our respective fields has been an exciting venture.

Third, we believe in the importance of thinking through the policy implications of our research. Social science inquiry often is done simply for the contribution that it may make to the academic discipline. It seems important to us to look also at its practical relevance. Therefore, in our final chapter we make suggestions based on our data and our values for both immediate and long-term change. Our hope is that the book will be useful not only to academicians but also to the many people who presently are trying to promote a more humanistic response to the rape victim.

LYNDA LYTLE HOLMSTROM
ANN WOLBERT BURGESS

Chestnut Hill, Massachusetts
January, 1978

Acknowledgments

We are indebted above all else to the rape victims whose situations are analyzed in this book and who allowed us to be with them through a very difficult part of their lives. We also acknowledge the cooperation of the many physicians, nurses, social workers, police officers, assistant district attorneys, judges, and court officials with whom we came in contact and whose behavior we observed. We would like to be able to thank them by name, but privacy dictates that they remain anonymous both here and in the text of the book. Names of all victims and institutional personnel used in the case examples have been changed.

Special thanks are due to Anne G. Hargreaves, Executive Director of Nursing Services and Nursing Education, Department of Health and Hospitals, City of Boston, and Pamela MacLean Johansen, Assistant Director of Nursing, Emergency Services, Boston City Hospital for their assistance in arranging for our project to be based in the Emergency Services of Boston City Hospital.

Key people in the research design were the clerical personnel assigned to the accident floor and the pediatric walk-in service. It was their telephone call in the middle of the night that alerted us when a rape victim was admitted. We hereby thank Beatrice Crews, Sally Harper, Doris Jackson, Margery Jones, and Priscilla Sequira.

We thank the following student research assistants who helped us do library work; accompany victims to court; make telephone calls to the police, the courthouses, and the victims; and assist with the follow-up home interviews: Marie Beatini, Mary Terrio Burroughs, Linda Evans, Thomas S. Gary, Dianne Kenty, and Anna Laszlo.

We are grateful to the following people who volunteered their time to help in the huge job of gathering fieldwork data at the many courthouses: Helen Foley Barry, Donella Berry, Dorothy Ann Cain, Patricia Casey,

Patricia Colpitts, Barbara Frates, Barbara Barth Frink, Marion Longo, Agnes Stumpf, and John N. Wolbert.

Boston College secretary Katherine Lydon must be cited for the innumerable telephone calls she made to ascertain the days and times of court sessions.

The librarians of the Boston College library system deserve our thanks: Mary L. Pekarski and Anne F. Lippman at the nursing library were especially helpful in locating works for us. The reference staffs of the law library and of Bapst, the main campus library, were highly efficient in tracking down references.

We thank the many people with whom we discussed aspects of the research and especially want to mention the following: Benedict S. Alper, Stephen T. Barry, F. Ross Holmstrom, Paula Goldman Leventman, Pamela A. Roby, and Stephen Schafer. We are especially grateful to colleagues who took the time to read and comment on selected portions of the manuscript: John D. Donovan, Sharlene J. N. Hesse, and David A. Karp (the courtroom scene); A. Nicholas Groth (civil commitment); Leslie Sebba and Leon S. Sheleff (alternative models of the criminal justice system); Barrie Thorne (linguistic strategies); and John B. Williamson (variables associated with legal outcome). The interpretations and conclusions presented are of course our own and the people to whom we are indebted should not be held responsible for any shortcomings in them.

We appreciate the support and advice received from Peter W. Peirce, our Wiley-Interscience editor, and from Eric Valentine, formerly of Wiley-Interscience.

Many thanks are due to Lorraine B. Bone, Alice L. Close, and Shirley S. Urban for their careful and efficient typing of the manuscript, and to Deborah Blum for preparing the index.

Boston College granted a sabbatical to one of us during the time we were writing the book and thus considerably hastened the completion of the manuscript.

Additionally, we wish to thank the following authors and publishers who permitted us to quote from their works.

Robert M. Emerson and Aldine Publishing Company for permission to quote from Robert M. Emerson, *Judging Delinquents: Context and Process in Juvenile Court* (Chicago: Aldine, 1969). Copyright © 1969 by Robert M. Emerson.

Wayne Law Review for permission to quote from David Libai, "The Protection of the Child Victim of a Sexual Offense in the Criminal Justice System," *Wayne Law Review* 15 (1969). Copyright © 1968-69 by Wayne State University Law School.

Leon S. Sheleff for permission to quote from Leon S. Sheleff, "Victimology, Criminal Law, and Conflict Resolution," paper presented at the Second International Symposium on Victimology, Boston, Mass., September 1976.

An early version of our analysis of the courtroom scene appeared as "Rape: the Victim Goes on Trial," in Israel Drapkin and Emilio Viano, *Victimology: A New Focus, Vol. III. Crimes, Victims, and Justice* (Lexington, Mass.: D.C. Heath, 1975), pp. 31-47, with the prior agreement that the material could be used in the present book.

L. L. H.
A. W. B.

Contents

CHAPTER 1

■

The Lot of the Rape Victim

Our society makes the lot of the rape victim difficult. Often it is assumed that the rape was the victim's fault or that it makes the victim less worthy as a person. Furthermore, when the victim reports the crime or when someone else reports it, a difficult process usually lies ahead.

A series of institutions—including law-enforcement agencies, hospitals, and courts—deal with the crime of rape. When an attack is reported, these institutions are put into motion, and both the offender and the victim are processed through them.[1] Studies of the course of the criminal through this institutional maze are numerous, but little scholarly attention has been given to how the victim proceeds through the same maze.

Our study is an attempt to correct this oversight. It focuses on victims and follows them over time, especially as they go through the criminal justice system. This focus on the victim has practical import as well as academic importance. Crime statistics show clearly that reported rapes have been on the rise. FBI uniform crime reports show that both the number of rapes and the rate per 100,000 inhabitants have increased dramatically in recent years. Thus, from a pragmatic point of view, it seems more important than ever to understand what happens to the victims of this crime. By documenting and analyzing their experience, we will be in a better position to recommend constructive change.

To investigate this issue, a study was done of all 146 victims with a complaint of rape admitted during a one-year period to the emergency wards of a large municipal hospital. In addition, a smaller number of victims from other sources were studied. We interviewed victims when they were admitted to the hospital, often in the middle of the night; did weekly follow-up interviews on their emotional problems; and accompanied them to court to observe firsthand all the courthouse proceedings. The study thus follows

1

the victims from the time they arrive at the hospital until the final outcome of the legal process. It looks at the initial contact with the criminal justice system—that is, who is involved in reporting the rape and why; the experience in going to the police; the decision to press or not press charges; the hospital exam to gather evidence; how cases get dropped at each stage of the legal process; the court experience; and the results both legal and psychological, of this court experience.

This is a study of institutional processing. We take seriously Everett Hughes's suggestion that, as social observers, we should pay attention to the connection between the institution and the person.[2] We look at the victim's course—or, to use the sociological term, the victim's "career"[3]—as she goes through the police, medical, and court systems. And we look at how these long-established work systems are structured and what impact their structure has on the victim who is briefly "going through." Police, hospital staff, and court personnel often remain in their jobs for years, forming lasting relationships with these institutions and with each other. But victims, like defendants,[4] are merely "passing through."

Law-enforcement agencies, hospitals, and courts are large bureaucracies. Many of the problems rape victims face are related to this fact. Staffed by bureaucratic officials and by professionals, these institutions can contribute not only to the comfort and security of victims, but to their depersonalization and control. The problems victims face include feeling lost in the system, lack of privacy, being kept in ignorance, and being caught in the conflict between victims' rights and organizational responsibilities.[5]

Victims often feel lost and neglected. Arriving at the police station, the emergency ward, or the courthouse they find that the organization has its own time schedule and procedures that are often set up more for the convenience of staff than for the public it is to serve. Victims who arrive at the emergency ward of a hospital may have to wait a long time for an exam, especially if more life-endangering cases than theirs are ahead of them. In some hospitals one must wait alone, since rules forbid the presence of a friend or family member. At the courthouse, the victim may sit unnoticed for hours in a crowded, noisy, depressing corridor. For serious crimes such as attempted murder and rape the victim waits to be interviewed by an assistant district attorney. These DAs, often working under hectic and unpredictable time schedules, dash out into the corridors in between appearances in court on various other cases to try to sandwich in an interview with the victim.

The rape victim may also find that she has little privacy. One of the victim's main concerns may be whether people will find out what has happened. Yet often the police, medical, and court personnel as they do their work make the victim's situation known to the community. News of the crime may be spread by the manner in which the police arrive in the community—driving a marked car with siren or flashing light on. Physicians may tell the victim's parents or spouse the results of the medical examination. The court process is one of the least private aspects of all. The victim, unless very young, must give testimony in a hearing or trial open to the general public. Usually, spectators are present. The victims are asked to state their name and address openly before strangers. Victims are asked about intimate details of the alleged crime, as well as details about their private lives. Some spectators may be present on official business, awaiting their turn in court. But others are there just for the show. They are "court-watchers"—voyeurs in search of sex and violence.

The victim is often kept in ignorance. Police, physicians, and district attorneys tend to not inform the victim about what is happening. Police often ask embarrassing questions without explaining why they must do so. Physicians who examine victims are still, for the most part, following the traditional professional model in which the professional decides for the client what he or she needs. And DAs sometimes fail to inform victims of crucial aspects of the case. The victim may be sitting in the courtroom in the middle of the trial before suddenly realizing—due to comments of the lawyers—that the rape charge has been dropped and is no longer an issue.

Victims may find that there is a conflict between their rights and the responsibilities of the organizations. Hospitals, for example, are responsible for giving care that meets certain standards. If they fail to do so, they can be held legally liable for negligence. Rape may cause gynecological damage, venereal disease, and pregnancy, so adequate treatment typically requires doing an internal pelvic examination. Some victims do not want to be examined, however, and may wonder if they have the right to refuse. If they do try to refuse, they may be subjected to pressure by hospital personnel to submit, since the hospital must protect itself.

These and many other problems that rape victims face as they come into contact with institutions designed to deal with rape are discussed throughout this book. What the procedures have in common is that they often further victimize the victim. Ironically, the institutions that society has designated to help victims may in fact cause further damage. Although such procedures may be distasteful to any client, they are especially upsetting to the rape victim who has just been through a life-threatening situation.[6] Already humiliated and depersonalized by the assault itself, rape victims are in a psychological state of crisis[7] and are thus hypersensitive to any slight. The neutral stance of the record keeper who talks to patients as they arrive at the hospital or the calm detachment of a professional on the emergency ward may be perceived by the victim as an attitude of callousness.

The experiences of the particular victims reported in this book are of interest not only in themselves, but more importantly for their theoretical and practical implications. The findings have theoretical importance for criminologists and sociologists. They raise the basic analytic question of whether victimization can be increased by those groups and institutions that are supposed to protect citizens. If this is so—and we believe our data show that it is—then, in addition to looking at the crime, the perpetrator, and the victim, we can add a fourth element to our analytical framework: the part played in victimization by those groups and institutions that are supposed to protect the victim.[8]

The findings also have practical implications. Analysis and documentation of the difficulties victims face in the present system can suggest changes one could institute that would promote more adequate help for rape victims. Many groups around the country—including concerned social scientists, clinicians, former victims, attorneys, feminists, and law-enforcement officials—are interested in helping to bring about more humanistic treatment for rape victims. We hope that our analysis of the experiences of a sample of rape victims will be of use to them.

NOTES

1. Lynda Lytle Holmstrom and Ann Wolbert Burgess, "Rape: The Victim and the Criminal Justice System," paper read at the First International Symposium on Victimology, Jerusalem, Israel, September 2-6, 1973; published in *International Journal of Criminology and Penology* 3 (1975), pp. 101-110.
2. Everett Cherrington Hughes, in *Men and Their Work*, "Institutional Office and the Person," (Glencoe, Ill.: The Free Press, 1958), pp. 64-67. (First published 1937 in *American Journal of Sociology*.)
3. Ibid.
4. Abraham S. Blumberg, "Covert Contingencies in the Right to the Assistance of Counsel," in *The Triple Revolution Emerging: Social Problems in Depth*, Robert Perrucci and Marc Pilisuk, eds. (Boston: Little, Brown, 1971), pp. 479-480. (First published 1967 in *Law and Society Review*)
5. Lynda Lytle Holmstrom and Ann Wolbert Burgess, "Victimization by Government: Failure to Help the Victims of Violent Crime," paper read at the American Society of Criminology Annual Meeting, Chicago, November 1-4, 1974.
6. Ann Wolbert Burgess and Lynda Lytle Holmstrom, *Rape: Victims of Crisis*, (Bowie, Md.: Robert J. Brady Co., 1974), pp. 37-39.
7. Ibid. This analysis uses Gerald Caplan's definition of crisis as a psychological disequilibrium in a person who confronts a hazardous circumstance that for that person constitutes an important problem which he can for the time being neither escape nor solve with his customary problem-solving resources.
8. We would like to thank Stephen Schafer for a discussion that helped clarify the theoretical implications of victimization by such institutions.

CHAPTER 2

■

How We Did the Research

This book represents the finished product—the outcome of our research and analysis. But any research project has a history that the reader is entitled to know about to assess more accurately its results. Before presenting our findings, we want to review the process we went through as we worked together on this project.

HOW WE GOT STARTED

It is hard to know exactly what makes one decide to study a certain topic. Although rape has recently been much talked about, when we started our research almost nothing was being said or done about it as a social problem—especially from the point of view of the victim. One of us (Holmstrom) had just finished a research project and was searching for a topic that had some impact on women's lives and on the relationship between the sexes. She remembered having heard many reports by women at consciousness-raising groups in the late 1960s about physical assaults that had been made upon them by men. And yet, it seemed that despite its common occurrence and its apparently strong impact on the people involved, that, researchers seldom picked up on this assaultive behavior as a research topic.[1] Thinking about this phenomenon led Holmstrom to the idea, initially only vaguely formulated, of studying rape and especially rape victims. The next step was her decision to meet with Burgess, with whom she had done interdisciplinary teaching, to discuss how to go about such a study. Burgess's immediate response was, "If you want to add a counseling aspect to your study, I'd be interested in going in with you on it." We discussed how an interdisciplinary project might be an especially fruitful way to ap-

5

proach the problem, and how the academic skills of a sociologist and the clinical skills of a psychotherapist and psychiatric nurse might well complement each other. We decided to become a team.

Holmstrom's impression at the time of this preliminary discussion was that little existed in the scholarly literature on rape victims. Burgess's impression was that little existed in the way of counseling services for them. We checked out our impressions and found that they were accurate. The scholarly and professional literature on sexual offenses, including rape, was voluminous, but it had overlooked the victim.[2] The literature had focused on the person committing the crime (an example is the well-known book, *Sex Offenders*, by Gebhard and his colleagues.[3] Or, the literature had focused on the circumstances under which the crime took place and characteristics of victim and criminal that can be obtained from official records. Amir's widely cited analysis of rape is an example of this type. Using information from police records, he analyzed the situation in which the crime occurred, such as place and time of day, and characteristics of the victim and offenders, such as age, race, and whether they were strangers to each other.[4] Only in clinical case histories written by psychologists and psychiatrists did one begin to get some insight into the experience of the victim. But because they were reports of isolated and scattered cases, they remained only suggestive. Clearly what needed to be done was to collect such information from a sample of victims in a systematic way. Counseling programs, like the scholarly literature, had also neglected the victim. Although programs existed for hundreds of problems—from drug abuse to divorce, from alcoholism to widowhood—almost none existed for victims of sexual assault.[5] Clearly there was a need here, too.

Having decided to work as a team and having ascertained that information on and services for victims were indeed lacking, our next step was to gain access to a population of victims.

GAINING ACCESS TO A SAMPLE OF VICTIMS

Now that we have gathered information on several hundred rape cases, it seems obvious to us how one locates victims. But in the beginning of our work, it was not so self-evident. We knew that victims who reported the crime would be concentrated in various places—at police stations, hospitals, or courts. Thus these seemed to be likely places to start looking for a sample.

Preliminary Inquiries

Our initial inquiries did not meet with success. First we tried locating victims through the courts. It soon became clear that it was very difficult to
track down cases this way because of the innumerable delays before any
particular case came to trial. We also realized that such cases would be
representative only of that very small percentage of victims whose cases
came to trial.

We next asked some criminologists for advice, and through them made
contacts in the criminal justice system. Preliminary discussions suggested
that these officials might help us in the future when we were certain of the
approach we wanted to take.

Our third approach was to the police. Two or three days of telephoning
to the office of the psychological consultant to the police produced no
results. We never got through and our calls were never returned.

Fourth, we tried the medical hierarchy of a large municipal
hospital—Boston City Hospital—where a high percentage of the rape victims in the area are taken. The initial contact was with a colleague in the
Department of Psychiatry who referred us to medical personnel on the
Emergency Services. This referral resulted in an interview with the physician who was the medical director of the pediatric emergency service. She
expressed polite interest, but also thought of various reasons why we could
not begin right away.

After trying these four possible entry points into the system, we still were
not getting very far. No one had refused us, but neither had anyone really
offered to help. And certainly no one was moving very fast.

Impatient with delays, we tried a fifth approach—the nursing hierarchy
at this same hospital. They moved with utmost speed. We contacted the Executive Director, Nursing Services and Nursing Education of the Department of Health and Hospitals for the City of Boston. She immediately put
us in contact with the Assistant Director of Nursing for the Emergency Services of the hospital—the person with the authority to determine who
would or would not be allowed to work in the emergency wards in connection with the nursing service. We arranged an appointment and exchanged
ideas. The Assistant Director made arrangements for us to meet at once
with the three shifts of staff nurses, the people who would be most in contact with us as we worked. She introduced us to these nurses, emphasizing
in her presentation that we were interested in doing "some clinical work."
The research aspect was noted, but not stressed. We exchanged ideas. The
staff nurses expressed polite interest, asked some questions, told us what
they had done with rape victims in the past, and told us some of the problems they thought we might face—for example, that the police are often in a

hurry and might rush us. They agreed to telephone us each time a rape victim was admitted. Two days later a rape victim was brought to the hospital and the nurses called us promptly. And they, as well as the administrative staff, continued to do so for an entire year. Without their tremendous and conscientious help, we could not have done the project.

The result of gaining access to the system through the nursing hierarchy was that we were officially defined as an extension of the nursing service. For those interested in the sociology of professions and formal organizations, it should be pointed out that the nursing hierarchy had the authority to give us permission to work in the hospital under its auspices. Once nursing had given us permission, our presence on the emergency ward was a fait accompli so far as the other services in the hospital, such as medicine and social services, were concerned.

Access to Individual Victims

Access to the hospital was just the first step. We still needed the cooperation of the individual victims. Often the nurse or physician on duty told the victim about us. Their explanations varied, depending on their perceptions of us. Some stressed that we did counseling, others said we were "doing a study."

We presented ourselves to the victims as part of the hospital system, although we also told them we were affiliated with Boston College. We wore street clothes (dresses) rather than hospital attire. We presented ourselves in a professional role, saying for an introduction something like, "Hi, I'm Dr. Holmstrom and this is Dr. Burgess. We're called on all cases like this and we'd like to talk to you a little about how you're feeling." Often this explanation was sufficient. If not, we sometimes added that we did the follow-up on the emotional aspect and that we wanted to talk to them about their feelings so that we would have a baseline for comparison when we contacted them later to see how they were doing. We also informed them that we were studying the problems that rape victims faced.

Since it is difficult to introduce oneself to a person who is in a psychological crisis (for example, some victims were sobbing uncontrollably when we arrived), we also had handouts printed that repeated all this information. We gave one to each victim.

Victim Counseling Program

The Victim Counseling Program is a collaborative effort between Boston College School of Nursing and Boston City Hospital. Any victim of rape, attempted rape, sexual assault or molesting will be seen by the staff.

The aims of the program are:

1. To provide a counseling program for the victim through initial visit at the hospital and by telephone for follow-up.
2. To study the problems a victim experiences as a result of being assaulted.

Staff

Ann C. Burgess, R.N., D.N.Sc. Associate Professor, Boston College   Phone: 969-0100 Ext. 2111.

Lynda Holmstrom, Ph.D. Assistant Professor, Boston College   Phone: 969-0100 Ext. 2182 or 2391.

A notice containing this same information was posted on the wall of the gynecological examining room; a number of victims commented on having read it. In cases of child and adolescent victims, we discussed what we were doing with victims and their parents.

Access to the Courts

To observe what happened at court, we simply accompanied the victim. Arriving with the victim was seen as sufficient explanation for our presence. An occasional defense lawyer expressed displeasure at our being there. But other court personnel, including district attorneys, clerks, sheriffs, and judges, were usually quite accepting. Occasionally we were interviewed by a judge before a trial about why we wanted to stay. We replied that we came from the hospital, provided counseling services to rape victims, and studied rape victims' problems. After this explanation, the judges ruled that we had a direct interest in the case and could stay.

THE SAMPLE

Main Sample of Victims

Our primary sample consists of 146 persons who were admitted to the emergency wards of Boston City Hospital during a one-year period from July 1972 to July 1973 with a complaint of rape.[6] It includes all the adult victims that were admitted during that time, and most of the child and adolescent (16 and under) victims. We decided on using an entire year's sample for two reasons—to obtain a sufficient number of cases, and because the existing literature suggested that rape rates might vary with the season of the year.

The City Hospital Emergency Wards provide emergency care to various social classes, races, and age groups, as well as both sexes. They are thus an especially good place to do research if one wishes to study a population that may be heterogeneous. And indeed, our sample of 146 victims turned out to be very heterogeneous. It included women of varying employment status—career women, housewives, college students, and women on welfare. Occupations represented included schoolteacher, business manager, researcher, assembly-line worker, secretary, housekeeper, cocktail waitress, and health worker. Various ethnic groups were represented. There were 81 white and 60 black victims, plus five who were Oriental, Canadian-Indian, or Spanish-speaking. Marital and family status varied. There were single, married, divorced, separated, and widowed women, as well as women living in consensual relationships with men. There were virgins and sexually experienced women. There were victims who had no children, who were pregnant (as much as eight months) at the time of the attack, who had very recently given birth, and who had anywhere from 1 to 10 children. As for age, 109 victims were adults and 37 were children or adolescents; the age range was from 3 to 73. In physical appearance they ranged from very pretty to very plain. In dress they varied from high fashion to hippie garb. And there were not only female victims, but three males as well.

Supplementary Samples of Victims

Referral Cases.   In addition to working at City Hospital, we obtained cases through other means: at other hospitals, from the district attorney's office, from colleagues, and through self-referral. There were two research reasons why we accepted these cases. First, they give us some comparative information. Although the study is not comparative in the strictest sense, we nevertheless do have considerable information about how rape victims are treated in a variety of settings beyond the main ones in which we made observations. Second, these referral cases make it possible to report the results more anonymously. Many of our statements are based not only on our work at City Hospital, but on our information from these other settings. We often specify the sample we are discussing, but in other places we do not indicate the source and there is no way for the reader to know if the case is from City Hospital or from some other medical facility.

For the most part, the referral cases are similar to those in our main sample. However, they differ in one important way: often they were the more "extreme" or more "dramatic" cases. For example, in our main sample many victims were raped by more than one assailant. But only in our referral sample was there a case of rape by nine men who transported the victim through two counties and who later telephoned such explicit threats to the victim's office that she was placed in protective custody.

Second- and Third-Year Cases in City Hospital. We followed intensively the cases admitted during one year to City Hospital. Since then we have continued our connection with the hospital and have, on a volunteer basis, trained staff nurses to be victim counselors and supervised their counseling. In this supervisory and consulting capacity, we have systematically discussed the cases admitted for rape during the second and third years with the nurses who now are doing the counseling. Thus we have indirectly gathered a considerable body of data on these cases, too.

In summary, we have gathered information on a total of several hundred victims: on 146 victims intensively and over time; on at least 45 referral cases; and on 191 second-year and an estimated 200 third-year cases indirectly through case supervision discussions with nurses presently doing the counseling. We find that the data from these latter groups confirm our findings from the first 146 victims.

Sample of Courts and Defendants

Courts. We followed the victim to whatever court her assailant was taken to. The majority of cases were heard in two district courts and one superior court close to City Hospital's catchment area. However, all told, we observed cases in eight district courts located in four counties, and in one superior court.

Defendants' Hearings and Trials. It is important to emphasize that we observed the hearings and trials of the specific assailants who were accused of attacking the victims in our sample. It would have been far easier simply to go to court and obtain a sample of trials of defendants who were not connected to our victim sample. However, we believed it was essential to follow particular cases from start to finish. Thus, in each case, we followed the victim and the proceedings against the assailant alleged to be involved in her assault.

The result is that it took three years to collect the data reported in this book. During the first year, we were still accepting new victim cases for intensive study. The time between assault and trial is easily two years. Thus, at least three years are required to follow such a group.

DATA COLLECTION: THE MAIN SOURCES

The main sources of data were participant observation and interviews when the victim was admitted to the hospital, weekly follow-up interviews on the emotional problems, and participant observation and discussion at the courthouse.[7] The data thus obtained resulted in 2,900 pages of notes.

The Hospital Scene

We decided that if we wanted to understand how victims felt right after the attack (which is when institutions begin to deal with them), if we wanted to see how victims were treated, and if we wanted to establish a relationship with them, then we had better *be there*. This is why we arranged to be telephoned when the victim arrived at the emergency ward. We both went to the hospital immediately, usually arriving within 30 minutes of the call. We interviewed the victim and also talked to anyone else we could find on the scene—physician, nurse, policeman, relative, friend.

Victim.   In interviewing the victim, we focused on the following areas and in each area encouraged her not only to tell what happened but to express her emotions about it as well.

The assault

Circumstances.   When and where was the victim approached? Why was she there? Where did the rape itself occur?

The Assailant.   Who did it? Was he of the same race? Was he known to the victim? Was he a stranger? If there was more than one assailant, how many were there?

Conversation.   What kind of conversation occurred between the victim and her assailant prior to the rape? Did he try to "charm" her or offer to help her? Did he threaten her? Did he make humiliating comments? Did he talk during the rape? What did he say? Did he offer to pay her? What did she say back to the assailant?

Sexual details.   What type of sex did the assailant demand (i.e., vaginal, oral, or anal intercourse)? What type of sex did he actually obtain from her? What other degrading acts did he perform, such as urinating on her or pulling her breasts? How did she react to what she was forced to do?

Physical and verbal threats.   Did the assailant have a weapon? Did he threaten the victim physically or verbally? What kind of violence did he inflict, such as slapping or hitting her?

Struggle.   Did the victim struggle or not? How does she feel about this?

Alcohol and drug use by assailant or victim.   Does she think the assailant was under the influence of drugs or alcohol, and had she been using drugs or alcohol?

Emotional reaction. How did the victim feel emotionally at the time and how does she feel emotionally now? What is the most painful part to think about?

Sexual reaction. How did it feel sexually? What does the sexual assault mean to her? Is this her first sexual experience, or what has been her normal sexual style? What are her feelings about sex? Has she been attacked or raped before?

After the attack

Seeking help. Where did she go for help? Did she clean up or change clothes before seeking help? Whom did she talk with to help her decide what to do, and did she decide to seek help or was the decision made for her by others?

Encounter with police. If the victim reported the rape to the police, what was her reaction to this experience? Did the police encourage or discourage her from taking it to court, and how did she feel she was treated by the police?

Encounter with the hospital. How does she feel about being in the hospital? How did she feel about the gynecological examination? What concerns her most medically as a result of the rape, such as possible pregnancy, venereal disease, or feelings about the rape?

Pressing charges. Is the victim willing to press charges, and is she willing to cooperate with the police and testify in court? How does she feel about this?

Social network

Family and friends. Who is the victim's family, and which people are important to her? Whom will she tell in her family? What friends are there at work or school, and what friends will she tell? Is there some other person she might tell—employer, counselor, therapist, minister?

Possible prior difficulties.

Has the victim had prior psychiatric or social difficulties (e.g., drug use, suicide attempts)? If so, has she had contact with a therapist or counselor for them? How does she usually handle stress or crisis situations and what have these situations been?

We made systematic observations of the victim as well: body movements that would be clues to anxiety and distress—smoking excessively, breathing deep sighs, holding arms and rocking slowly, change in breathing, flushing, perspiration, and tears; silences as well as what the victim would say; the style and condition of her clothes; recent injuries such as bruises and lacerations that might be related to the attack; older injuries such as trace marks or slash marks that might be related to some other incident.

Usually both of us were present for the interview, and often one interviewed while the other took detailed notes. Afterward, we each wrote up a set of field notes. Thus for most cases we have two accounts that can be checked against each other.

Incidentally, we do not recommend such an interview with a person in crisis solely for research purposes or without some contact with a person trained to work with emotional issues. Inquiries about such painful issues can be either damaging or therapeutic, depending on how they are made and the type of follow-up that occurs. In our case, there were counseling reasons as well as research reasons for each of the questions.[8] And follow-up counseling was provided.

Victim's Network: Friends and Relatives. We interviewed family and friends whenever possible at the hospital. We asked them what happened, how they were feeling about it, and what they planned to do. We looked to see if they were concerned about the victim or were focusing on their own problems instead. In addition we made observations, noting who came to the hospital, who failed to come (for example, some victims telephoned relatives from the hospital but they declined to come in), with whom the victim left the hospital, and how these people treated her.

The Hospital Staff and Setting. We talked informally to physicians and nurses and asked their opinions of the case and what they had found out. We observed how they treated the victim and what they said to her. We also observed the general atmosphere of the hospital—whether it was a quiet night or whether it was a busy one with even the corridors filled with injured and sick people waiting to be seen.

The Police. We chatted informally with police, asking their opinions of the case. We observed what they said and did with the victim. And on a number of occasions, we observed the officer's interview of the victim.

The Main Problems. The main difficulty interviewing at the hospital was that it was often a busy scene. It was not always possible to do an interview completely uninterrupted and in a private room. We had to be flexible in approach and able to talk to victims even under harried circumstances.

Follow-Up Interviews

The Questions Asked. We did follow-up interviews with victims for a number of weeks, usually by telephone, and asked about the following areas.

Physical problems.

Disturbing thoughts: the painful parts of the experience.

Feelings; what kind of moods they were in.

Their activities—were they getting back to their normal routine of work, school, social life?

Resumption of their normal sexual style.

Reactions from people in their network—family, friends, employers, peers—to the rape.

The legal process—had they talked to the police again, had they identified the assailant, how did they feel about this, did they receive threats to make them drop charges, were they pressured into going to court, how did they feel about getting ready to go to court, reactions to what happened at court.

Evaluation of services received—from police, hospital, and counseling program.

The average number of follow-up interviews with rape victims themselves was five. In addition to talking to the victim, we also talked to family or friends.

Telephone.   The acceptability of the telephone to victims for follow-up interviews was discovered by accident. We had originally intended to have the victims return to the hospital to meet in a group with other victims and share experiences. We had difficulty getting them to return and so telephoned them to see if we could get them to come. In so doing, we found out that victims felt quite comfortable on the telephone. This chance discovery was useful indeed, since doing interviews by telephone is obviously far less time-consuming than doing them in person.

The Main Problem.   The main difficulty in doing follow-up is the tendency of victims to disappear after the sexual assault—they move, go away on a trip, or stay with friends and relatives for a while. Thus, we always tried to get enough information from them about various places they might be so that we could later track them down.

The Courthouse Scene

We made 159 trips to courthouses to observe their procedures. Typically we met the victim when hearings and trials for her alleged assailant were scheduled. We often went many times with one particular victim and waited with her for hours, only to be eventually told that the case would be "continued". We went to the courthouse many times when the defendant failed to appear, as well as times when the victim failed to show up. Thus we saw not only the actual hearings and trials, but also experienced the long waiting periods and observed the action that occurred during them.

Observations Made.   Once at the courthouse, we focused our attention on the following areas.

Basic background data

Dates scheduled for hearings and trials; continuances and postponements.
The charges.
Amount of bail.
Whether defendant was out on bail or in custody.
Whether stenographic record and/or tape recording of testimony was made and if so by whom.
Whether defense lawyer was court-appointed or privately retained.
Personnel—names of victims, defendant, police officer, district attorney, defense lawyer, and judge.

Informal scenes—in hallways, waiting in courtroom.

Who accompanied the victim to court and who accompanied the defendant to court; interaction between these two groups of people; any threats made from one group to the other.
Conversations and interaction that occurred prior to court session, during recesses, and after court.

District attorney's preparation of the case

Where he conducted the interview—in the hallway or in his office.
The issues that were of concern to him.
His demeanor vis-à-vis the victim.

The hearing or trial itself

The testimony, opening and closing arguments, judge's instructions to the jury, judge's ruling on objections. Field notes written as verbatim as possible, often while the court was in session and if not, then immediately afterward.
The number of spectators present.

The dress and demeanor of the people in the courtroom.

Jury composition by sex, race, and age.

The verdict and sentence.

The victim

Informal conversation with her and systematic observation of her testimony and of her physical appearance and behavior.

The Main Problems.   One of the most difficult parts of the project was to determine exactly when the hearings and trials were to be held, since they are postponed over and over again. Thus, despite accompanying rape victims on their many trips to court, and despite the cooperation of and constant telephoning to victims, police, court clerks, and district attorneys, we still sometimes missed finding out when a case was to be heard. However, by constant checking, we usually found out in time. It was possible to make observations at 28 of the 39 hearings and 12 of the 17 trials. We (Holmstrom and/or Burgess) attended most of these hearings and trials. When it was not possible for us to be present (usually because of teaching schedules), observations in court were made by Boston College students trained by us.

DEVELOPING DATA-COLLECTION PROCEDURES

Open-Ended Goals

We had chosen to study a problem—what happens to rape victims—about which little was known. When we began we had very general goals. We knew only that we wanted to do two things: study the problems these victims experienced, and provide counseling services to them. Because our goals were so open-ended, we decided to keep the data collection procedures open-ended, too.

Decision to Use Flexible Interview Guides

We decided to gather the interview data by means of flexible interviews. We thus opted for the type of interview guides described above—guides consisting of general topics and questions to be discussed with each rape victim, rather than a questionnaire schedule consisting of rigidly specified questions. The interviews were standardized, however, in the sense that the same list of topics was to be discussed with each victim.[9]

There are several advantages to using such a flexible approach. First, people can often remember better and discuss issues more easily if they are allowed to talk as their thoughts come to them, rather than in an arbitrary manner and order predetermined by the investigators. Permitting people to talk in the style they find most comfortable is especially important when discussing a sensitive issue. Second, it allows the investigator and the person being interviewed to discuss things that the investigator had not thought of—things that may be crucial to an understanding of the problem. For example, when we began we did not realize the extreme degree to which victims would emphasize their distress over going to court. It was the open-ended nature of the interviews that allowed us to discover that victims find court as upsetting as the original rape itself. This potential for discovery is extremely important when one is studying a problem about which there is little preexisting knowledge.

Development of the Interview Guides

The first few cases were used to develop the interview guides. When we began we hardly knew what to ask about. We agreed, prior to talking with the first victim, that we would ask about three broad areas: the details surrounding the incident, including the details of the rape itself; the emotional reactions of the victim; and how the victim felt about the institutions that dealt with her after the rape. We did this with the first few victims, and we also let them talk about anything else that seemed important to them. We then went over these early cases and made up a list of topics for the guides. Some of these topics came from our initial questions and some came from the new issues the victims brought to our attention. These lists of topics then became our interview guides for all subsequent interviews.

Completing the Interviews

Using the guides, we interviewed each victim. The sequence of topics varied from person to person. In many cases, victims themselves spontaneously mentioned many issues that were on the list—for example, their feelings about pressing charges or their reactions to the defense lawyer. When they spontaneously mentioned the issues we followed up on the topic in a manner approximating that of a conversation. With talkative victims, much of the interviewing consisted of listening to what they had to say and probing further only after they volunteered much information. With less verbal victims, we had to be more active in interviewing style since they did not provide information spontaneously. In all cases, great care was taken to keep notes as verbatim as possible of all the victim's comments.

Observation Guides

We did not want to rely on interview statements alone. Because there are many things people either cannot or will not tell you, we also wanted to see with our own eyes how victims were treated. To do so, we developed the observational sections of the guides described above. These parts were developed in the same way as the interview questions. In the early cases, we simply wrote down every single thing we could remember that we had observed. We then went over these notes and developed a list of things to observe systematically for each case.

Two Sets of Data to Compare

For most of the issues we studied we had two types of data: interview statements and observations. The observational data were used to confirm or to question what the person said.

Very often the observations made supported what the person told us. For example, victims complained again and again about having to wait untold hours at the courthouse. With interview statements alone, one might wonder if this complaint was an exaggeration reflecting frustration with the system. But with observational data as well, we knew that these complaints about waiting were accurate. Like the victims, we sat hour upon hour in courthouse corridors. The exact hours and minutes were logged into our field notes.

Observational data were also used to question and to reinterpret interview statements. For example, in one case a young girl told us that she was upset at court when she looked and saw that people in the courtroom were crying. We had been there and knew that the people in the courtroom were not crying. This discrepancy plus some other bizarre statements led us to conclude that this victim was actively hallucinating under the stress of the court experience.

Uncertain What Data Will Pay Off

When we began we were not sure which data would "pay off"—that is, turn out later to be important. Doing research in an open-ended way means making a commitment to keep careful notes on some types of data for which you are not certain there will be a payoff. For example, one thing we observed was the physical layout of the courtroom. We always drew a sketch of the floorplan and where each individual was sitting or standing. It seemed to us in some vague way that this information might be important. Some victims talked of how it unnerved them to have the defendant so close to them when they testified. And indeed our sketches of the rooms showed that in some district courts the distance between victim and defendant is very slight—a few feet at most.

DATA COLLECTION: SUPPLEMENTARY SOURCES

The interviews and observations already described constitute the main sources of data for this book. However, we gathered information from other sources to supplement the above.

Analysis of Records

We analyzed the medical records of each victim, looking especially at the following areas:

The chief complaint of the patient.

The physician's observations. What style were his or her observations recorded in, what was included, what was excluded, what adjectives were used to describe the patient, what clues were given about attitudes (e.g., was she called "uncooperative" if she refused an exam)?

Medical findings. Presence or absence of bruises, lacerations, sperm.

Treatment given. Medication, Xrays, hospitalization.

Diagnosis. What terms did the physician use when asked to make a judgment about whether the victim was in fact raped.

Information damaging to the patient. What did the record reveal that was not directly related to the rape but could be damaging in court (e.g., a history of previous pregnancy or abortion, psychiatric history)?

Interviews with Professionals and Activists

We informally talked with and also formally interviewed physicians. We asked them how they felt about treating rape victims, what they thought the definition of rape was, how they felt about testifying in court, and what suggestions they had for improving the treatment given to victims. We talked informally with other professionals—nurses, hospital executive officers, medical examiners (especially about rape victims who are murdered), defense lawyers, psychiatrists, school counselors, and university counselors. And we also had discussions with activists and action-oriented people from various cities throughout the United States including Berkeley, Seattle, Las Vegas, Chicago, Cleveland, New York, Washington, D.C., Memphis, Tuscaloosa, Miami, San Juan, Houston, and Honolulu. These people included members of rape crisis centers, hot line organizers, victim assistance programs, self-defense teachers, and NOW (National Organization for Women) rape task force members.

Analysis of Our Own Experiences in the System

We used our own experiences in the system as still another source of data.

Testifying. One of the difficulties of doing a research project such as ours is that one comes to have information about criminal cases and therefore one can be subpoenaed to testify in court. Sociologists do not have privileged communication with their research subjects, nor do psychiatric nurses enjoy privileged communication with their clients.

We were called to testify several times and actually did so three times. When one of us testified, the other took notes of the questions asked and the answers entered into evidence. Also, the person who testified later wrote notes about her feelings of having to go on the stand. The great anxiety we experienced being called to court gave us some insight into the amount of stress the victims experienced.

Reaction to Our Research. We kept track of everything that was asked us or said to us about our project—whether by colleagues, friends, or by audiences when we gave talks. Again and again, for example, we were told the joke about how "you can't put a peg in a moving hole." These reactions to our work gave us some notion of what public attitudes are toward the rape victim.

Rap Sessions with Rapists

To see the rapist's as well as the victim's side, we accepted the invitation of a colleague to meet with convicted sex offenders he was treating at Massachusetts Treatment Center. Although we did no formal data gathering at these sessions, we nevertheless were able to gain some insight into the situation of these men—how they perceived the rapes they had committed, their experiences in courts, and how they felt about the institution in which they were confined.

EFFECT OF OBSERVER ON THE OBSERVED

One cannot observe without affecting whatever it is one wants to observe. This dilemma occurs both in physical and social science. You cannot do a study without making observations. But when you observe you change the object of your observations. There is no way out of this dilemma completely. A partial solution is to try to take into account what effect you as researcher may be having.

How We Were Perceived

We have clues—from casual comments and in some cases from interviews—about how we were perceived by the people we wished to observe.

By Hospital Staff. The staff dubbed us "the rape ladies." Since for the most part they went out of their way to help us, we assume that our presence had some legitimacy in their eyes. Perhaps the thing that established us at the hospital more than anything else was our willingness to be called to the hospital on a moment's notice at any hour of the day or night. We were subjected to good-natured teasing about whether we had the stamina to last an entire year. But later, when the staff knew we were writing up our findings, they said in all seriousness, "Be sure to emphasize that you were on call 24 hours a day."

Many nurses helped us, not only by their telephone call but in other ways as well—giving us information on patients' reactions prior to our arrival or locating a missing record for us. Only one nurse actively resisted our efforts; she had herself recently been a rape victim. One night as we arrived she told us point-blank how awful it was that we talked to victims when they were upset; the doctors and police harassed them enough, and they certainly didn't need us talking to them too. She was also horrified at the fact that we did follow-up interviews by telephone. "It's so impersonal," she said, regarding as irrelevant our explanation that victims, having once met us, seemed comfortable using the telephone. The nurse later became a "convert." In the second year she wanted to be and was trained as a victim-counselor.

The physicians who examined victims—gynecologists and pediatricians—accepted our presence on the emergency wards. Many went out of their way to help us. Others were more detached from our work, neither helping nor interfering. Only one put any obstacles in our way.

The physicians most attuned to the emotional needs of patients also seemed to be the most inclined to talk to us about patients. One of them referred to us positively as "part of the team." Another asked to observe an interview so that he could learn the kind of questions and approach we used.

Although we were careful to explain to the physicians our credentials and what we were doing, we were often misperceived by them. One physician kept thinking we were from the hospital's Social Service and sometimes wrote that on the patient's medical record. Another assumed we were nuns because we taught at Boston College; he informed us, laughing, of this assumption one night after suddenly realizing one of us was very pregnant. And still another thought we got paid to do this kind of work and must be doing it "to earn a little extra money on the side."

By the Victim.   Victims saw us as part of the hospital system. Despite our careful explanations, our exact training and position were not always understood. Victims called us, or asked us if we were, social workers, "workers," psychiatrists, "shrinks," doctors, counselors, or religious women. Several asked if we were rape victims ourselves.

In general, victims accepted our presence. Almost all were willing to talk to us at the hospital and 85 percent talked to us on follow-up as well. Those who went to court let us go with them. A few victims did not want to see us or were outraged by our presence. One told us so in no uncertain terms, shouting at us to go away. She later telephoned us and talked to us, but still maintained her hostile style.

By the Criminal Justice Personnel.   People in the criminal justice system perceived us as being associated with the hospital and "helping victims." They asked us to read semilegible words on medical records to them and asked us questions about how the hospital worked, thinking that we should know. Police and district attorneys often helped us by putting a victim in touch with us or letting us know when a case was going to be heard.

Defense lawyers were the least enthusiastic about our presence. Some did not seem to mind, but others put up barriers. Occasionally one raised—unsuccessfully—a formal objection to the judge about our presence. One or two seemed greatly displeased by the fact that we remained; a nurse at the hospital, for example, briefly dated the defense lawyer in one of the cases we were following and told us he complained to her at great length about our presence in the courtroom.

Several defense lawyers tried to use us against the victim. One defense lawyer told the jury we had put the victim up to testifying. Another subpoenaed one of us to testify in superior court about what occurred in district court. Still others tried to make us divulge information about the victim to them.

Effect of Our Presence on the Research Findings

Effect on Psychological Trauma and Dehumanization.   We presumably lessened the amount of psychological trauma and dehumanization that occurred. First, we provided crisis intervention counseling to the rape victim.

The point of doing such counseling was to try to prevent long-term psychiatric problems from developing. Psychological and psychiatric theory as well as case histories of untreated rape cases suggest that if the victim does not deal emotionally with the rape at the time it will stay with her as an unresolved issue—she will continue to carry it with her. Second, as time went on, we possibly lessened the amount of dehumanization that occurred. For example, as the year went on, the nurses became more and more interested in the project. As they saw what we did, their behavior sometimes changed. For example, a nurse might be more apt to go out of her way to make sure that a victim did not get left alone.

This influence is important to keep in mind in interpreting the findings reported in this book. It means that, if anything, our data and analysis of the institutional victimization of victims *understate* rather than overstate the problem.

Effect on Legal Outcome.   We tried to be alert to what impact, if any, we were having on how far a case went legally, the verdict, or the sentence. We did not wish to have any impact on the legal outcome of the cases we observed. However, we think that our presence as researchers did affect the result in a small number of cases.

A few cases went further in the legal system than they would have without our presence. We never put any pressure on a victim to press or not press charges. We explicitly told victims that we would support whichever decision they made. However, we think that a few victims might not have been willing to testify if they had not had someone such as us to talk to about their emotional reactions. For example, in one referral case the victim came to us because she was in a state of psychological crisis over court. She had testified and the case resulted in a mistrial. She was terribly torn between wanting to forget the whole thing and wanting to testify at a second trial so that the assailant would not go free. She came to us for help, and presumably having someone to talk to made it possible for her to pursue the case. She told the district attorney she would testify again, the case went into plea bargaining, and a conviction was obtained. Also, in a few cases police officers told us they pursued a case farther than they normally would have because they knew we were interested in helping the victim. This influence also is important to keep in mind in interpreting the results of our study. Our data show a high attrition rate and a low conviction rate. Without our presence, if anything, the attrition rate would have been even higher and the conviction rate even lower.

We do not think we influenced the verdict in any trial. We did testify three times, but fortunately the questions put to us were innocuous and the testimony we gave did not seem to become an issue in the trial. References to us never seemed to become a focal point in any trial.

We do not think we had much influence on the sentencing. Twice after a case was heard, the judge asked us what we thought should be done with the defendant. In each case, we recommended psychiatric care along with whatever decision the court might make regarding imprisonment. However, in neither of these cases did the court's ruling touch upon the issue of psychiatric intervention.

MUTUAL EXCHANGE BETWEEN OBSERVER AND OBSERVED

The older model of doing research was for an investigator to arrive someplace—at a community, an institution, or wherever—and then to collect data, leave, and write up the findings without ever giving anything back to the people who were studied. Increasingly, the public has become sophisticated about the process that researchers use. As a result, people studied now often believe that research should not be just a one-way street with the investigator taking all and giving nothing in return. Fortunately, in this project we were able to give something to many of the people studied in exchange for their cooperation.

With victims, we exchanged counseling for information. Victims, by telling us their experiences, provided us with much of the raw data for our research. In return, we provided them with crisis intervention counseling. This was a nonmonetary exchange. We neither paid victims nor did anyone pay for our services.

With the hospital, we exchanged our consulting services for permission to work on the emergency wards. This exchange also was nonmonetary. The hospital gave us access to a population of patients. In return, a year later we trained staff nurses to do victim counseling and we still act as unpaid consultants to the Victim Counseling Program.

THE EXPERIENCE OF INTERDISCIPLINARY RESEARCH

Can a sociologist and a psychiatric nurse work together? In the beginning, we did not know if we could. We came to the project with very different backgrounds.[10] Holmstrom brought to the project training in sociology and anthropology, research experience analyzing the careers of professional couples, an interest in the sociology of the professions and medical sociology, a knowledge of feminist literature, and experience in the women's movement. Burgess, in contrast, brought training in nursing and psychiatric care, previous work with a wide range of emotional problems including suicide, depression, and drug abuse, knowledge of long-term and short-term psychotherapy as well as crisis intervention counseling, and experience in many hospitals, in private practice, and in the training of other clinicians.

We each had to learn the language, concepts, and methods of the other. Basically, we taught each other the relevant aspects of our respective fields. Holmstrom initially felt uncomfortable asking interview questions that might make a person cry, not realizing that such release might have a therapeutic effect; would never have considered touching a patient and was shocked to observe Burgess walk in and comfort a sobbing victim by the laying on of hands; was not attuned to making certain types of bodily observations—for example, did not know what drug trace marks, cigarette burns, or razor scars from suicide attempts looked like; was less conscious of the need to remember types of medication prescribed; observed but did not realize the psychiatric significance of certain types of behavior—for example, a patient huddled over and rocking back and forth; did not know what to do when a victim expressed suicidal thoughts; and felt anxious when interviewing a rape victim who was also a chronic psychotic and actively hallucinating. Burgess initially was unfamiliar with the methods of participant-observation fieldwork; was not accustomed to recording raw data in the fantastically detailed and meticulous way that good field notes require; was less practiced in using open-ended interviews as a basis for later developing interview guides; had given less thought to the variety of life-styles that victims might have; was less attuned to making systematic observations about the structure of institutions and the way patients would react to different occupational groups; and was less aware of why it would be important to follow victims to court and make observations in that setting too. Thus we found it necessary to teach each other these respective items. By a process of mutual education we each expanded our range of skills and our conceptual framework. And by a process of countless discussions, we came to make analytical sense out of our data. The resulting conceptualization—for example, the typology of sexual victimization described below—is very much a joint product.

TYPOLOGY OF SEXUAL VICTIMIZATION

Rape, Accessory-to-Sex, and Sex-Stress

As we listened to victims admitted to the hospital with a complaint of rape, we began to realize that these cases were not all alike. We then spent considerable time trying to think of what made them different and what criterion would be useful for separating them into subtypes. In doing this analysis we utilized two main sources of ideas—the existing literature and our data. We were aware of the importance that the literature we read and the legal system we observed place on *consent* in defining rape. As we reviewed what victims had told us, it became clear that the cases were not all the same as regards consent. They fell, instead, into three groups.

First, a large group of victims clearly did not consent to the sex. The sexual acts were against their will and they were forced by the assailant to do them. We labeled these cases rape.

Second, another group of victims, often children, did not have the cognitive or personality development to be able to consent or not consent. They therefore aided or contributed in a secondary manner to the sexual activity. The main person involved, the assailant, stood in a relationship of power over the secondary person, the victim, because of being older, being an authority figure, or for some other reason. The assailant then gained access to the victim by pressuring her to take material goods (candy or money); pressured her to accept human contact (if she was extremely socially deprived); or pressured her to believe the sexual activity was appropriate, enjoyable, and not counter to the norms in the community. We labeled these cases *accessory-to-sex.*

A third group showed still another type of victimization. These were cases in which the male and female initially agreed to have sexual relations, but then something "went wrong." Usually what went wrong was that the male exploited this agreement—became violent, demanded acts the female considered perverse, robbed her, or, if a financial contract for sex had been made, failed to pay. In some cases, what went wrong was that the parents or other authority figures came upon the consenting couple and defined it as rape or caused the female to say it was rape as a way out of getting caught. And in some cases, the person who said she was raped actually just wanted some service from the hospital (such as a morning-after pill) that she felt she could not directly ask for. We labeled these cases as *sex-stress.*

Choosing Labels

We had to decide what to call the different types of victimization. Creating the categories did not automatically commit us to any particular word for each one. In selecting terms, we were guided by two aims. The first was to select words that would reflect the essence of the category. We utilized the term *rape* for the first category since it is widely accepted that this term means sex without consent. We developed the term *accessory-to-sex* for the second type because in each of these cases the victim contributed to the incident in a secondary way, that is, as an accessory. And we thought of the term *sex-stress* for the third kind because we wanted to show that these victims, even though they consented to sex, did later find themselves in a sexual situation that was stressful to them.

Second, we gave considerable thought to the connotations of the labels we chose. All terms have value connotations and it is impossible to avoid implying judgments. No term is neutral. However, we tried to pick labels that would not be a "put-down" for the victim. We could, for example, have used the term *false-accusation* cases instead of *sex-stress*. After all, these victims claimed rape even though they had consented. However, as we looked at the data again we realized that these persons were victims too, although of a different set of circumstances, and that they too had a request to make of the emergency ward. Since we wanted to present the situations from the viewpoint of the victim, we chose to call this group *sex-stress* cases. This term does not define the statement made by the victim in a negative manner but describes instead the situation the victim was in.

Obsession with the "Legitimate" Case

In the chapters that follow, we will be referring to people as rape, accessory, or sex-stress victims. Our main focus will be on the rape cases. However, it is important to understand the other types of victims too because of their impact on how the system deals with rape. Staff expend much energy trying to determine whether—to use their words—a case is "legitimate." In other words, they constantly wonder whether the person in question was really raped. Knowing that other types of victims present themselves to authorities with a complaint of rape makes staff suspicious of all victims. Furthermore, these other victims are of interest in themselves. They too are making requests of the system. They too want something from the hospital and from the criminal justice system.

NOTES

1. Exceptions would include Clifford Kirkpatrick and Eugene Kanin, "Male Sex Aggression on a University Campus," *American Sociological Review* 22 (February 1957), pp. 52-58; and Randall Collins, "A Conflict Theory of Sexual Stratification," *Social Problems* 19 (Summer 1971), pp. 3-21.
2. For exceptions see John H. Gagnon, "Female Child Victims of Sex Offenses," *Social Problems* 13 (Fall 1965), pp. 176-79.
3. Paul H. Gebhard, et al., *Sex Offenders* (New York: Harper & Row, 1965).
4. Menachem Amir, *Patterns in Forcible Rape* (Chicago: University of Chicago Press, 1971).
5. For an example of an early victim program see Charles R. Hayman et al., "A Public Health Program for Sexually Assaulted Females, *Public Health Reports* 82 (June 1967), pp. 497-

504; Charles R. Hayman, et al. "Rape in the District of Columbia," *American Journal of Obstetrics and Gynecology* 113 (May 1, 1972), pp. 91-97.

6. Almost all were complaints of completed forcible rapes, although some were of attempted forcible rape or molestation.

7. For a discussion and example of the participant-observation approach, see the study by Hughes and his colleagues of medical student culture, Howard S. Becker et al., *Boys in White: Student Culture in Medical School* (Chicago: University of Chicago Press, 1961). For examples of the usefulness of this method as applied to the study of courtroom procedure and the hospital, see Robert M. Emerson, *Judging Delinquents: Context and Process in Juvenile Court* (Chicago: Aldine, 1969); Stephen J. Miller, *Prescription for Leadership: Training for the Medical Elite* (Chicago: Aldine, 1970); and Nancy Stoller Shaw, *Forced Labor: Maternity Care in the United States* (New York: Pergamon, 1974).

8. Ann Wolbert Burgess and Lynda Lytle Holmstrom, *Rape: Victims of Crisis* (Bowie: Md: Robert J. Brady, 1974), pp. 127-41.

9. Stephen A. Richardson, Barbara Snell Dohrenwend, and David Klein, *Interviewing: Its Forms and Functions* (New York: Basic Books, 1965), p. 45.

10. For discussions of the experiences of interdisciplinary research teams, see Elizabeth Bott, *Family and Social Network*, (London: Tavistock Publications, 1957), pp. 30-39; Raymond S. Duff and August B. Hollingshead, *Sickness and Society*, (New York: Harper & Row, 1968), pp. 11-13.

CHAPTER 3

■

Entering the Criminal Justice System

It will be hell [pressing charges]
if they catch him and hell wor-
rying if they don't.

RAPE VICTIM

Rape cases are the worst. . . .
The girls won't go through
[court] or else things are so
tough . . . the case isn't given a
conviction

POLICE OFFICER

The act of reporting a rape starts in motion a complicated process.[1] A number of institutions immediately swing into action. There are many stages and the victim may drop out at any one of them. But frequently she finds herself swept along by the day-to-day workings of these institutions. She finds she is caught up in a protocol that is routine to the authorities since it constitutes their daily work, but new to her and thus not fully understood by her. At the very least, she will be questioned by authorities and her statement, describing what is often one of the more painful and embarrassing moments in her life, will be forever recorded in official files. These things may not be done exactly against her will. But still, more may be done to her than she bargained for. It thus becomes especially important to learn how she became involved in the process.

REPORTING THE RAPE[2]

To understand how a rape gets reported, one must look not only at the victim herself, but at her social network and at the community. A striking finding in the present study of reported rapes is the degree to which people

Table 1. *Who Reported the Rape to the Police (by Age of Victim)*

Who Contacts Police			Age of Victim		
			Adult Victims 17 and over	Preadult Victims 16 and under	Total
Someone other than victim makes decision to contact police, acts as intermediary, or gives advice			57	21	78
	Adult Victims	*Preadult Victims*			
Member of victim's social network contacts police	26	18			
Stranger contacts police	22	3			
Network's advice leads to victim contacting police	9	0			
Victim herself contacts police on own initiative			22	2	24
Rape never reported to police			6	0	6
Other			1	0	1
No data			8	0	8
Total			94*	23	117*

*Total includes one victim counted twice because she was raped in two separate incidents during the study and one victim counted twice because her rape was reported independently two different ways.

other than the victim are involved in the chain of events leading her to the police. In more than half the adult cases,[3] someone other than the victim was involved in reporting the rape to the police: someone other than the victim made the decision to contact the police, acted as intermediary at the request of the victim, or persuaded the victim herself to call. (see Table 1).

In the confusion surrounding a rape, it is hard to determine exactly who makes the decision to notify the police. However, it is clear that in a considerable number of cases people took it upon themselves to make the decision *for* the victim. Sometimes they simply assumed she would approve. For example, in one case as soon as the assailant left through the backdoor, the woman, who was hysterical, ran to her neighbor for help; the neighbor simply went ahead and called the police. Sometimes a person explicitly went counter to the victim's will, as in the following case.

> As soon as we got to [the hospital, he] marched up to a police car that was sitting in the emergency ward yard and said, "Sir, my girl friend has just been raped." [How did you feel about that?] I was furious. I didn't want to report it and to have him do it really made me angry.

Sometimes tactics of persuasion were used. The nine cases in this category are especially interesting because they show the long and twisting path a victim may travel before deciding to report the crime inflicted upon her. One such woman spoke as follows:

> I walked into the apartment, took off my coat, and told my roommate. . . . When I told her, she was freaked out. We went to a friend's home. . . . The home is in the woods and we sat there and talked about what I should do. It reminded me of Vermont and the woods. It was very peaceful there. We came back to the city and went to the Women's Center to discuss what to do. They advised reporting it to the police and coming to the hospital. At the Center I was emotional and crying. I thought coming to the hospital was a good idea, but wasn't certain about the police.

The victim eventually did come to the hospital. Two friends came with her. While there, she talked with a police officer.

Often it is someone in the victim's social network—family or friends—who contacts the police, as the above cases illustrate. But almost equally often it is a stranger, someone in the community whom the victim happens to run into after the rape or who has heard the victim scream. In the following case, it is a cab driver who "knows what to do":

> [The assailant] let me out of the car near Symphony Road. Up to then I had been very calm and cool. But as soon as I got out of the car I went to pieces—got sort of hysterical. A cab was passing and the cab driver helped me. I was crying and I told him what happened and asked him what should I do and he said that I should go to the police and so he took me there.

Only a minority of women in our study contacted the police completely on their own (see Table 1). Some acted decisively right away. One tricked her assailants and called while they were still there:

> There was a telephone in the bedroom. So while they were in the living room I said I had to check the baby. I picked up the phone and dialed 911, told the police I was raped, and gave them the address and apartment number.

Others hesitated and took a while to collect their thoughts. One said:

> He told me to stay in the bathroom. I waited 'til I was sure he was gone. . . . I heard the window go up. . . . I passed out on the bathroom floor. . . . I woke up and I wondered if I had dreamt it all. Then I realized I was on the floor and realized I didn't. I went into the bedroom and saw mud on the carpet [that he tracked in]. But I didn't want to seem like an idiot and call the police if nothing happened. I decided it had happened and to call them.

And another said, "I didn't know if I should call the police. I wasn't injured. . . . I never had to call the police before for anything."

The preadult victims showed an even more pronounced pattern of network involvement than the adult cases. In almost all the young cases, someone other than the victim made the decision to contact the police or acted as intermediary. Most of the time it was a family member—parent, sibling, or grandparent—who called. The young victim returned home and either told what happened or, as in the following case, showed by her appearance that something had happened:

> She was out walking the dog. . . . She didn't come in. She came in screaming three hours later. . . . Had marks on her neck. . . . It was horrible.

Here, the grandmother notified the police. In a few cases, a stranger made the report—for example, after hearing a child's screams. In only two cases, did a young victim reach the police completely on her own; these two victims were 16 years old and flagged down police cars on the street.

The hesitation of many victims and the tendency for friends and family to discuss whether to report the rape can be discouraging and sometimes bewildering to the police. They cannot do their work unless the rape gets reported. They also know that any delay "looks bad" in court. Some members of the criminal justice system have even labeled victims "collaborators" when they did not immediately report the crime.

Socially and psychologically, however, the need of many victims in the present study to seek out others for support or for advice makes sense. Talk of "mass society" may have led us to think of people as isolated individuals.

But in fact numerous sociological studies confirm the continuing importance of the primary group—that is, the importance of informal, interpersonal relations. Studies show the influence of the primary group in such diverse areas of activity as the production rates of workers in the factory, the combat motivation of the soldier, the way people confer status in the community, and how people respond to the mass media.[4] It is not surprising that it should turn out to be important for the rape victim as well. It is not surprising that the way victims deal with the crime inflicted upon them—including the decision about whether to report it—is influenced by their social network.

Psychologically, turning to others for support or advice makes sense, too. Rape victims typically experience rape as an attack that threatens their very lives.[5] As a result, they are in a psychological state of crisis. They have experienced an overwhelming danger that they could neither escape at the time nor solve with their customary psychological resources.[6] People in crisis typically have difficulty making any decisions at all. It is thus understandable that victims should turn to others. One might add that some victims of rape also are physically incapable of making a decision. The assailant may have beaten them so badly that their faculties are not completely available to them—a fact not always appreciated by professionals, as a case history in the next chapter on the hospital will indicate.

Many writers have stated that rape reportage rates are low and have speculated on reasons why. Recently, there have been some systematic investigations of factors affecting the decision to report or not report a rape. Smith and Nelson, working with a sample of victims, first excluded those under age 18 and those whose victimizations were reported to the police by someone else. Looking at the 49 remaining cases they found that the probability the victim would report the rape varied directly with the amount of danger to the victim during the rape, social distance between offender and victim, and perceived probability of compensation from significant others for reporting. Nonreporting was apt to occur among victims whose offenders were acquaintances, of approximately the same age and social class, and who did not use a weapon or commit another crime at the same time. This nonreporting "illustrates the widespread internalization among the sample of cultural stereotypes which tend to legitimate rape to the extent that appropriate reportage responses are forgone."[7]

THE POLICE ENCOUNTER

The police typically are the first officials that a victim of a reported rape encounters. Being interviewed by the police is an important step in the victim's career through the criminal justice system. The nature of the material that is discussed—the details of an extremely frightening and humiliating sexual experience—mean that the encounter may be unsettling for many victims even under the best of circumstances.

The Interview

The questions police were observed to ask fall into three categories. Most often police interviews focus on "who-what-when-where" questions: Where did it happen, who was there, what time was it when you got in the car, what happened, what time did they let you go. Second, police frequently ask questions about any relationship or agreement between the victim and assailant: "You went there with him?" "Did you and he have an 'arrangement'?" Third, they may ask questions about the victim's background: "Were you ever in a hospital?" In addition, they sometimes make statements impressing upon the victim the seriousness of the charge she is making. It is a "cooling out" tactic since in context the implication is that maybe the victim should not make such a charge. It is a test of the strength of her motivation.

The style of the questioning, however, is as much a component of the interview as are the particular questions that are asked. The police officers observed in the present study were all male. The demeanor of these officers ranged from low-key and nonjudgmental to harsh and moralistic. This range is broader than that observed by Sanders among detectives. He states, "During the period of observation of rape investigations, I never did observe a detective be anything other than gentle, discreet, and 'understanding' during sessions when he talked with victims."[8] Sanders notes that this approach may have been simply a practical one to elicit information. Police occupational culture emphasizes the practical accomplishment of goals and hence "mistreatment of rape victims is simply bad police work."[9] However, he also notes that a lack of sympathy would go against the police's public statements claiming a concern for the victims of crime.

The way the officer chooses to begin the interview is extremely important. His opening statement is of crucial importance in setting the tone. Some officers begin the interview with a statement designed to put the victim at ease. They begin with a brief explanation of why they need to ask the questions. It is their way of trying to help the victim "make sense" of what they are going to do. For example, one officer began by saying, "I need to know some information about what happened. And I have to ask some questions." Or they begin by saying they have heard these kinds of things before. It is their way of acknowledging to the victim that they realize that the interview may be embarrassing for her. For example, one officer began by saying, "I've been doing this for many years and have heard these kinds of things before. I'm here to help you." Other officers, in contrast, simply start asking questions without any introductory comments.

The police interviews of Veronica and of Melissa provide examples of all three types of questions that may be asked, as well as the importance of the demeanor of the officers. Veronica, age 28, was interviewed at the hospital by a sergeant in a very low-key tone of voice:

Sergeant:	What happened?
Veronica:	It was one o'clock. There were three or four guys. Only one attacked me in the car—the guy wearing a multicolored shirt.
Sergeant:	Have you seen him before?
Veronica:	I saw him before at [the bar]. But I didn't speak to him. I saw him a long time ago, too.
Sergeant:	Was the multicolored-shirt one the ringleader?
Veronica:	Yes.
Sergeant:	Was there a weapon?
Veronica:	No.
Sergeant:	Did you accept a date with him?
Veronica:	No.
Sergeant:	Was there conversation?
Veronica:	No.
Sergeant:	Where did all this take place?
Veronica:	In the car.
Sergeant:	It must have been a big car. I see you have some scars there—burns?
Veronica:	Yes.
Sergeant:	Were you ever in a hospital?
Veronica:	No, except four months for burns.
Sergeant:	Can you tell me anything else that would help me?

The case of Melissa provides an illustration of a more overbearing approach by police officers.

Melissa, age 20, was taken back to the police station after leaving the hospital. The detectives sent out for coffee for everyone and then began to interview the victim. Detective Paley asked Melissa about the incident. He spent quite a bit of time getting her to talk about the unnatural act that had occurred; she said she was embarrassed, but she finally did talk about it. There was discussion about why she went with the assailant. The detective then went on to ask questions about her background, including a prior rape.

Detective:	Have you ever tried committing suicide?
Melissa:	Yes, I took pills right after my mother died.

Detective:	Is the scar on your wrist from the suicide attempt?
Melissa:	No, it's from the [first] rape.
Detective:	Did you try to commit suicide after the rape?
Melissa:	No, [the scar] was part of the rape.
Detective:	Have you run away from home?
Melissa:	No, not now. When I was age 13 I did.
Detective:	You take drugs?
Melissa:	No. I tried them once.
Detective:	What did you take?
Melissa:	"Ups."
Detective:	Ever been in a hospital?
Melissa:	Yes.
Detective:	What for?
Melissa:	Abcess.
Second *Detective:*	You know, it's a life sentence for this.

In both interviews, the officers asked about the incident, the relationship to the assailant, and the victim's background. But the tone and the demeanor of the officers was very different. In the first case, the officer was low-key and ended the interview with a supportive question. In the second, the officers asked more confronting questions specifically about her past behavior in a way that sounded abrasive to the listener. They also ended the interview with a statement about the most severe consequences possible for the assailant; they seemed intent to impress upon her the assailant's side and thus test the strength of her motivation.

The Police Officer's Evaluation of the Case

Professionals tend to categorize clients, preferring to work with some types more than others. They hold an image of a set of characteristics that would comprise the "ideal client," as well as what characteristics make a client less desirable. This sorting occurs whatever the profession, be it teaching, medicine, nursing, or any other. Everett Hughes called attention to the process in his studies of occupations. Writing of the medical situation, he states:

> There are conceptions of the ideal patient: about what is wrong with him, about his social and economic characteristics, about his acceptance of the physician's authority and prescriptions, his understanding, his co-operation and his gratitude.[10]

Hughes has urged those who wish to understand *any* occupation to ask what clients are considered the most desirable. Numerous studies have confirmed the importance of looking at this issue.[11] If such a sorting process occurred with police and rape victims, too, it would not be surprising. And indeed, our data show that such a sorting does occur—although it is a far more complicated process than the mass media accounts of rape would have one believe.

Are Rape Victims Less Desirable than Other Victims?   The police treatment of rape victims has received much publicity in the mass media. The stereotype is that police find something especially distasteful about rape victims as compared to victims of other crimes. Supposedly, they typically say victims were asking for it, make moralistic and negative comments about victims, and do not believe their claims.

Table 2. Police Reaction to Victim by Type of Case

Police Reaction	Type of Case						Total
	Adult Rape	Preadult Rape	Adult Accessory	Preadult Accessory	Adult Sex-Stress	Preadult Sex-Stress	
Positive	32	9	0	3	2	4	50
Mixed	4	0	0	0	1	1	6
Reservations	6	2	2	0	5	1	16
Negative	9	5	0	1	2	1	18
Total	51	16	2	4	10	7	90

To see whether this image held up in fact, we rated—whenever possible—the police in their "overall" response to each victim in the sample who came to the hospital with a complaint of rape. Police were not always on the scene or available for comment. However, sufficient data were gathered on 90 of the 146 cases of sexual assault to make a rating. Four categories of response were developed: (1) *positive* (police were polite and showed some sympathy for the victim's situation, listened seriously to her claim of rape, and did not make any derogatory comments about her); (2) *mixed* (one officer was positive and another negative, or the same officer expressed both positive and negative responses); (3) *had reservations about the case* (talked in a matter-of-fact way, rather than a moralistic way, about it being a weak case; said it was an emotional problem rather than a police problem; or said it was some kind of crime other than a sex crime); (4)

negative (showed complete lack of sympathy for the victim's situation, did not take seriously the claim of rape, or made derogatory and moralistic comments about the victim.[12]

The stereotype of the police as antirape victim does not gain much support from the data. Negative reactions by police were observed, but their occurrence was not as frequent as the stereotype would lead one to believe. Looking at the totals for the rape, accessory-to-sex, and sex-stress cases combined, one sees that in slightly more than half the cases the police responded positively, and in only one-fifth did they respond negatively (see Table 2).

Although negative responses are in the minority, one should not gloss over the fact that they do exist. The fact remains that one-fifth of the time, officers' responses to victims who said they had been raped were negative. These instances have an influence far beyond their numbers. *These* are the cases that one *hears* about. It is the "horror stories" that make interesting news. Thus, these are the cases that help perpetuate a negative image of the police and contribute to the reluctance of victims to report the crime inflicted upon them. As one victim told us, "In a way, I think I should have gone to the police. But I had heard stories about how the police treat women. I've seen TV and read stories that really scared me."

Police Response by Type of Case.   It is also of interest to look at the police response by type of case: rape, accessory-to-sex, and sex-stress, as well as age (see Table 2). It should be emphasized that these are categories *we* developed. They are not identical with the ones the police use. Later we discuss a typology police themselves use in differentiating cases.

Looking at adult rape victims, in almost two-thirds of the cases the police responded positively to the victim. For example, in one such case, the officer treated the woman as follows:

> The officer who brought her to the hospital came and got her after the medical exam. He was an older man—in his fifties—and very paternal. He put his arm around her and asked how she was. He said they would talk to her and help her all they could.[13]

In approximately one-fifth of the adult rapes, the police responded negatively. For example, in one case the officer—learning of our interest in the emotional problems after rape—said:

> This girl won't have any problems. . . . [It's not right] for a girl to go into a stranger's apartment, drink beer, and then be upset when the guy makes advances.

In another case the officer said loudly, with derision and contempt in his voice, "Her boyfriend did it. He rapes her every Monday, Wednesday, and Friday—when she wants it."

In half the preadult rape cases, the police responded positively. Their reaction was especially positive as the age of the child decreased. In one case, the victim was 13 but looked even younger. The police officer stationed at the hospital said, "I called you right away—even before calling the doctor." He commented on her age and said, "It's different if it's an old married woman of 22." And in the case of a 5-year-old girl, both hospital staff and police were somewhat shaken. They seemed impressed both by the victim's tender years and the extent of the phyiscal damage done. The officer who came to collect her clothes for evidence said, "God help us." The nurse broke the tension, saying, *"He* needs the valium."[14] The five young rape cases where the police reacted negatively were all teenagers, 15 to 16 years old. All had considerable freedom to be out on their own at night. And the police raised questions of being "promiscuous" or "asking for it" or of "being drunk." For example, in one case the police officer telephoned the victim's mother from the hospital and said, "I think your daughter is asking for it." In another case the police told us they responded to the call but that both the victim and the man "were incoherent and not cooperating" with them. They planned on talking later with the victim's mother and said, "We hope they all have sobered up a bit [by then]."

The reaction of police to adult accessory-to-sex cases is of interest. These two cases were women who we—the researchers—thought were incapable of making a judgment of consent. They were so impoverished socially and emotionally that the mere hope of minimal contact with another human being was enough to let them drift from man to man—any man, no matter how abusive. In these cases the police response was a rather matter-of-fact statement that the woman had not been raped and that it was an emotional problem rather than a police problem. In one case the victim came in and said she had been raped. The officer interviewed her at the hospital in a very calm, low-key manner and tried for some time to get a coherent story from her. He became somewhat frustrated in his efforts since her story kept changing (we heard at least four versions) and she was vague about the details. After talking to her, he spoke to us rather matter of factly as follows:

> Does she have a psychiatric history? She's changing her story. She's lying. She's vague. . . . [That bar] is a rough place—no Caucasians go there. . . . Has she a mental history? Maybe suicidal. She needs help.

His perceptions were accurate. She did have a long psychiatric history (although she would not admit it to him), did change her story, was vague, told of two suicide attempts, gave numerous other examples of self-destructive behavior, had been at a notoriously rough bar frequented mainly by racial groups other than her own, and by current clinical standards certainly did need help.

In the adult sex-stress[15] cases, the most common police reaction was to express reservations. Police were apt to say it was another crime (e.g., assault), but not rape. In one sex-stress incident, the victims were two prostitutes who had been subjected to violence and to acts they regarded as perverted. The following scene occurred when the policeman came to the hospital to get them.

> [They're in the waiting room. Do you know them—know what they look like?] I know them well. (slight laugh). They work the street—Park Square and when it gets hot there, they move to Boylston, and when it gets hot there, they go back to Park Square. How badly were they assaulted? [We weren't the ones who did the medical exam—we just talked to them.] I want to know so I can tell the sergeant.

He said that what had been done to the women by the men was definitely illegal. Sometimes police were especially harsh in an adult sex-stress case. In one incident, the police were openly hostile as they interviewed the victim at the hospital. Afterward, the officer, explaining why it was not a reportable case of rape, said in a disparaging tone of voice:

> She's a known prostitute and junkie. She stated she took drugs with her consent prior to the experience. She didn't struggle. She knew the men and the woman involved. Her facts kept changing.

In preadult sex-stress cases, the most common police response was positive. Presumably one reason for this reaction is that in most of these cases one does not have to raise the issue of consent. The victim's age alone makes it a crime. It is a statutory, even if not forcible, rape.

The Ideal Rape Victim. Police officers differ in the degree of enthusiasm they express for pursuing cases legally. This response is somewhat different from their overall reaction and demeanor described above. For example, an officer can express sympathy for the victim's situation, listen to her claim seriously, not make any derogatory comments about her, but still not see it as a rape case worth pursuing through the courts.

Police officers do not see all claims of rape as being equal. Instead they have in their minds an image of what constitutes the ideal rape victim—the ideal client—and what constitutes an ideal rape case. Police officers themselves speak of cases as being "strong" or "weak," or sometimes of being "good" or "weak." By keeping track of all the comments they made and the questions they asked as they began their investigations, it was possible to see what criteria they used in making this distinction. The criteria fall into four types: (1) the quality and consistency of the information they can obtain, (2) the characteristics of the victim—her behavior and her moral character, (3) the relationship between victim and offender, and (4) characteristics of the offender.

First, police look at the quality and consistency of the information they can get. To be strong, the case cannot rest on the victim's statement alone. Instead, there must be corroborating evidence. Furthermore, there cannot be inconsistencies. Police look to see if the information from the woman "checks out." Describing a strong case officers will say, "everything fits together so well." Conversely, describing a weak case, officers say, "She used a fake name. She's a runaway. . . . Everything she said was a bunch of lies." Police also like to have witnesses—especially police witnesses—to the crime. In one case, the officers arrived while the assailant was still at the scene and were so enthusiastic they said, "We'll testify even if the girl doesn't." Police hope the victim can provide a good description of the assailant or of his belongings, such as his car. One officer told a victim, "You got the license number, right? . . . We've got a good case." In another instance the officer said it was a good case because "the girl had a length of time to really observe the guy" and gave a "complete physical description," including a tattoo she saw while he was naked. Officers look for corroborating medical evidence. The question they ask again and again of physicians is, "Was there penetration?" And they ask if sperm were found. One officer said of a case, "The medical report is good. It's positive for sperm." They are also interested in injuries. The thing officers seem most impressed with, however, is a consistent and unchanging story. One officer gave a victim the highest possible praise by saying, "Even when you ask her the questions differently, she gives the same story. She knows what happened." The worst thing a victim can do is change her story. Any change makes the case weak. In one instance, the victim's statement to the district attorney differed from what she had told the police. The victim divulged to the district attorney that the assailant actually had raped her not once but twice. The police officer, upon hearing this, was so highly antagonized that the district attorney had to calm him down.

Second, police officers look at characteristics of the victim—her behavior and her moral character. In a strong case, the victim was forced to accompany the assailant, and in a weak one, she accompanied him willingly or asked him to accompany her. One officer said of a victim, "She won't have much of a chance in court. I doubt if it will get to court. . . . She invited him to stay over." A case is strong if the victim was not exposing herself to risk. An example is the victim of whom an officer said, "Here you have a girl minding her own business, going into her own apartment." A case is weak if she was taking chances. In one instance the officer said, "She does not have a good case. . . . She was hitchhiking. . . . The judge will not look with favor [on that]." A case is especially strong if the victim was a virgin and weak if she is unmarried but sexually experienced. Describing the merits of one case, the officer explained, "She's been playing house since she was nine." A case is strong if the victim is sober, but weak if she was drinking or high on drugs. A case is strong if the victim is stable emotionally, but weak if she has "emotional problems"—if she's "not all there," has a psychiatric history, was a runaway, or attempted suicide. A case is strong if the woman is upset ("She's shook up"), but weak if she is not ("She's too unconcerned"). An officer comparing the relative merits of two cases said, "This is a stronger case than the [other] one. . . . [Here] the victim was shook up."

Third, police look at the relationship between victim and offender. They ask whether she "knew the guy." It is a strong case if the assailant is a stranger. One officer told a victim, "You didn't know the guy, right? We've got a good case." Officers are also impressed with the relative ages of victim and assailant, especially in cases where the victim and assailant know each other. If, for example, both are teenagers with only a year or so difference in their ages, the police may not be too enthusiastic. But if the victim is in her early teens or younger, and the assailant in his twenties or thirties, the police are more enthusiastic about pursuing the case.

Fourth, police look at characteristics of the offender. Nothing makes them more enthusiastic about a case than to find out the assailant has other charges against him or a prison record. In one case where the assailants had a series of rape and robbery charges against them, the police were positively gleeful about making the arrest. The officers kept saying, "They're going away for a long time." In another case, the assailant had one rape but many armed robbery charges against him; the police said, "We're glad to get him and stop all the robberies." In another, the assailant not only had a rape charge but a charge of armed robbery on a male victim who was severely injured during the crime. In the latter incident, a knife was thrown into the victim's back, breaking two ribs and puncturing a lung. The victim was taken to the hospital where a team of surgeons worked on him. Complications occurred, and he was in the hospital a month and had a medical record "an inch thick." The robbery victim and the rape victim both made a positive identification of the assailant. The police were anxious to see him sent away and kept saying, "He's really a goner."

In summary, police have in their minds an image of the ideal rape victim and the ideal rape case. They are most enthusiastic about legally pursuing a "strong" case. Putting their criteria together into an "ideal type" composite, the perfect case would be one in which all the information checks out, there are police witnesses to the crime, the victim can provide a good description

of the assailant, there is supporting medical evidence including sperm and
injuries, the story remains completely consistent and unchanging, the victim is forced to accompany the assailant, was previously minding her own
business, a virgin, sober, stable emotionally, upset by the rape, did not
know the offender, and the assailant has a prison record and a long list of
current charges against him.

The Police Officer's Concerns

Much publicity recently has been given to the emotional difficulties rape
victims face in dealing with the police. But the emotional difficulties the
police face in dealing with this crime have received less attention. In addition to keeping track of police officers' reactions to and evaluations of
specific individual cases, we kept track of their comments about rape and
rape cases in general. We found that many officers have strong feelings on
the subject.

Rape Is a Heinous Crime: A Gut Reaction.   Police officers talk of rape as
being a "terrible thing." One officer who sees rape as a very traumatic experience said he treats it "as if the victim were in a state of shock." An older
officer said, "I have come to the conclusion that rape is the most heinous of
crimes." They talk of the rapists as being "perverted" or "animals." They
say, "Something is wrong with these guys," and "You don't want a guy like
that around." Some say they have difficulty understanding why men rape.
One officer commented.

> Being normal—I don't know if one can be normal after being on the force for
> so many years, but I think I'm normal—and I just don't see why they *do* it.
> They must *want* to do it. After all, they can buy it on the street.

Police officers, as should be clear from these quotes, believe in the existence of rape. And they talk of it as causing suffering. It is true that officers distinguish between "weak and strong cases" and that some go so far
as to say most claims are false. But we did not hear officers deny the existence of the possibility of rape. It is true that officers occasionally may say
a particular victim gets raped whenever she wants it. But we did not hear
them talk about rape in general as being a pleasant activity. Indeed, in looking at the police officers' comments, there is a striking *absence* of statements
to the effect that women in general want to be raped, women enjoy being
raped, and you can't rape a woman unless she wants you to. Yet, in many
other circles, such statements are common.[16]

We can only speculate on why the police take rape more seriously than many others do. We suspect it is because police officers are the one group that sees rape cases firsthand. They are often the first to arrive on the scene, occasionally even arriving while the rapist is still attacking the victim. They see with their own eyes victims screaming, bleeding, injured, sobbing, and with their clothes in disarray. Furthermore, police are the one group of people who stay with the victims as they go through the criminal justice system. Other professionals such as physicians, nurses, and district attorneys are with the victims for a few minutes or possibly a few hours. But usually the same team of police officers follows the victim through the system. They take her to the hospital, talk to her during the investigation, sit with her during parts of the long wait at the hospital or courthouse, and attend the court sessions. Thus they come to know certain individual victims better than other groups do and they also observe firsthand much of the aftermath of rape.

Officers tend to have punitive attitudes toward the rapist. Talking about what should happen to the rapist, officers often express a fantasy of what they would *like* to do to him; namely, make a direct physical attack. One said:

> You know, I have a daughter. In fact I have four daughters. If one of them had this experience . . . I would go after the man myself, maybe. And you know what I would do? I would castrate the beast. He would never do that again.

Another said, "If it was my sister, the guy would be dead already." And still another said, "I think these guys who rape should just be shot—that is my personal opinion." Others talk more of an institutional response. One said, "[Prison's] where they belong." And another—commenting on a strict decision made by a judge—said, "That's what you *want* to hear—that's a vote for law and order!" Officers are much less apt to think of rehabilitation as the solution—either because they know that in the present system little treatment exists or because they do not think treatment will work. One said:

> The state will have to spend a lot of money to bring him to court so many times. Best thing they could do with him is to shoot him while he is in jail. He is no use to anyone. [You don't think there will be any chance of rehabilitation? Will he get any therapy at all?] As much as any of them get in there— *not much!*

Another believed that psychiatry cannot help the rapist. He said, "Once the mind is damaged, it stays damaged."

Other researchers also have commented on the negative attitudes police officers hold toward persons committing sex crimes. Niederhoffer states that policemen "exhibit an exaggerated hatred of sex offenders."[17] Westley found that among policemen, sex cases were "an area of intolerance and of difficulties." Their intolerance "manifests itself in extremely rough treatment of the offender, the 'take him out in the alley and beat him up' attitude."[18] Niederhoffer, in a pilot study, asked 22 patrolmen to rank 16 major crimes with regard to seriousness. The crime they considered most serious was carnal abuse, that is, the sexual fondling of a child short of sexual intercourse. They thought such an attack on a child deserved more severe punishment than the crimes of murder or kidnapping—crimes that at the time called for the death penalty.[19]

Checking It Out: The Fear of Being Wrong.   The police officer, in deciding which cases to pursue, is putting his professional competence on the line. He is asked by the system to check out which are the "real" rapes. He is expected to make a judgment as to whether a crime has occurred (is the claim of rape indeed true). And if it has, he must make a further judgment as to whether he thinks the perpetrator of the crime can be correctly identified. The concern for "checking it out" was expressed by one officer as follows:

> I worked for several hours for [the defendant]. . . . I thought maybe she was trying to get him on something. But everything she said has checked out, so she has a good case.

In context, their fear of being wrong seems to have two components: a concern for the person who might be erroneously convicted ("Better 100 guilty persons not in jail than one innocent person in jail"), and a fear of appearing professionally incompetent ("I'm embarrassed to have that case in court").

Officers talk a lot about the ambiguity and "messiness" of rape cases, a concern that seems to be related to their fear of being wrong. They feel that in rape cases it is especially hard to make a judgment. One officer told us about discussions he has had with doctors to the effect that "if a woman has been having regular intercourse, then it's almost impossible to prove forcible entry." They talk about rape cases as being so "complicated" and as being "messy" affairs. One said:

> I prefer five clean murders to one rape case. The more you investigate and get into it, the stickier it gets. . . . Give me a murder any day rather than a rape. Murder I can understand, but I can't really understand rape.

And another said, "The biggest problem [in rape] is a lot of false accusations, and it's hard to tell who's telling the truth."

These observations on "checking it out" and mistrust of statements seem to fit with comments of other researchers. Several have noted the general skepticism of the police. Manning reports that recent studies of police occupational culture suggest that one assumption among police is that people cannot be trusted.[20] Niederhoffer notes that during an investigation the officer runs into conflicting reports of what occurred. "His wisest procedure is to trust no one. Cynicism improves his technique as an investigator."[21] Sanders has stated, "Police are skeptical of almost anything and anybody, and rape and rape victims have no special status of being the subject of such skepticism."[22] However, Sanders also notes that "unlike most other criminal investigations, the question of authenticity looms disproportionately large in cases of sexual assault."[23]

Investment of Time and Effort: It Often Comes to Naught. Police often talk of aspects of rape cases that make their efforts come to naught. One such theme is the difficulty of getting the rape victim to court. Again and again they talk of how "the girls don't show." One said:

> The girls don't want to testify. . . . We go to so much trouble to work up a case and then take it to court and the girl doesn't show and the judge gets mad and throws it out and it makes us look foolish.

Another, talking about a victim who did not want to go through the court process, said, "It is really tough on us. This is a good case." Sometimes they express their concern directly to the victim. One said to a victim, "You can't back out on me after all the work I did to arrest him." Another said, with regard to being at court, "Don't let me down."

A second, related theme is the difficulties rape cases face in the court system. Officers know that it is "hard on the girls when they get on the witness stand" and that the "questions are pretty rough." As one said, "It is like she is on trial and not the man." They acknowledge that "the victim rather gets lost" in the proceedings, and state that "no one looks at the rights of the victims." One said:

> No one cares about the victims. It is a defendant's world. . . . All the police do is bring the guys in and the judges let them walk out.

They complained about "how bad the sentencing was" in sex offense cases—meaning it was too lenient in their view.

Police officers' difficulties with the court system are reflected in the stories they choose to tell about their work. Officers often have a favorite lack-of-conviction story they like to relate. The theme in these stories concerns a case in which they were sure the woman was raped, but there was no conviction. Usually this outcome occurs because the jury would not believe the victim, sometimes because of a technicality. One officer related the following story:

> There was a case where a stewardess got raped. I'm *sure* the guy did it. But, no conviction. In court they asked her things like do you live with your parents and no, she had an apartment. They asked do you go to parties. There were objections, but the jury had already heard the question. . . . The case was dismissed.

Another told of a rape-murderer who got off on a legal technicality "even though everyone knew he was guilty."

As the above comments indicate, officers sometimes feel a sense of futility working on rape cases. One officer summarized these frustrations well:

> Rape cases are the worst. For all the work that is put into them, I only remember one prosecution [leading to conviction] in the 17 years I have been on the force. I can get cases to superior court just on my testimony. But then [either] the girls won't go through with it or else things are so tough at that level that the case isn't given a conviction.

Development of Professional Armor.   Society expects certain people to engage in work that is potentially very emotionally upsetting. Physicians perhaps have been written about in this regard more than any other group. As Parsons long ago so astutely observed, physicians are expected to deal with certain issues that have enormous potential for disturbance: sex, death, suffering, access to the body, confidential information about private lives, and uncertainty. It is Parsons's conclusion that what enables physicians to carry out this work is a set of institutionalized roles—including an expectation that physicians will be "affectively neutral"—and special mechanisms of social control.[24] Various studies have dealt with ways in which physicians and other clinicians protect themselves from the emotional onslaught of their work.[25]

Police officers, like physicians, are asked to engage in work that can be emotionally disturbing. Their involvement with rape is a good case in point. Here they must deal with sex and violence, sometimes sex and death. They see the suffering of the victim. They need access to information about the body; they must ask about the results of the pelvic examination conducted by the physician, and they must ask the victim questions such as "Did the assailant penetrate?" They must obtain information about the private lives of the victims. They need this information for investigative purposes and also for preparing the case for court. Always they are working in the realm of uncertainty—what really happened, who is telling the truth?

And indeed, it should be clear from the above quotes that officers do have strong emotional reactions to working with rape.

Thus one would expect to find institutionalized roles and social control mechanisms operating to facilitate the carrying out of police work. Professional protocol is a case in point. Parsons comments on medical protocol. He notes, for example, that physicians do not watch a woman disrobe—a process that has strong sexual connotations—but observe her only after she is disrobed and on the examining table. Various aspects of police protocol also serve as control mechanisms. Even though the results of the medical exam of the victim may be crucial to their case, police in this study were careful never to be present in the examining room when the exam was done; the door of the room often was open, but officers were careful to stand an appropriate distance away. Likewise, it is not surprising that police officers should develop what might be called "professional armor" to protect themselves against the constant emotional onslaught of their work. An officer who at first seemed totally unsympathetic to the situation of the victim told us:

> I take the attitude that it is my job and I do not get involved in these cases. I bring them in and that's it. You'd go soft if you really thought about the cases you see every night.

Another officer told us, "After six years on the force, I believe no one."

The development of professional armor occurred before our very eyes in one case. A woman was brought to the emergency ward saying she had been raped by four males. The officers assigned to the case included a veteran sergeant of 11 years on the force and a young officer who said it was his first rape case. They displayed a marked contrast in how they dealt with the victim. The veteran sergeant was openly suspicious of her, strongly suspected she was a prostitute, and questioned her repeatedly on whether she had been soliciting. Although he did take the case to court, he had strong doubts all along. The young officer, in contrast, believed the victim. He behaved as follows as the case unfolded:

> The young officer was sympathetic to the victim. He was enthusiastic for her to press charges—indeed, so enthusiastic that he pressured her to do so despite her many protests and statements that she wanted to drop charges. He stayed with her through much of the wait at court. He chitchatted with her to pass the time and asked about her job hunting. He was very sympathetic, supportive, and—in general—had a calming effect on her.
>
> The testimony started. The woman, once on the stand, said she could not tell a lie. The boys had asked if she was working the street and offered to pay her

$80. She agreed. But after the last one had finished, he held a gun to her head, took back the money, and asked for her to get going.

Hearing this testimony, the seasoned veteran got a now-we-really-know look on his face. The effect on the younger officer was more dramatic. He was visibly upset as she testified and said, "Oh, no." It was clear that her words had changed his feelings. His sympathies had gone over to the other side.

Talking about the case afterward, he expressed concern for the boys involved. "Think what it did to those kids." The boys were found guilty of taking her money and also of shooting at a person who had tried to help her. The officer made no mention of these offenses except to say it was too bad that the incident would remain on their records. He focused mainly on the false accusation of rape. He said, "I thought she was telling the truth. I didn't know why she didn't want to testify." Walking away, he shook his head and said rape cases "are a messy business."

Clearly, having been "taken in" made a big impression on this beginning officer. One can only wonder how this case will affect his reaction to the next victim. Surely he will not allow himself to be so vulnerable next time. He may well come to echo what the veteran officer on the case told us—that he thinks most of the charges are untrue.

The officer who is "too good" to victims gets teased. All work groups develop norms that exert pressure on individual workers. Workers' norms of productivity—what the informal group feels constitutes a fair day's labor—perhaps have received the most attention; the "rate buster" gets a scolding from his fellow-laborers.[26] But since a similar group phenomenon occurs with any aspect of work, it is not surprising that it should occur with police officers, too. One can observe a kind of "group armor" in the camaraderie among officers that distances them from victims and encourages them not to take cases too much to heart. In this context, the officer who is "too good" or "too serious" gets a ribbing. One young officer, for example, had a reputation for being especially considerate to victims. He did so at the price of comments now and then from his fellow workers. One night the teasing went as follows:

> The officers were standing around waiting. There was some general chitchat in a jesting way about Officer Brandon. They said he takes these cases very seriously and "believes all of them." We said that women found him very helpful and that he listened carefully to what they had to say. The group just laughed. "That's Brandon, our upstanding officer."

He was put down for his careful attention to victims and his humanistic approach.

Victim's Reaction to the Police Encounter

Newspaper articles and TV programs on rape have tended to picture mistreatment at the hands of the police as one of the victim's main problems. The stereotype is that the police treat them badly—degrade them, do not believe them, focus beyond the call of duty on the sexual details—and that victims have negative reactions to police. Such stereotypes are supported by various published case accounts.[27] The question is, however, how widespread are such occurrences and such reactions?

Positive Reactions Common. Contrary to stereotype, the majority of sexual assault victims in the present study spoke favorably about the way the police had treated them. With regard to victims' immediate reactions to the police, 31.5 percent of victims had a definitely positive reaction; that is, they cited some specific attribute or action of the police that made them feel better.[28] One of the strongest statements was:

> The police have been outstanding. I have the utmost respect for this police force. They've been unbelievably kind. . . . My feeling is, What can I do to repay them?

Another woman said that, in general, she had a negative image of how the police treated rape cases; however, after reflecting upon how the police had treated her own case, she added, "I think that [image] is just prejudice [on my part]."

Fifty-two percent gave more neutral replies about how the police had treated them. These victims made statements to the effect that "Everything was fine," "I was treated well," or "I had no problem with them." In other words, their statements were mildly favorable. But these victims did not elaborate on any specific aspect about the service received that made them feel better. Nor did they complain about the treatment.

Only 10.3 percent of the victims had a negative reaction to the police treatment. These victims made some negative comment such as "Everyone just stood around staring at me," "There wasn't any privacy in talking with them," or "I felt pushed into pressing charges and they made wisecracks like 'you can't rape the willing'." One of the most negative comments made was:

> They didn't sound like I had a chance. I tried to tell them he would keep on doing this kind of thing. They said he probably just likes young girls. The officer was laughing, not taking it seriously, sounded as though he didn't care.

Negative reactions were in the minority. However, they could be very painful when they did occur.

Themes of Concern.   The rape victims' replies were analyzed in more detail for their themes of concern. By far the most commonly mentioned issue was the general "style" of the police officer—that is, whether the police were "nice" to them. Forty-nine of the 115 rape victims mentioned this issue. Almost all of them (45 of the 49) spoke positively of the officers. They said of the officers: "Very nice—treated me well," "Very nice and kindly," "Sympathetic," "Very understanding," "You hear stories about how police act, but they were very kind with me," "He was really great—just a doll," "He couldn't have been nicer to me." The few who discussed this issue in negative terms said the officers did not care or were cold. "They weren't so nice. . . . Seemed very cold."

Receiving explanations was very important to victims. Those who reported that police explained procedures to them spoke of it in positive terms. In contrast, when victims saw that explanations were not forthcoming, they tended to respond negatively: "They don't tell me anything!" Occasionally a victim reported that the police officer prefaced the questioning with an apology for having to do it. Victims saw such an approach in positive terms. As one said:

> I had heard that [the police] would be rough and tough. But before they asked
> me questions, they apologized and warned me that some of the questions might
> be embarrassing. I didn't mind that at all and the police were really very
> good with me.

Such an apology seems to be a way of acknowledging to the victim that the officer knows the questioning may be difficult for her. Explanations and apologies are ways that police officers can prepare victims psychologically for what is to follow. And victims react well to such preparation.

"They asked lots of questions" was the reply victims often gave when asked about the police encounter. This comment was said often in a neutral way—not in a positive or negative tone, but as an objective description of what had occurred. Victims did not necessarily object to being asked questions per se. What victims did complain about, however, was the *repetition* of questions. A number made comments such as "They were always asking the same questions over and over. They kept asking if I knew the boys and they asked me so much I wasn't going to talk to them anymore," "It was very confusing to answer questions over and over," "I began to get hysterical when they made me go over the story again," "They kept asking the same questions over and over. . . . The constant repetition got to me." A few victims complained about specific questions that they were asked. One said:

> They asked so many questions such as "Did you know him?". . . "Had you ever dated him?" Those questions really upset me. It was as though they didn't believe me.

And another victim reported, "The sergeant asked me if I climaxed. I just felt trampled. I didn't understand why they asked that."

Privacy was a concern of a number of victims. Those who mentioned the issue complained about the lack of privacy in police procedures, either in the neighborhood or at the station. Regarding police behavior that alerted neighbors, one victim said:

> I said [to the police] . . . to please not make a lot of noise to call attention to the neighbors. The first car that arrived was OK—it was unmarked and made no noise. But before we could drive away another one arrived with its siren blaring.

In another case, the mother of a young rape victim complained about how police behavior made it necessary for her to make up a cover story:

> The police were here. . . . I could have killed them. I had company. I told the women there was a . . . guy hanging around and the police wanted us to look at pictures.

Regarding police procedures that diminished privacy at the station, victims indicated that it was easier to talk to one or two officers. As the number increased, victims became increasingly ill at ease. One victim explained how she had felt comfortable talking with one officer. But back at the station there were a number of officers around and "it was like standing in the foyer of the Sheraton."

A number of victims complained about the attitude of the police—about their not believing the victim, blaming the victim, lecturing, emphasizing the seriousness of the charge, or saying they would enjoy being raped. Victims reported that officers said such things as, "It's a serious thing to make such charges, you sure this really happened?" "That's stupid—you shouldn't be out driving around at that time of night." "Do you know he could be sent up for life?" "If some bunch of girls raped me I wouldn't complain."

Striking in its absence were comments about the sex of the officer. The police officers were male, but only three rape victims made any comment about how they felt talking to a man about such matters. These three said they would have preferred talking to a woman.

As time went on, many victims continued to report favorable reactions to the police. Complaints, however, were prevalent in two areas: lack of action and lack of information.

A number of victims complained about lack of action. They said things such as, "The men came back . . . [but] the police didn't seem to want to do anything about it." "[The police] never came back. . . . The police are more afraid to come here than the people who live here." "They still haven't picked him up. I think that is terrible. . . . His apartment is almost across from the [police] station." "I have given up on the police department. I'm not that important and a rape isn't that important to them."

Many victims, including those whose cases went to court and those whose cases did not—complained about lack of explanation and lack of information. They wanted to know what was happening. They felt that police did not inform them. One victim whose assailant was never found by the police said repeatedly, "You know, the police never contacted me after that one time." Another victim—whose case went to court—spoke as follows:

> When I got back there was a summons in my mail box to come to court on June 19 at 9 A.M. Just form-type paper. . . . I am really angry at the detective that he just left that notice and hasn't told me a thing.

In the first case, the victim seemed to feel there was "unsettled business." The police never called even to say that nothing turned up. Hence there was no closure to the event. In the latter case, the victim was upset because she was asked to go through the criminal justice system without being consulted and without being informed of what was happening.

Other research suggests that victims' reactions to police may have important consequences. Bart's study based on questionnaire data from a sample of 1070 women who had been raped suggests that the victim's experience with the police may affect her emotional reaction to the rape and her future cooperation with the police. About a third of the victims reported that as a consequence of the rape they felt "hostility to men in general." One factor that was significantly associated with such hostility was the "attitude of the police." "If the police were sympathetic only 26% of the women reported 'hostility towards men,' while if police were unsympathetic, 37% of the women reported they were hostile as a result of the rape."[29] One victim in that study, for example, commended the Seattle police she talked to and also reported, "'My feelings . . . are of anger and rage against the man who raped me; *not against all men*'"[30] A case example presented by Bart suggests a link between the victim's experience with police and her subsequent willingness to cooperate with police. "'From the moment the police came it was just one question after another. This went on for about one hour. . . . So help me God if I ever get raped again I'll never lift a finger to help the police. It's just not worth what you go through."'[31]

THE DECISION TO PRESS CHARGES

Once the victim talks with the police, she is faced with making a decision about whether to press charges. Sometimes the victim is more keen than the police to pursue a case. Sometimes it is the police who are more keen. In the latter situation, the victim may get entangled in the legal process before she has a chance to get her own thoughts straight. Victims who do go to court sometimes talk about feeling caught up in the system or about this decision being predetermined. One such victim, who was wondering if she could drop charges, said, "But I don't know how legally involved I am now." Another said:

It all happened so fast. Only once was it mentioned that it would go to court. It wasn't a thing that I thought about—it was almost prearranged.

Another, talking about how she ran into a fire station and asked them to call the police, said, "I knew I was starting something big." She was right.

The Authority of the State

Victims quickly learn that the state has an interest in what happens in a rape case. Legally, rape is a crime committed against the state rather than against the woman. She is a witness. This definition often comes as a surprise. One victim, laughing at the irony, said, "What kills me is that the Commonwealth got raped and we're only witnesses."

The victim, who is defined as a witness, can be arrested and made to come to court. Police officers will say, "If a woman didn't show for court, I'd have to arrest her." In practice, they seldom do so. It never happened during the present study, although officers did talk of cases in their careers where they had made such an arrest. Victims also can be fined if they do not show up on the appointed date. It is common for court officials to give them instructions, saying something like, "You are to pay $100 if you do not show up as a witness. You may go on personal recognizance. Be here January 12 at nine o'clock."

Once the rape is reported, the victim need not be the one to sign the complaint. The police officer can go ahead and sign the papers with or without the victim's permission. In the present study, some complaints were signed by victims and some by police.[32] Once the process is started, neither the victim nor the police officer can drop the charges on their own. Instead, there must be an appearance in court and one must request permission of the court—in practice, the permission of the judge—to drop charges.

It is a rude awakening to many victims to find out that the rape they thought was committed on them was really against the state, that they can be arrested and/or fined if they do not appear in court, that someone else can sign the complaint without their permission, and that they may have to go to court even to drop charges. These procedures all contribute to the victim feeling a sense of being "processed" through the system and of having little say in what is happening. It is not surprising that one victim, when asked her opinion by a sympathetic judge, replied softly, "When I was at court before I was told I was just a witness for the state. I'm not very important in the case."

The Victim's Feelings About Pressing Charges

The criminal justice system puts pressure on many victims to press charges. Once the police are convinced a rape did occur, they generally would like to see a conviction. Nevertheless, only on rare occasions do they insist on taking a case to court if the victim is completely opposed to it. The police know it is hard to prosecute a rape case with a willing witness, let alone an unwilling one. They realize that although they can coerce a witness into appearing in court, they cannot coerce her into giving a credible story on the witness stand. Officers acknowledge that, in fact, if the woman will not testify, there goes the case. The victim's feelings about pressing charges are thus one key factor that determines what happens to the case and to her.

Victims' Initial Feelings. Victims have strong feelings about pressing charges. The issue of whether to press charges is often as salient as the rape itself. In our study, the rape victims were divided as follows in their initial reaction. A substantial minority (41%) clearly and unequivocally wanted to press charges. Another substantial minority (31%) were ambivalent. And a small minority (15%) definitely did not want to.[33]

The ambivalent victims are especially interesting because the issue is such a "heavy" one for them. They find themselves torn, as the following quote indicates:

[How do you feel about pressing charges?] Do I have to? (sobbing) Can I not? . . . Rape is awful serious. . . . If I could just get him on assault and battery [I would feel better]. . . . They'll put him behind bars so long. It bothers me what he did to me. I don't want it to happen to others. But I don't hit back—I'm a passivist. . . . It will be hell going through it if they catch him and hell worrying if they don't. I'm afraid he will end up on my front doorstep. I'll be afraid to walk out of the door. . . . I'll always be thinking that maybe he'll be there.

These victims find themselves in a double bind—no matter which choice they make, it seems to be the wrong one. As another victim said, "I'm scared to [press charges] because of what he might do to me; but I'm scared not to because he might do it again to me if he knows that I won't tell."

Victim's Reasons. Many people would like to influence victims' willingness to testify in rape cases. Thus, the reasons victims give for wanting or not wanting to go to court are of special interest. In our study, victims gave three major reasons for wanting to press charges (see Table 3).

Table 3. Reasons Given for Wanting to Press Charges. [34]

To protect others from him	27
Outrage at what he did	26
To punish him, have justice done	19
Afraid not to press charges	5
He's sick	4
Other	12

One main reason was the victim's wish to protect other women and to prevent the same thing from happening again. Over and over victims made statements such as, "I'd press charges for others' sake," "Next time it might be someone's little kid," "I keep thinking that he'll do someone else in."

A second reason was outrage at the assailant's behavior. They thought rape was a horrible thing and they had been hurt by it. As one victim said, "[He's] given me an experience I'll never forget. . . . I can't think of anything worse than rape." Another said, "This man had no right to disrupt my life."

A third reason was that the assailant deserved to be punished and that justice should be done. "He should pay his debt to society," "The men did wrong and should be punished."

A few victims said they were afraid and therefore wanted to press charges. They thought they would increase their own safety by going to court. As one said, "It's survival. . . . The way to protect yourself is to get it on the record." This line of thinking is of interest since fear is more commonly given as a reason to not press charges.

The reasons victims gave for not wanting to press charges included three main ones (see Table 4).

Table 4.   *Reasons Given for Not Wanting to Press Charges.*[35]

To avoid ordeal of court	29
Afraid of assailant taking revenge	26
To avoid sending a person to jail	17
What's the use—he'll get away with it anyway	9
Feel sorry for the guy	9
Just want to forget the whole thing	9
Scared of identifying wrong guy	5
Would look bad on my record	3
Other	16

One main reason not to press charges was the wish to avoid the ordeal of court. Again and again victims talked of how court would upset them. Most often they talked about the kinds of questioning they would have to undergo and how they would be made to look bad. Victims said, "They will blame me," "It will be me on trial," "They will say I am guilty." As one said, "I've heard of what they do to people who go to court. . . . I know how those trials go and I am not going to be humiliated." Victims talked about how they would be asked "personal questions" and "embarrassing questions." Some victims had something in their past—hospitalization, abortion, trace marks, lesbianism, a court record—that they thought would be used against them in court. As one said, "They'll bring up my past—that I had an abortion, that I was on birth control, that I slept around. I don't want to . . . have all that brought out." Also mentioned were the trouble of going to court ("It would be a hassle"); suffering more in court ("It would hurt me more"); and the aggravation of having to see the assailant there ("Looking at him would be awful").

A second major reason to not press charges was fear. They were afraid of what the assailant or his family and friends would do to them in retaliation if they testified. As one said:

I'm very scared (victim becoming visibly upset). I really believe he'll kill me
if he finds out I told and if he goes to jail and then gets out.

A third major reason was unwillingness to send a person to jail. They said
it was hard being responsible for someone's arrest and possible imprisonment, they didn't like having the guy in jail—he needed treatment instead,
and that sending him to prison might make him turn out worse. One spoke
as follows:

I don't want to put the guy in jail the rest of his life. I've been into psychology
. . . and know how many fucked-up people there are. Maybe it could happen
to me. . . . Prison would be such a frustrating experience for anybody. I
wouldn't want to go to prison—I'd kill myself rather than go. . . . I have
guilt feelings about prosecuting.

Some victims felt it would be futile to press charges ("He'll get off with a
suspended sentence—he had just got out of jail before he raped me," "It isn't
worth the slim chance [of getting a conviction]"). Others felt sorry for the
rapist ("I feel badly for him") or wanted to forget ("I wanted to put it out of
my mind"). A few victims were extremely worried about identifying the
wrong man ("I've read so much about misidentification") or worried that
going to court would look bad on their own record ("I'm trying to get a job
with the school department—will it look bad on my record?").

Changing One's Mind. Victims' feelings about pressing charges do not
necessarily remain the same. A fourth of the victims in the present study
changed on this issue as time went on.[36] Most of these became less willing to
press charges, usually because of their increasing concern about what court
would entail. They either thought more about what court would be like or
they experienced the beginning stages of the court process and felt that they
"just couldn't do it." One victim who went through the early hearing for
probable cause said:

I just couldn't go through with the questioning again. They make you feel
guilty while that guy just sits there with his arms folded and he's the one on
trial. . . . [The defense lawyer would] ask what time did this happen and what
time did that happen. What did he expect, that I kept checking my watch all
the time? . . . I'd never go through with that again. I just didn't know better. If
anyone gets raped, I'd tell them not to press charges.

Sometimes victims were influenced by pressure, either from the rapist's
friends and family or by their own friends and family, to drop charges.
Eight victims became more willing to press charges. Learning more about
what the assailant had done, especially finding out that he had raped others,

seemed to be the most important factor in this change. One victim, for example, began by talking of how her assailants were "just kids" and "wouldn't grow up to be aggressive killers." Later she found out they had raped several women. She said, "I wasn't going to [press charges], but knowing I wasn't an isolated case made a difference."

Since the tendency is for victims to become less enthusiastic about court over time, one might ask who displays an interest in pursuing the case. Very often it is other people—officials who represent the state or people in the victim's network. In approximately one-fourth of the cases, people in the victim's network were more emotionally involved in pursuing the case than was the victim herself. This pattern was even more pronounced—occurring more than half the time—with preadult victims. For adult victims, it was almost always males—boyfriends, husbands, fathers—who were more emotionally involved in pursuing the case than was the victim. For preadult victims, it was almost always the parents who were more involved.

The general picture that emerges is of the rape victim as a reluctant, or at least ambivalent, witness. It is the rare victim who is unequivocally determined to press charges and who remains so throughout the entire court process.

POLICE REFERRAL TO THE HOSPITAL

After talking to police, the next step in the career of many victims is going to the hospital. It is part of police protocol to refer or take them there. In our study, almost all the victims seen on the emergency ward were there as a result of police action.

In looking at the experience of victims in the hospital—the topic of the next chapter—it is important to remember that they are often there not completely of their own choosing. The general picture that emerges is that not only do many rape victims hesitate to report their victimization to the police and hesitate to press charges, they also hesitate to seek medical attention.

NOTES

1. Lynda Lytle Holmstrom and Ann Wolbert Burgess, "Rape: The Victim and the Criminal Justice System," *International Journal of Criminology and Penology* 3 (1975), pp. 101-110.
2. It should be remembered that this study deals with reported rapes and how they are processed; it does not address the question of how many rapes go unreported or of what happens to those victims. Almost all cases in the present sample were reported to the police; a few were reported to the hospital, but at the victim's request, police were not notified.
3. For victims, we follow the age division used by City Hospital to define adult and pediatric cases. Adult means 17 and older; preadult or "young" means 16 and under.

4. For a discussion of the "rediscovery" of the primary group in such diverse fields as industrial sociology, sociology of the military, sociology of the community, and communications research, see Elihu Katz and Paul F. Lazarsfeld, *Personal Influence: The Part Played by People in the Flow of Mass Communications* (New York: Free Press, 1964), pp. 32-42). (First published 1955 by Free Press.)

5. Ann Wolbert Burgess and Lynda Lytle Holmstrom, "Rape Trauma Syndrome," *American Journal of Psychiatry* 131 (September 1974), p. 982.

6. This definition of crisis follows closely the pioneering work of Caplan. See Gerald Caplan, *Principles of Preventive Psychiatry* (New York: Basic Books, 1964), p. 53.

7. Linda C. Smith and L.D. Nelson, "Predictors of Rape Victimization Reportage," paper read at the American Sociological Association annual meeting, New York, August 1976, pp. 15-16.

8. William B. Sanders, "Rape Investigations," paper read at the American Sociological Association annual meeting, New York, August 1976, p. 7.

9. Ibid., p. 12.

10. Everett Cherrington Hughes, "The Making of a Physician," in *Men and Their Work,* (Glencoe, Ill.: Free Press, 1958), p. 124. (First published 1955, in *Human Organization.*)

11. As an example see Judith Lorber, "Good Patients and Problem Patients: Conformity and Deviance in a General Hospital," *Journal of Health and Social Behavior* 16 (June 1975), pp. 213-25.

12. The question of whether police find rape victims less desirable to work with than other victims could be more adequately answered by systematically collecting data on police attitudes toward victims of various types of crime, something that was not done in the present study. What the data collected do show is that the public's stereotype of how the police react to rape victims does not hold up in fact. Sanders's work suggests one way in which a rape case may be seen as desirable. "A rape case is considered important, and therefore, solving a rape heaps status on the officer who solves it" (Sanders, op. cit., p. 7).

13. In context, this gesture seemed to be intended and taken as a supportive act; of course there are victims who would find such paternalism objectionable.

14. Valium is a prescription drug used in emergency settings to treat an acute stress or anxiety reaction in a crisis situation.

15. We defined sex-stress cases, it will be recalled, as ones in which both parties initially consented to sex, but then something "went wrong." Some were prostitutes who had contracted for sex and what "went wrong" was that violence, "perversion," nonpayment, or robbery occurred.

16. We have no systematic data on how these statements are distributed in the population. However, whenever people talked to us about our research, whether at a professional meeting or a cocktail party, we kept notes on what they said to us about rape. Again and again we were given opinions and told jokes by businessmen, academicians, physicians, strict psychoanalysts, and others to the effect that you can't rape a woman unless she wants it or that the woman enjoys the rape experience.

17. Arthur Niederhoffer, *Behind the Shield: The Police in Urban Society* (Garden City, N.Y.: Doubleday Anchor Books, 1969), p. 129. (First published 1967 by Doubleday.)

18. William A. Westley, "The Police: A Sociological Study of Law, Custom, and Morality," (unpublished doctoral dissertation, University of Chicago, 1951), p. 116, quoted in Niederhoffer, op. cit., p. 129.

19. Niederhoffer, op. cit., p. 130. Niederhoffer's interest in such attitudes is somewhat different than that in the present study. He is asking whether policemen have an authoritarian personality. He notes that one statement on the F scale measuring authoritarianism

is #75. Sex crimes, such as rape and attacks on children, deserve more than mere imprisonment; such criminals ought to be publicly whipped. See T. W. Adorno, Else Frenkel-Brunswik, Daniel J. Levinson, and R. Nevitt Sanford, *The Authoritarian Personality* (New York: Harper, 1950), p. 240.

20. Peter K. Manning, "The Police: Mandate, Strategies, and Appearances," in *Crime and Justice in American Society*, Jack D. Douglas, ed. (Indianapolis: Bobbs-Merrill, 1971), p. 156.

21. Niederhoffer, op. cit., p. 64.

22. Sanders, op. cit., p. 6. For material on the context of rape investigations see also William B. Sanders, *Detective Work: A Study of Criminal Investigations* (New York: Free Press, forthcoming).

23. Sanders, "Rape Investigations," p. 13.

24. Talcott Parsons, *The Social System* (Glencoe, Ill.: Free Press, 1951), p. 450.

25. Morris J. Daniels, "Affect and Its Control in the Medical Intern," in *Medical Care: Readings in the Sociology of Medical Institutions*, W. Richard Scott and Edmund H. Volkart, eds., with the assistance of Lynda Lytle Holmstrom (New York: Wiley, 1966), pp. 335-43 (first published 1960 in *American Journal of Sociology*); Fred Davis, "Uncertainty in Medical Prognosis, Clinical and Functional," in Scott and Volkart, op cit., pp. 316-17 (first published 1960 in *American Journal of Sociology*); Renée C. Fox and Judith P. Swazey, *The Courage to Fail: A Social View of Organ Transplants and Dialysis* (Chicago: University of Chicago Press, 1974).

26. Melville Dalton, "The Industrial 'Rate-Buster': A Characterization," *Applied Anthropology* 7 (Winter 1948), pp. 5-18; Van Dusen Kennedy, *Union Policy and Incentive Wage Methods* (New York: Columbia University Press, 1945), pp. 105-145; Donald Roy, "Quota Restriction and Goldbricking in a Machine Shop," *American Journal of Sociology* 57 (March 1952), pp. 427-42.

27. Anonymous, "When a Woman is Attacked," *Rape Victimology*, LeRoy G. Schultz, ed. (Springfield, Ill.: Charles C. Thomas, 1975), pp. 13-18. (First published 1973 in *Sexology Magazine*.)

28. Ann Wolbert Burgess and Lynda Lytle Holmstrom, "Accountability: A Right of the Rape Victim," *Journal of Psychiatric Nursing and Mental Health Services* 13 (May-June 1975), p. 15.

29. Pauline B. Bart, "Rape Doesn't End with a Kiss," (unpublished manuscript, Department of Psychiatry, Abraham Lincoln School of Medicine, University of Illinois, Chicago, 1975), p. 18. (Abridged version published June 1975 in *Viva.*) There are, of course, problems of interpretation. It is possible that a woman prone to hostility to men in general might be prone to view the police negatively.

30. Ibid., p. 18. (Emphasis added by Bart.)

31. Ibid., pp. 31-32. This victim also reported other negative experiences, for example, at court.

32. In cases of young victims, parents often sign the papers.

33. There were no data for the remaining cases.

34. Victims could give more than one reason.

35. Victims could give more than one reason.

36. In addition, for some victims whose assailants are not apprehended, the issue may become too hypothetical for them to know how they feel about it.

■

CHAPTER 4

The Hospital As Healer and Detective

I didn't want to come [to the hospital] because of the stigma.

RAPE VICTIM

We seldom get a really legitimate case, and this, unfortunately, is one.

GYNECOLOGIST

THE HOSPITAL STAFF'S CONFLICTING DUTIES

Hospital staff, in the case of rape victims, have two duties. They must provide medical care and collect legal evidence. The aims in these two tasks are somewhat contradictory. The clinician's duty is to help the patient no matter what the patient has done, but the clinician is also asked to gather evidence that may legitimate or throw into question the patient's claim of rape. Thus the staff is expected to be both therapeutic and investigative at the same time.

Expectation of Nonjudgmental Care

The hospital is expected to give care nonjudgmentally to all patients. Staff are expected to make medical judgments, but to remain nonjudgmental in the moral sense. Decisions about treatment are supposed to be made without reference to whether the patient is rich or poor, with or without good moral character. Parsons refers to such a nonjudgmental ideal when he states that the medical role is to be universalistic rather than particularistic. He uses the example of a potential heart patient to explain:

> So far as the decision [whether to take on a person as a heart patient] is taken on technical professional grounds the relevant questions do not relate to *who* the patient is but to *what* is the matter with him. The basis of the decision will be "universalistic," the consideration of whether he has symptoms which indicate a pathological condition of the heart. Whose son, husband, friend he is, is in this context irrelevant.[1]

No matter how many concrete instances one can cite of departures in practice from this norm, it remains present as an ideal. An instance observed during the present study is a case in point. The physician "slipped up" and made a moralistic judgment based on who the patient was. Later others called him on it, and he admitted he was wrong.

Departures from the ideal of universalistic care are common and have been well documented. Research studies on a variety of types of cases show that medical decisions often are made not only on technical grounds, but on economic, social, and moral grounds; that is, not only on what is wrong with the patient, but on who he is. Sudnow's work shows that "two persons in similar physical condition may be differentially designated dead or not."[2] At the county hospital Sudnow studied, the amount of effort made to attempt revival when clinical death signs were observed was related to the patient's age, social background, and his perceived moral character. Roth's work shows how medical decisions regarding tuberculosis patients are influenced by socioeconomic considerations; "the poor patient . . . tends to be regarded by the medical staff as irresponsible and requiring additional hospitalization."[3]

If medical attitudes and even decisions in fact are affected by social, economic, and moral considerations in such cases as "dead on arrivals" and tuberculosis patients, it would not be surprising if one found a similar process occurring with regard to rape victims. Given the general antivictim attitudes of the broader society toward rape cases, there is tremendous pressure on staff to incorporate social factors—whether the victim knew the assailant, her moral character, and so on—into their interpretation of the clinical signs and symptoms they observe. In other words, there is pressure to make decisions and judgments not on the basis of universalistic criteria—signs and symptoms of rape—but on the basis of who the patient is.

Collection of Evidence: An Extraneous Task

The duty of hospital staff to collect evidence to be used in proceedings in the criminal justice system is extraneous to medical treatment per se. The hospital is to gather facts that will be used by agencies external to it and for purposes that are irrelevant to medical care, especially to the physical care of the victim. One does not need to raise the question of whether the victim was raped in order to prepare a treatment plan for bruises, possible exposure to venereal disease, and possible pregnancy. But this question is the fundamental concern when one is recording evidence.

Many hospitals and practitioners presently are reluctant to gather evidence. As one police officer explained to us:

> I take all my rape cases to City. Other hospitals don't want to get involved, in case it becomes a legal case. Like just this morning I took a woman to Central because it was more of an assault case. And they didn't want to have anything to do with the possible rape aspect.

Victims occasionally told us of being denied care elsewhere. One victim, for example, arrived with her parents at Memorial Hospital. The hospital said they did not treat rape cases and referred them to City. Clearly, there is a division of labor between hospitals, with certain types of cases being sent from one institution to another.

Collection of evidence has been seen, to use Hughes's term, as a kind of "dirty work." He notes that in professional, as in other types of work, there comes to be a "conception of what the essential work of the occupation is or should be." Some tasks are nearer to the ideal work of the profession. "Some tasks are considered nuisances and impositions, or even dirty work—physically, socially or morally beneath the dignity of the profession."[4]

STAFF ATTITUDES AND BEHAVIOR

Overt Reaction: Professionally Polite

Overwhelmingly, the emergency ward personnel observed in the present study are "professionally polite" when dealing with sexual assault victims. They concentrate on accomplishing the technical job at hand, and often do it with a pleasant smile or comments designed to put the patient at ease. They do not go out of their way to show a great deal of sympathy for sexual assault victims, but neither do they indicate overtly any negative feelings toward them. Gynecologists examined adult victims; pediatricians typically examined preadult victims and then requested that a gynecological consultant do a gyn exam. It was possible for us to observe the interaction between these physicians and patients in 65 of the 146 cases. For the overt reaction of the physician in the presence of the patient, see Table 1.

Table 1. Physician's Overt Reaction to Sexual Assault Victims

Especially positive (went out of his or her way to provide extra help in some concrete way)	9
Professionally polite (concentrated on the technical task, often with a pleasant smile and reassuring talk; category includes both the more neutral and detached style and the more open style)	42
Conscientious harassment (out of a sense of professional duty, tried hard to pressure an unwilling patient into accepting treatment)	5
Indifferent	2
Negative (did some concrete negative act in the patient's presence)	6*
Other (mixed—positive and negative with same patient)	1
Total	65

*If one wishes to define total lack of communication as a concrete negative act, two more cases would fall into this category.

Professional politeness clearly is the main response. The main variation within this category was simply the individual physician's personality style. One doctor, for example, was cool and detached with all his patients; another was more open in demeanor. Each physician observed, however, was consistent from patient to patient. The nurses' overt responses were similar to those of the physicians. Their main reaction was to be professionally polite. In comparison with physicians, however, nurses leaned somewhat more toward the positive end of the continuum. They were more apt to treat victims in an especially positive way. And in no case was a nurse observed overtly treating a victim in a negative way.

Positive Reactions. It was unusual to see a physician deviate from "his style." However, this sometimes did occur. Physicians were especially positive to a few victims. A handful of adults was singled out for special treatment. They were all rape victims rather than some other kind of sexual assault victim. Many of their other characteristics varied (e.g., their marital status, age, race, type of assailant). But they had two things in common: they all were pretty and articulate.

The others singled out for especially positive treatment were young victims. Indeed, pediatric cases were disproportionately apt to be treated especially well. This finding matches with the global overall difference one can so easily observe between adult and pediatric emergency wards. In general, pediatric areas have a "warmer" feel about them. Pediatric clinicians as a group seem more attuned to the emotional and social aspects of illness than are those persons accustomed to working with adults. They are also more aware of the need for follow-up care than are persons who work with adults. The following accessory-to-sex victim is a case in point:

Suzanne, age 13, was brought to the pediatric walk-in clinic by her father and the police. The pediatrician and nurse dealt very carefully with both the patient and the father. The pediatrician thought it very important that her father be with her during the blood test and had him stay. He also talked with the father to make the necessary financial arrangements for obtaining the medication since the father had said the family could not afford it. The gynecologist responded positively to the case, saying, "He would have murdered her if he got into her, she is such a small girl." No medical findings of assault were found on exam and everyone seemed very relieved at that news. The nurse was careful to explain the need for the penicillin and to explain the exam results to the father. The girl said she was hungry and the nurse brought her ginger ale and crackers. The pediatrician wanted to have a social service consult and also thought it important that follow-up be done on the case. Indeed, several months later when Suzanne missed a subsequent appointment with him, he took the initiative and telephoned various staff to make sure that they got onto the case to find out what had happened.

There is a special feeling when a very young child is attacked. The vulnerability and innocence of such a victim make an emotional impact on staff. Word of such an assault passes quickly through the hospital grapevine, and many people tend to get involved. One of the most dramatic and most provictim staff reactions observed in the study was in the case of a raped 5-year-old.

The police said they responded to a report that crying noises were coming from a vacant building. They arrived and found an 18- to 20-year-old man on top of a young child. The child was badly beaten. Her clothes were all off. There was blood on her pants and her white shawl. The man started to run away. Police fired, and although the man crouched down, a bullet grazed and stopped him. Police took both assailant and child to the hospital.

The child was admitted to the pediatric walk-in clinic. The physicians and nurses on duty there that night happened to all be white. They thought she might be frightened if surrounded only by white faces and so took pains to have a black aide talk to her. The girl responded best to this aide. This person is the one who found out where she lived—thus enabling the hospital to locate the mother and other family members—and that her name was Ella.

When we arrived, Ella was lying on the examining table with a sheet over her. Her top lip was extremely swollen and dried blood outlined her mouth. Bruises were on her face and forehead. The mother stayed in the room with the child during the exam, and even held the labia of the child for one of the photographs that was taken as evidence. The exam revealed multiple bruises on the child's vagina and blood on her inner thighs.

Many staff people quickly became involved. The aide was the most successful in obtaining early information from the child. The executive officer from the adult side came over and took charge of loading the film for the camera. A pediatrician and also a gynecologist examined the victim, the pediatric nursing supervisor came down and stayed quite a while, and also the pediatrician from the floor to which the child was later admitted was down to examine her. Others stood around talking, and word about the case went quickly through the grapevine. When we walked beside the stretcher taking her to Xray, a staff person in a wing we passed through whispered to us, "Is that the little girl who——?" Staff reaction to the victim was overwhelmingly positive. As the night nurse who was most involved said, "I'm shaken."

The assailant was admitted to the adult emergency ward. The nurse there reported that when the assailant was getting examined in the bullet room he kept pulling the sheet off himself and exposing himself. He yelled at one of the attendants, "Leave me alone or I'll do it to your kid, too."

The child's family was asked if they could identify the assailant since it seemed he was a member of the community. They went over to the adult side and did so. With that, the assailant jumped down off the table, dragging his intravenous tubing with him, and bolted through a windowpane. The police recaptured him. He had lacerations from the glass but refused to have the staff suture them, and the staff did not push to have the sutures done. He was handcuffed at the ankle and wrist to the bed, and then placed in the prisoners' room.

Staff reaction to the man was totally negative. They made remarks such as, "Should have just shot the bastard," "If he hadn't bent over, it would have got him in the heart," and, "Too bad it wasn't the fifth floor he jumped out of."

Negative Reactions. Only six victims received especially negative treatment. The physicians were overtly exasperated at what they labeled as these patients' "lack of cooperation," or they made moralistic or degrading comments to their faces. In one such case, the physician ended up shouting at the victim about her lack of cooperation during the pelvic exam. In another, the victim was lying on a stretcher in preparation for being wheeled to Xray. A physician said in a rather loud voice, just a few feet away from her, "What do you think of *that* one—she's nutty!" In another case, the scene went as follows:

A rape victim age 25 was brought to the hospital by police. She worked as a stripper. After work one night she went home, still wearing her long, black, sexy gown. When she arrived, there were two guys in the hallway of the apartment building. One said, "Honey, can we use your phone?" She let them into her apartment, and one of them raped her. At the hospital after the gynecological exam, the victim was quite upset. She told us, "I can see why women don't go to hospitals or report this type of thing. [The doctor] couldn't see how I was raped; he didn't believe me. . . . He said, 'How can a chick like you get raped when you let the guys into the apartment?'" We talked with the nurse who confirmed the conversation. The physician later told the nurse he realized he had made a moralistic judgment and that he should not have.

The victims who elicited negative staff reactions had, as a group, somewhat mixed characteristics, but several were less physically attractive than most victims, at least two were very inarticulate, and at least four had "discrediting" moral backgrounds or circumstances of attack.

Conscientious Harassment. A handful of victims met with "conscientious harassment." These cases are more complicated to interpret because they indicate two somewhat opposite things and do not fall neatly into categories of positive vs negative response. In these cases, the physician (and often other staff as well) was trying to persuade, pressure, or coax victims into consenting to some medical procedures that in their duty as clinicians they believed the patient should have, but which the patient was dead set against having. The physician and staff saw themselves as conscientious. They took time to talk to and try to persuade the patient. They showed that they really wanted to give good care as defined by the standards of current medical practice. But this behavior, from the patient's point of view, constituted harassment. Depending upon how hard the health workers pushed, their behavior began to infringe upon the patient's freedom of choice. The physicians were saying, in effect, "I deny you emergency ward care unless I get to try to pressure you into the whole treatment protocol, not just part of it." If the patient, for example, wanted to have a pelvic exam, she had to be willing to get—or to put up with being pressured to get—painful penicillin shots as well. A simple no will not do. The result is a bargaining process between staff and patient, as illustrated by the cases of Ronnie and Lotte.

Ronnie, a 59-year-old rape victim, came into the emergency ward. She was somewhat reluctant to have a pelvic exam, but after a little teasing and negotiation, this exam was accomplished. The "hard bargaining" came over the penicillin shots. Physician and patient each had their own clear-cut request.[5] Her request was for Nembutal pills so she could sleep. His request was to treat her for possible exposure to venereal disease, that is, to give her penicillin shots. She refused the shots, and the dialogue went as follows:

Physician:	What if you get an infection?
Patient:	I'll come back and tell you. You are a hard man to get along with.
Physician:	I'm just trying to help. If you get a disease you will blame me.
Patient:	No I won't. I don't like shots. Just give me my Nembutal.
Physician:	You go to [your regular doctor] for that.
Patient:	I don't go until October. I don't have any until then. . . . Ronnie doesn't like shots, Ronnie likes pills.

The physician and nurse tried to get her to accept a "package deal"—she would agree to the shots and he would agree to give her some pills. This proposal did not work, and the dialogue continued:

Nurse:	We won't force you.
Patient:	Will I get my Nembutal?
Nurse:	Will you take the shots?
Patient:	No, I just want to sleep and forget [the rape].
Nurse:	Do you understand about the clap?
Patient:	Yes.
Nurse:	We can't force you. It's your body.

The patient never did agree to the shots. She just kept saying she hated needles. Finally, the physician gave her penicillin in pill form (regarded as a less effective form for preventing VD), and gave her one and only one pill for sleeping.

Lotte provides an even more dramatic case of conscientious harassment because staff felt strongly that she should be examined. Their request was to treat her—to give her shots and, above all, to be allowed to do a pelvic exam. Her request was for no medical care at all. Rather, she wanted to be allowed to see her injured boyfriend. The bargaining went as follows.

Lotte, a rape victim age 15, was brought to the hospital by police. When we arrived the nurse explained that the staff was having quite a bit of difficulty talking with her. Lotte had refused to be examined. They had not even been able to get as far as having her put on a hospital gown. Staff thought she should be examined. There was blood visible in the crotch of her long white pants; they were concerned that this might be from an injury sustained during the rape.

The pediatrician and nurse had spent a very long time with her, trying to persuade her to agree to a pelvic exam. The gynecologist called as a consultant also tried talking with her. He then waited around patiently for a while, watching TV, still hoping that other staff could persuade her to change her mind. All agreed, however, not to force her to be examined if she refused.

We went in to talk to her. Much of the time we sat in silence. When asked about the incident, she gave only the briefest of answers. Asked how she felt about the hospital she said explicitly, "I'm scared of doctors." At one point she said simply, "Can I leave now?" Much of the time she remained mute. After one such long period of silence, Lotte suddenly asked, "Did they tell you about Robert?" It took quite a while to find out why Robert was important to her and who he was. Finally, she said, "He was with me tonight —he's my boyfriend. They cut him. The police said he's in the hospital— the other part of the hospital." Lotte then asked several times if she could see Robert.

The nurse, hearing about Robert, called over to the adult side to check out this information. She also wanted to give Lotte penicillin and finally was able to get the patient to undo her pants just enough to have a place for the needles.

Regarding Robert, word came back from the adult emergency ward that there was no such patient. The girl was so visibly upset at this news that the pediatric nurse went over to check it out. She found that Robert had been admitted as an unknown male and later taken upstairs to another ward and admitted as an inpatient. He was put on the danger list as a precaution, but they felt he was in good condition. He had been hit over the head with a bottle during the rape, and he had sutures to the scalp and ear lacerations and was sleeping. The pediatric nurse thought the girl would want to see him and *maybe also he would be able to talk her into being examined.* Staff, now knowing more about the nature of the attack, were even more concerned that damage had been done to the girl, and felt strongly she should be examined.

We walked over with Lotte to see Robert. The nurse there prepared her for the shock of seeing him, saying, "He's been cut. He's not as handsome right now." The nurse asked him to tell her she should be examined; he did, but she still refused. She left the hospital without ever being examined. The pediatric nurse sighed and said, "Well, we tried." In a follow-up interview, Robert explained Lotte's refusal to us, saying, "Lotte doesn't like to be touched by others."

By enduring great pressure to submit to treatment she did not want, the patient eventually got what she did want, namely, to see her boyfriend. The hospital staff did get to give a minimal amount of treatment, namely, two penicillin shots.[6] However, mainly what the staff gained was the knowledge that, from their point of view, they had done their best. As the nurse said, "Well, we tried."

Bargaining is not peculiar to the treatment of cases of sexual assault, but rather is a common component in clinician-patient relationships. Balint long ago called attention to bargaining. Patients, he writes, in the first phases of becoming ill may *"offer or propose various illnesses,* and . . . they have to go on offering new illnesses until between doctor and patient an agreement can be reached, resulting in the acceptance by both of them of one of the illnesses as justified."[7] The two parties then settle down to some definite "organized" illness. Roth, in his study of the treatment timetables in tuberculosis cases, notes that there is a "continual process of bargaining between patients and physicians over the question of when given points on the timetable will be reached." Patients press to be moved along more quickly on the timetable. Physicians attempt to resist these pressures and maintain control.[8] The cases of "conscientious harassment" in the treatment of sexual assault victims described above are another manifestation of clinical bargaining between practitioner and client.

Professional Politeness.   Despite the dramatic staff reactions discussed, it must be remembered that overwhelmingly the overt reaction of hospital personnel to sexual assault victims is one of professional politeness. How are they able to maintain such an evenhanded demeanor? There are at least three possible contributing factors. One is that the ideology is strong that patients should be treated nonjudgmentally. No matter how many exceptions occur, staff still remind one another that that is the way they are supposed to treat patients. Second, although they are to gather evidence, they see their *main* duty as patient care. Third—and very important—they see most victims only for a few minutes. In contrast to police who may follow the case through the entire system, and district attorneys who may spend several days in court on a given case, the physician or the nurse sees the victim very briefly. One would expect that a contrast between public and private behavior would be easier to maintain for a short, rather than a prolonged, period of time.

Behind the Scenes: The Ideal Client

The overt treatment of victims by hospital staff may be evenhanded, but the behind-the-scenes conversation is filled with judgmental statements. Physicians and nurses both reveal that they have images of what constitutes the ideal client. The categories they use to label patients are somewhat different from those used by police, but the process is the same. They too have an image of the ideal victim.

Legitimate or Not.   Much staff energy goes into trying to decide whether the case is "legitimate". By legitimate they mean the victim was "really raped" and that therefore she has a legitimate complaint to make. Staff comments on specific cases included: "It seems legitimate," "It's true blue," "It did seem real," or, "It's legit." On the more skeptical side, they said such things as, "Half of them just don't get paid"—meaning that victims are "just prostitutes" who did not get their money.

Hospital staff do not seem to have the list of characteristics of what they look for in making their distinction so neatly defined as have the police. But in looking at cases they feel are legitimate they seem to go by consistent story, age (most impressed by very young and very old victims), affect (whether the victim is visibly upset or is calm or smiling), clinical evidence (bruises, hematomas), and whether the victim knew the assailant (it is more legitimate if he is a stranger). When an elderly, badly bruised victim came in, one nurse commented to us, "This is the first real rape case I have seen since I have been here." A 14-year-old victim was brought in. She had very visible red marks on her neck from being strangled. The pediatrician on duty expressed her belief in the girl's account by wondering out loud how someone could assault a young kid, and then added, "Doesn't it just make you sick?" A woman, smiling out of nervous tension, arrived at the emergency ward. The nurse took us aside and said, "She came in smiling—I don't know what the story is. That's her husband by the desk, so I didn't want him to hear." A very upset, badly beaten woman (right eye very swollen and purple, many black-and-blue marks on mouth and jaw) raped by a stranger came in. The gynecologist who examined her said to us, "We seldom get a really legitimate case, and this, unfortunately, is one." Staff may be more skeptical in cases where the victim knows the assailant. In one such case, the nurse on duty first "warned us" that it was someone the woman knew, and added, "I didn't know if you wanted to come in for that." In another such case, the pediatrician on duty said, "Any girl who [knows the guy] isn't raped."

Staff members sometimes make an effort to get over the biases they hold. One gynecologist talked to us about this process.

> Those who come in and say they've been raped are of two types. They're either upset or they're defensive. It took me a long time to get over my bias with regard to the latter, and I don't think all of the personnel here have.

If [a victim] says [she went out because] someone called at three in the morning, who am I to question that?

Asking for It.   Another, but less common, theme is whether the victim was "asking for it." Hospital staff talk about how the victim should not have exposed herself to danger. Regarding one risk-taking rape victim, the nurse told us in a very punitive tone:

She was hitchhiking. She said, "Next time I'll know better." Humpf! She should have known better *before.*

The Victim's Perceived Moral Character.   Rape and other sexual assault victims are an extremely varied lot. They include not only young adult women—the type of victim perhaps most often portrayed recently in the mass media—but a whole range of types. They are affluent and poor, old and young, married and single, prim and risqué, stable and unstable. They include victims with prior emotional problems, victims who get drunk, and prostitutes. Behind the scenes staff have strong reactions to the victim's perceived moral character: to victims who are "mental," to those who arrive intoxicated, and to members of the world's oldest profession.

When victims with emotional problems—for example, psychotic or actively suicidal victims—arrive at the emergency ward, the main staff reaction is that of being uncomfortable. At first glance what one notices is that in these cases staff make judgmental comments. They say things like "she's a mixed-up lady," "a crazy lady," "has lots of hang-ups," "you'll fill your notebook on this one," or "lots of luck on this one." One nurse always indicated to us nonverbally—with a slight smile and raised eyebrow—whenever she thought a case was "a little off." But if one listens more carefully to staff, these judgmental comments and reactions seem to be a kind of defense. Their underlying reaction is that of discomfort around such patients. Emergency ward staff are primarily trained to give acute physical care. They often say explicitly that they simply do not know what to do with the emotional problems. Two cases provide illustrations.

Rachael was a 44-year old rape victim. She also happened to be psychotic. Staff reacted strongly to her presence in the emergency ward.

As we arrived at the hospital, it was immediately apparent to us that "something was up." Even the receptionist had moved from her desk. That had never happened before. We figured it must be something important!

The nurse stopped us and "warned"us saying, "Do you want to ask the doctor about her background?" It was obvious, even prior to our seeing this woman, that she had impressed people with her mental status.

We saw that she was sitting in the small interview room, neatly dressed in a brown pants suit, short hair carefully brushed into place, makeup meticulously applied, and we went in to talk.

Rachael immediately smiled a very noticeable smile. Her eyes had a slightly odd look and she would stare at you, putting her face directly into your line of vision. Her nails had a brownish stain on them. She took out her Lucky Strikes and began smoking in a stylistic way characteristic of old state hospital patients—very intense in manner and burning the cigarettes down to the very end. Her opening statement was, "I can't get married now. He must have broken my cherry."

Throughout the interview, Rachael kept repeating our professional titles in a very ritualistic way, tacking the phrase "Dr. Holmstrom" or "Dr. Burgess" onto the beginning or end of many sentences. She also inserted statements about our appearance.

Holmstrom:	Would you recognize the assailant if you saw him again?
Rachael:	Oh, yes. (leaning forward again) Dr. Holmstrom you are pretty.
Holmstrom:	Thank you. Did he have a weapon?
Rachael:	He said he had a gun.

Her associations were often loose.

Holmstrom:	Then what happened?
Rachael:	I called my parents and sister. Oh, something just dripped from me, from my vagina, blood from my vagina. There was blood on my pants. I had bladder trouble as a child, had to go to the hospital for that.

She told us of her mental history from age 16½ to 44, and said she had heard voices for years.

Burgess:	You mentioned hearing voices. How often do you hear them?
Rachael:	I hear them all the time. But I ignore them. They bother me.
Burgess:	What do the voices say?
Rachael:	To grow up and that I have duck feet.

Throughout much of the interview, Rachael's speech was strained, and her tone of voice did not necessarily match the content of what she said.

The emergency ward staff did not know quite how to react. The nurse on duty had become interested in talking to rape victims. But regarding this case she told us, "I knew I was in over my head talking to her." The gynecologist was taken aback initially by her behavior. He said:

I knew something was wrong. I went in to see a woman with an alleged rape complaint. I sat down on the stool to examine her as I always do. She sat right up and looked down at me and said, "You are very handsome." She tried to seduce me. I knew something was very wrong.

The gynecologist also admitted not wanting to inquire about the victim's psychiatric problems. Asked if he had talked to her about her mental history, he laughed slightly and said, "No, *she* talked to *me* about her mental history." He did, however, request a psychiatric consultant.

Behind the scenes, the gynecologist expressed discomfort, detachment, and amusement. But in the patient's presence he "kept his cool" and managed to mainly "play it straight."

The family wanted to see the gynecologist. He announced, through the nurse, that he would meet with one member of the family, a representative. One member, the mother, got up to go see him. But the sister decided she would go, too. Then Rachael suddenly got up and went, too. They all stood in a circle. The mother treated Rachael like a child. She said, "Maybe the doctor doesn't want you here while he talks." Rachael stayed. The gynecologist said to them, "There are no bruises, everything is still intact, her hymen is intact." The mother said several times, "How wonderful." The sister then asked, "Did he break her?" The doctor restated that everything was intact. The sister said, "Thank God. That's wonderful. Thank God." After these responses had gone on for a while, the physician's eyes caught ours, and there was ever so slight a smile on his face indicating his detachment from the scene. However, by then, the family was oblivious to him and the family members were talking among themselves about the good news. They soon departed.

Clearly, the staff had been more uncomfortable with Rachael than she with them. This pattern of events is usually the case, and it is not surprising. After all, it is the patient with an obvious psychiatric history who is upsetting the staff's expectations, rather than vice versa. For people not used to talking to patients with such acute psychiatric problems, the experience can be disorienting. Such a person, for example, does not follow the normal daily rules of interaction. Constant smiling, mannerisms such as leaning forward and staring intensely, the unusual content of some statements, and loose associations all throw the uninitiated listener off guard. And when the patient does not follow the everyday rules of interaction, the staff's normal reactions are thrown off. They do not know how to respond.

Teresa, a victim admitted to the pediatric side, provides a second illustration of staff reaction to emotional problems. The pediatric staff are more attuned to these aspects of illness, but still may feel uncomfortable with a patient who has pronounced emotional problems. They may believe it is important to help the patient, and yet not know exactly how to do so.

Teresa was the first victim we interviewed on the pediatric side. It was her second visit to the hospital. She was a 15-year-old sex-stress victim. She had been brought to the pediatric walk-in clinic by her mother and the police three days before. She had run away from home to be with a 23-year-old man she knew, and had been found with him. She was given the standard medical exam, and sperm was found. After three days, the mother brought her back to the hospital because "she was sleeping so much and seemed dizzy."

Staff knew there were emotional problems involved in Teresa's case, but they were not sure in what way. Regarding Teresa's first visit, the nurse told us, "When she was here before, they just didn't deal with [the emotional part]." Regarding the second visit, the nurse said, "The staff didn't know what to do." So they decided to call us.

When we first saw Teresa and her mother, they were sitting at the far end of the waiting area. The TV was blaring above them. Teresa was staring straight ahead. She did not register any affect when the nurse approached her. We were introduced. Holmstrom stayed with the mother, who seemed very relieved to have someone to talk to. Burgess, experienced in psychiatric interviewing, talked to the young girl in a separate room. There was no breakthrough for 10 long minutes. Teresa sat in silence and stared down at the floor. Finally, she talked some about the incident. She had been seeing the man for six weeks. She liked him and wanted to continue seeing him, although she did express some ambivalence about what had happened. She talked of the trouble of his being in jail now as a result of the incident. She said she was worried about everyone at school knowing. After a long time, information came out on why she was so sleepy. Her main thought had been, "I want out." Or, as she said in her own words, "I wanted to end all the trouble." So the morning after the incident she had gone to her mother's medicine chest and "took all the pills I could find." Thirty-six hours after the pills she was still very lethargic. With her permission, staff were informed of the pills she had taken. They said they would do an evaluation and take care of it.

Staff, in this case, knew the girl needed help, but had been unable to break through her detachment. As they said, "You could wave your hand in front of her face and she would not flinch." They were willing to see a person experienced in psychiatric interviewing arrive on the scene, if only because they had reached the point of desperation. Clearly, Teresa was a challenge to all concerned.

That staff react in a special way to sexual assault victims who have psychiatric or emotional problems is not surprising. Other studies have also found that staff see patients with such problems in a special light. Roth, writing of emergency wards, notes that "psychiatric cases are commonly regarded as nuisances, and the tendency is to get rid of them quickly, either to the psychiatric ward or to the outside world."[9] Hughes and his colleagues, in their study of student culture in medical school, found that students wanted to learn about physical pathology. Hence they disliked "crocks"—patients with "all of these vague symptoms and you really can't find anything the matter with them."[10] The medical students also thought of psychiatric patients as especially likely to present difficulties. One student, commenting on such a patient, said, "Boy I really don't know what to do with this one. I think she's a real schizophrenic. . . . I certainly don't want to have any more to do with her if possible. Frankly, I'm afraid of her. She scares me to death."[11]

Thus various studies show that patients with psychiatric and emotional problems are seen as nuisances, as a disappointment and waste of learning time, as presenting difficulties, and even as frightening. In our study, judgmental comments were made about such patients, but the main staff reaction seemed to be discomfort.

Rape and other sexual assault victims also may arrive at the emergency ward either intoxicated or high on drugs. Staff typically assume that these victims got drunk or high from their own "choosing." Often this assumption is correct. However, we have talked to victims for whom alcohol or drugs were part of the attack—that is, assailants used these items as "weapons" against the victim.

The main staff reaction to victims who are high is either one of humor or of moralizing, as the following cases illustrate. Cheryl, a rape victim, arrived intoxicated and provoked a humorous response.

> A nurse talked to Cheryl about what happened. By the time we arrived, Cheryl had passed out. We first saw her lying unconscious on a stretcher in an examining room. Her shoulder-length hair was disheveled. There was a bruise on her right temple and a string of mucuous was running out of her nose and onto the sheet. Her blue jeans were torn at the left knee, and she looked a bit dusty all over. A medical chart was on the table. Beside it was a note printed on a paper towel that said the police wanted to be called after she was examined.
>
> We went to ask the gynecologist what the situation was. He said he wouldn't examine her until she could say it was rape. We implied that maybe we should wait. He said, "Well, let's see, maybe I can get some sort of history." He went to the room, called out loudly, "Cheryl," and shook her body, but she did not come to. He said, "No way!" We asked if he would examine her later. He laughed and said, "Well, if it's much later I'll really be angry."

Meanwhile, in the corridor, the nurse was explaining the EW routine and how Cheryl would be handled to a young physician. She said, "The gynecologist will do the GYN part, the surgeon will look at the bruise," but "the rest [including the intoxication] is up to you." There was much laughter over this.

Cheryl was left to "sleep it off." When she regained consciousness, she walked out of the hospital without being examined.

Sylvia, another rape victim who arrived intoxicated, provoked mainly a moralistic response among the staff.

Sylvia was known to almost all the EW staff for previous admissions of intoxication. This time she arrived at 11:15 A.M. quite inebriated, and stated that she had been "robbed, beaten, and raped." Throughout the day, she was seen by many staff members.

GYN was just finishing with her when we arrived at 5:00 P.M. She was lying on the examining table. Her head was badly beaten. Her face was bruised and swollen—the left eye almost closed due to swelling and the mouth quite twisted. Her breasts had fresh cigarette burns on them. She was in considerable physical pain.

The nurse on duty told us the gynecologist had been really moralistic and hard on her with such statements as, "Do you mean you were out on a street after drinking when this man approached you?" and "You mean you do not remember how you got to the man's apartment?" The medical record he wrote states she "does not remember last intercourse or LMP [last menstrual period]." He did not seem to appreciate the fact that she might have been knocked unconscious during the two days of her abduction and therefore might have retrograde amnesia. He treated her as if she should have had full presence of her senses—and she was sitting there so bruised right in front of him. Later a surgical resident commented, "She's pretty banged up," and she was kept for 24-hour observation.

The distaste of hospital staff for intoxicated patients has been noted by other researchers. Roth, commenting on the social atmosphere of emergency clinics, notes that "there is an almost universal hatred of drunks."[12]

The main staff reaction to victims who are prostitutes is one of humor. Ladies of the street are seen with amusement. There is often a guessing game among the staff—"Is she or isn't she?" Following is a case in point.

When we walked into the emergency ward, the nurse had a funny smile on her face. We teased her saying, "Now, now." She said, still with the funny look, "I didn't say a thing." All the implications were that there was something a little "off" with these two victims.

The gynecologist had just finished his exam. Seeing us in the corridor he said, "We have two ladies from the oldest profession in the world. They got a little more than they bargained for this evening. Your words may fall on deaf ears. . . .They may chew your ear off."

A second nurse asked us to wait until she had a chance to tell the patients about us. So we did. As she came out of the examining room she said to us, "They're both prostitutes, so they should be quite a challenge." Later, laughing, she said to the first nurse, "You were right!"

In another case, the victim's "brother" arrived and was waiting for her, dressed in a brown vest and slacks, fancy platform shoes, and diamond stud earrings. One nurse commented, "Did you get a load of the rags he's wearing? He has to be a pimp!"

Professional Armor. Like the police, the hospital staff develop professional armor. They often have strong personal feelings on rape. But in the context of their work with victims on the emergency ward—including victims whose stories turn out to be less than accurate—they become hardened. One physician reacted strongly regarding rape and said, "I don't think guys should get away with rape. I feel that's very wrong." But regarding his examinations of rape victims on the emergency ward he said, "I don't know, I've become such a skeptic." Another physician, regarding what he would do if rape touched his private life, said, "I have two daughters. I'd plead temporary insanity and blow the guy's brains out." Yet regarding his work on the emergency ward he said, "I've gotten hardened working down here."

THE VICTIM'S PERCEPTION OF THE HOSPITAL

As Goffman and others have so clearly shown, staff and patients live in two separate worlds.[13] Goffman, writing of the extreme case of total institutions, states that there is a "basic split between a large managed group, conveniently called inmates, and a small supervisory staff. Inmates typically live in the institution and have restricted contact with the world outside the walls; staff often operate on an eight-hour day and are socially integrated into the outside world."[14] Social mobility between the two levels is very limited, social distance is great, communication is controlled, talk across the lines is restricted, and so is the passage of information. "Two different social and cultural worlds develop, jogging alongside each other with points of official contact but little mutual penetration."[15]

The emergency ward is a less extreme institutional case than the one Goffman refers to. Most EW patients, for example, leave for the outside world after receiving treatment; they do not become "inmates." Nevertheless, Goffman's comments on the enormous split between the staff and patient worlds has relevance to the emergency ward setting. Clearly, EW staff have one set of concerns, and patients have another.

How does the emergency ward look to the client? To find out how rape victims viewed the hospital, we asked them very general questions, such as, "How do you feel about being at the hospital?" Later they were asked some evaluation questions about how they felt they had been treated. They also were encouraged to talk spontaneously about any aspect of the hospital experience they wished to focus on.

The most striking finding is how different the patients' concerns are from those of the staff—not so much in terms of whether they see the emergency ward as a place where good or bad care is given, but rather in terms of what issues they choose to talk about. Staff, as discussed above, have an image of the "ideal rape victim." They expend considerable energy behind the scenes deciding if a rape case is legitimate, and have special reactions to victims who are "mental," "intoxicated," or "soliciting." Patients sometimes pick up on these staff issues. For example, one rape victim picked up on the issue of having to prove her complaint was legitimate. She said, "I feel like I have to prove it happened—to the police, to the doctors, and to you." As another example, if staff do make moralistic comments openly to them, patients say they find it distasteful. But our main finding is that, by and large, patients choose to talk about a set of issues that is almost completely different from those the staff choose to focus on.

Rape victims talked in a general overall way about whether they had been treated well. In this global sense, most rape victims gave favorable answers about how they were treated at the hospital. They felt that in general things went well.[16]

Looking at the specific issues most salient for the adult rape victim, two items clearly stand out in importance. First in priority[17] is the issue of whether they want to be at the hospital. Second in priority is the issue of the manner in which the staff treats them—the "style" of the physician and possibly of other staff. (The frequency with which issues were mentioned is shown in Table 2.)

By far the most common issue mentioned by adult rape victims was whether they wanted to be at the hospital; specifically, 51 out of 92 adult rape victims volunteered comments on this concern. Half of these had negative feelings about having to go to the hospital. They said, "the hospital makes me nervous," "I was hesitant to come," "I didn't want to come—I

Table 2   The Adult Rape Victim's Hospital Concerns*

Want or do not want to be at hospital	51
Style of physician and/or other staff	31
Wait or not have to wait	20
Explanations given or not given	14
The medical procedures (found procedures upsetting)	12**
Image (pro or con) of being taken to "City"	11
Expense of the medical care	8
Competent treatment, its presence or lack	8
Being left all alone or not alone	7
The questioning (too many questions)	6
Race or sex of the physician	4
Other (miscellaneous issues)	18
No data (number of victims with no information on their hospital concerns)	11

*One patient might mention several issues.
**This figure comes from tabulating answers to general open-ended questions. A specific question was also asked about pelvic exam. A total of 32 adult rape victims found some medical procedure bothersome. When asked about the hospital in a general way they mentioned some medical procedure they found upsettting (e.g., shots, blood tests, the medication), or they said the pelvic exam hurt physically, or they said the pelvic exam upset them emotionally.

was so tired," "I don't like hospitals in general," "I didn't want to come because of the stigma," or, "The only other time I was in a hospital was for the birth of my child—it bothers me." A quarter had a more pragmatic or neutral answer: "It's necessary," "I didn't mind," or, "I knew it was part of the routine," Only a quarter had positive views—they felt relieved to be at the hospital. One said, "I was so glad to get here—to get in the little cubicle." Another said, "I feel so safe here, I wish I could stay forever. He can't get me here—too many layers of concrete, too many people who care."

Younger rape victims also focus on the issue of whether they want to be at the hospital. They are more apt to have negative than positive feelings about being there.

As for "style," victims talked of whether or not the staff was "nice" to them. Most adult rape victims who mentioned style praised the staff; specifically, 26 out of the 31 who mentioned the issue had positive things to say about the staff. They said, "The doctor was kind and gentle," "The doctor was gentle. . . . didn't make me feel like just a thing," "The doctor was very nice. He tried to calm me down," "The doctor seemed pretty aloof, but I think that was the best way to handle me then," "The doctor was fantastic and made me feel relaxed," "Everyone was nice." Only a few (5 out of 31) made negative remarks about the manner of the staff. One complained, "The doctor was so rough. . .and the nurse said, 'Do what the doctor says.' "

The lack of comments about the physician's ascribed characteristics—sex and race—is striking. Much ado has been made recently by some researchers and activists about the need for more female physicians, the reason being given that with present sex-role attitudes only females can give sufficiently sympathetic care to a raped woman. For example, Schultz states (without presenting any data) that "the need for female physicians. . .is very great in terms of putting the [rape] victim at ease."[18] Our data suggest that from the adult victim's point of view the style of the physician is the crucial variable and that the sex of the physician is not a major issue. All the gynecologists observed in the present study were male. Most victims reacted positively to them. And of all the adult rape victims, only two commented on the physician's sex. These two thought that "a female doctor would have been better."[19]

Preadult rape victims also frequently mentioned the issues of whether they wanted to be at the hospital and the style of the staff. There are, however, some differences when their concerns are compared to those of the adults. For young victims, the medical procedures (especially discomfort with needles and shots) loomed much larger. And they were more apt to comment on the sex of the physician saying that they did not like having to talk to a male doctor. They did not mention the expense of care (their parents, not they, were responsibile for payment) or whether they were left alone (the parents tended to be present). They did not comment on the image of being taken to "City" or on the availability of competent treatment.

The most striking thing about the sets of patient concerns is the predominance of social-emotional issues and the general absence of technical-medical issues. One should be careful not to interpret this pattern to mean that patients do not care about their medical treatment per se. Possibly their answers may be biased because they knew we were interested in hearing about their feelings. Possibly also they assumed that competent care was something so basic it was to be taken for granted and therefore did not require mention. But what the findings clearly show is that patients attach great importance to the social and emotional aspects of their medical experience. Further details on the issues they mentioned, such as the desire for explanation, are discussed in the sections below.

RISKS, HOSPITAL PROTOCOL, AND VIOLATION OF THE BODY

Risks

The assault of rape on the body does not end with the conclusion of the attack itself. Rather, bodily risks to the victim continue. The main ones are the risks of pregnancy, of venereal disease, and of injuries sustained during the attack. Some victims realize this constellation of factors immediately; for others the recognition of this aftermath dawns more slowly. Some victims who quickly see the dangers arrive at the hospital with a clear-cut request for medical care.[20] As one victim said, "I wanted to be sure everything was OK." Another said she wanted "to get to the hospital to get the morning-after pill." In other cases, the bodily dangers are pointed out to the victim by police (indeed it is often police who initially suggest the idea that medical attention is appropriate), hospital staff, or family and friends. For example, one victim was concerned by possible pregnancy and venereal disease—"neither of which I want at this moment"—but said she hadn't thought of these things until others mentioned them.

Pregnancy.   Whether it dawns on them right away or more slowly, the possibility of pregnancy clearly is one of the top concerns of rape victims. Most typically, the adult rape victims in the study said pregnancy was a big concern. They said things like, "I don't want one of those guy's babies, that's for sure," "I'd jump off a bridge if I were pregnant," "I'm going to school full time and working full time and pregnancy is not something I relish right now, especially this way." "I'd like to be pregnant, but not by this gentleman. . . . My husband and I *wanted* a child, so we tried (smiled and looked enthusiastic) and I had a miscarriage," and, "I don't want to get pregnant. My sons are 14 and 13 and I don't want any more children, certainly not an illegitimate one."

Some victims were visibly shaken at the thought of a pregnancy from the rape. One blanched when asked about it, another was visibly shocked when told that sperm were found, and another faltered as the possibility dawned on her:

> Mary Ellen was composed until the physician came back in and told her what to do if her period did not come—namely, to make an appointment at the clinic. At this point, it dawned on her that she could be pregnant as a result of what had happened. She faltered, lost her composure a little. She asked, with great distress, almost a kind of panic, "What am I going to *do*?"

For some women, the issue of a pregnancy from the rape was of overwhelming importance:

Eva was Catholic and had 10 children. She was really worried about a pregnancy. She could not sleep, could not eat, had no appetite, and kept thinking about it as well as about venereal disease. She thought she would be able to keep the problem all to herself, but she was more and more obsessed with it until she was frantic with what to do. She was relieved finally to be at the hospital. She talked about the "morning-after" pills she was given. She said, "I don't care how sick they make me. I need to take them. I can't stand to think of a pregnancy."

Especially poignant are those cases where the victim may be or become pregnant by a partner of her choice at a point very close in time to that of the rape. Here one difficulty is that of determining fatherhood. One such victim, raped by her boyfriend's uncle, spoke as follows.

I am worried about being pregnant and I don't know whose baby it would be. . . .My boyfriend Willie wants to marry me now. [The rape] has brought us so close. But I am so worried about being pregnant. . . .I'm not sure if this is his baby or his uncle's. [How will you know?] Willie said if he gets sick, it is his baby. We are so close, he gets what I get. Guess I will have to wait on him.

In a referral case, the victim and her husband had a child four years old and wanted another. One of her big concerns was the effect of the diethylstilbestrol (an antipregnancy medication). "I worried what if I was pregnant [by my husband] and what the stilbestrol did to it."

Victims sometimes want to think through what they would do if pregnant from the rape, even if objectively the chances of it happening are very small and even if the hospital has provided preventive treatment. The issue of abortion often comes to mind. Some say they definitely would have an abortion and are fairly matter-of-fact about it. One victim, a mother with a 2½-year-old child and a 4-month-old baby, said:

If I did get pregnant [from the rape] I'd get an abortion. I wouldn't want the child. And I wouldn't want to put my husband or my children through that either. What would be the point of having the child? I'd just give it up. I wouldn't keep it.

Other victims are ambivalent and torn over the issue of abortion. For example, one victim, raped after getting off duty at the hospital where she worked, viewed the issue as follows:

At work I have to watch the mothers come and have their babies and watch them have their abortions. I have enough difficulties handling [abortion] even at work. It bothers me even at work. The way I feel is that, with my luck,

I'll be pregnant. And I don't know what to do. I'll be scared for the next month even though the doctor said there was no sperm.

For some, abortion is not even seen as a possible alternative. One victim talked only about whether she would give up the child.

I wouldn't want to give the child up. I know women who have given children up and they regretted it. I know some priests advise keeping the child, saying that it is part yours. But still, I wouldn't want to keep the child. I would look at it and I would be unfair to it because it would always remind me of what happened, of how it came to be.

Even if pregnancy is not a concern to victims right away, it seems to prey on their minds in the next few weeks. Occurrence of the next menstrual period is a major demarcation in the process of recovery from the rape. As one victim said when asked how long she felt it took her to get back to normal, "up until I got my period." Its occurrence is required to settle the issue in their minds.

Another sizable group of adult rape victims indicated that the issue of pregnancy was more hypothetical. They said it was not a concern and cited some concrete reason that prevented it from being a concern. Sometimes it had to do with their life cycle—they were years past the age of conceiving. Sometimes it had to do with their monthly cycle—they were raped while having their period.[21] But most often it had to do with already being on some form of birth control (pills, IUD, tubal ligation) at the time of the rape. The technology of birth control has had an enormous impact on many aspects of women's lives, and rape is no exception. Were it not for such technological advances, most raped women would cite chance of pregnancy as a major concern.

For young rape victims, the parents' concern over pregnancy sometimes comes through even more strongly than the victim's. Perhaps this is because the adults are more aware of the consequences or perhaps they simply are more able to verbalize.

Venereal Disease.   The possibility of venereal disease is another top concern of rape victims. Most adult victims who worried about it were concerned about getting it themselves. They said things like, "I don't know what all he had on his penis," "The police were saying I might get VD, so I decided [going to the hospital] was a good idea," and, "I felt dirty and [the thought of] disease entered my mind." One victim who delayed coming to the hospital said, "I watched myself for signs [of VD]. . . . I didn't know if he was clean."

A few were worried that if they got venereal disease from the rape they in turn might give it to others. One 73-year-old rape victim said:

I feel much better—after the doctor told me there was nothing. I didn't want to be around my son's children—was worried about the toilet seat, the drinking glasses—that I might give something to them.

Occasionally a victim even though treated did contract venereal disease and pass it on to another person. In one couple studied, the wife passed it on to her husband. They spoke as follows about their physical problems resulting from the rape:

We both were infected with gonorrhea. I got the symptoms and went over to [the school] health services and they started both [of us] on 10 million units of penicillin. . . . Ellen gets her last shot today. In fact, she is lying on a hot water bottle now from the shot she got yesterday. The doctors are giving us so much to be sure we do not keep reinfecting each other. They said that way we can go ahead and do whatever we want without worrying who was giving it to whom.

Husband, 1½ weeks after rape

We went back to the doctor— both for cultures. They said they'd write us up in the medical journal if we still had it!

Wife, 2½ weeks later

[Do you have any suggestions for the hospital?] I wish someone had warned me to stay away from my husband. We ran into so many [medical] problems.

Wife, evaluation interview

The case emphasizes how rape can affect not only the victim, but others in her social network, not only on an emotional level but on a physical basis as well.

Physical Trauma.   Physical injuries are another concern of the rape victim. Twelve of the 92 adult rape victims studied focused their spontaneous comments on the physical injuries. They said things like, "I was bleeding so much that I knew I had to go to a doctor to be sure I wasn't all ripped up inside," "I wanted my [stab] wound sewed," "My legs [bruised knees] were really hurting." One victim, three months postpartum, said, "I just had a D and C and I was paranoid something would happen to me, that maybe the rape would have done something internal."

Data from the medical records of the rape victims studied reveal a high incidence of physical damage. To tabulate the information, a *sign* of injury was defined as objective evidence of injury that could be seen by a person other than the victim. The incidence is impressive: 63 percent of the adult and 73 percent of the young rape victims had at least one sign of *general* physical trauma noted on their medical records; 43 percent of adult and 59 percent of young rape victims had at least one sign of *gynecological* injury noted on their records.[22]

Severity of injury is another way of looking at the problem. The majority of rape victims had at most a "minimal" level of injury as regards either general physical trauma or gynecological trauma. But a substantial minority suffered more serious damage: almost one-third had moderate to severe general physical injuries, and almost one-sixth had moderate to severe gynecological injuries.[23] Of course it should be remembered that rape victims with the worst injuries—murder-rape victims—were not included in the sample.

Hospital Protocol

Historically, the medical examiniation of the rape victim has been dominated by the issue of false accusation. Only recently has there been a greater awareness of the actual trauma suffered by the victim. Thus, in looking at the practices of any particular hospital, it is important to see it in its historical context.

Protocol at City. The treatment protocol at City, the main hospital studied, was quite modern for its time. The staff treated rape victims for possible pregnancy by prescribing diethylstilbestrol and for possible exposure to venereal disease by prescribing procaine penicillin. They also treated for any additional injuries sustained during the attack. Compared to a number of other places at the time, this treatment package was relatively complete. Other hospitals in the city followed similar procedures, but some hospitals refused to treat rape victims. Others treated rape victims but omitted some major part of the care outlined above; for example, they treated for pregnancy but not for VD. A supposedly forward-looking article by Enos, Beyer, and Mann indicates their protocol for possible pregnancy was to refer the victim to her family physician or obstetrician.[24] (Research, of course, clearly shows that many patients do not have such a physician.)

The evidence collection protocol at City was also modern in orientation for its time. A review of the medical literature on the examination of the rape victim shows that historically there has been an antivictim bias. The preoccupation has been with the issue of false accusation: how to conduct an examination to protect an alleged assailant from a false charge of rape.[25] Even a relatively recent article, which ironically is reprinted as a model exam in a book[26] whose explicit aim is to strip away male myths about rape, falls into this older tradition. The authors of the article (three physicians) state:

> It is essential. . .that an experienced physician undertake the examination [of the rape victim], as the guilt or innocence of the accused may depend on medical findings. Misinterpretation of the history, physical observations, and laboratory findings can lead to a serious miscarriage of justice. A guilty verdict usually results in a severe penalty.[27]

This article makes no mention of the other side of the issue: of the victim's right to have evidence accurately recorded so that a careful prosecution of the case can be made.[28]

By comparison, the orientation to evidence collection at City was progressive. The thinking of the staff was that they were recording evidence at least in part for the benefit of the *victim*. They sometimes talked about this aim with patients, especially if a woman initially was hesitant to be examined. The following is a case in point.

> The victim started to leave the hospital without being examined. Then the physician and nurse went to talk with her. They talked in very calm, low-key, matter-of-fact tones. The physician spoke first, saying the exam was important, especially for legal reasons. "They'll come and ask me about the evidence. Since you've come to the hospital you might as well let us get the evidence while you're here. Otherwise, it's just your word against his." Then the nurse talked to her a while saying similar things. The woman was persuaded. She decided to stay and to be examined.

Another physician reported that he was able to gain the cooperation of the victims by explaining to them that the exam, including looking for evidence, is for *them*.

Emphasis on Physical Condition.   Although treatment given at City was fairly complete on the physical level, like most American medicine it was meager on the emotional level.[29] The staff, especially on the adult emergency ward, saw their treatment role as being almost exclusively that of giving physical care. The 51 conversations we observed between physician and victim are revealing in this regard. The physician first obtained a history of the incident and a gynecological history. Aside from the history of the assault, the conversation focused overwhelmingly on technical aspects of physical care. (see table 3).

Table 3   Topics of Conversation Between Physician and Sexual Assault Victim

Explanation of medication or providing other technical information	21
Reporting findings	13
Conscientious harassment	5
Comments on emotional aspect of sexual assault	4
Orders to relax	4
Moralistic comments	3
Dramatic lack of conversation	2
Other	14

The most common topics of conversation were explaining the medication or giving other technical information, and reporting findings to the patient (the presence or absence of sperm, whether hymen was broken). It was rare to hear a physician talk to the victim about the emotional aspect of assault. All four instances recorded were from the one physician who took an active interest in the emotional aspects of gynecological care. In one rape case, he said to the victim:

> This may all hit you in a few days and you find that it's hard to have sex with your husband. You may find you're "gun shy." I told him that understanding helps. And if you have a good relationship, if you have a good thing going (patient smiled and gave a slight laugh), that helps.

These comments were supportive in tone, and in general victims tended to respond well to his concern. Other physicians, if questioned, would say that they thought the emotional aspect was important, but in practice they did not take the initiative to see that anything was done about it.

The "condition on discharge" notations written by the physicians are another indication that their focus was almost exclusively on the physical condition of the victims. Providing a description of the patient at time of discharge is considered optional, but physicians did so for 48 of the 115 rape victims. The tendency was to describe them in optimistic terms: 16 were "well," 10 "good," 13 "satisfactory," and 9 "stable." Such designations could only have been arrived at by thinking of the victim's physical condition alone. For example, among the victims who were listed as "well," several exhibited severe psychological symptoms from the rape.

The specific degree of wellness listed, incidentally, did not prove to be a very precise indicator even of the victim's physical condition; instead, the term chosen correlated more with which physician did the examination. (see Table 4).

Table 4. *Condition at Discharge by Physician Conducting Examination*

Condition at Discharge	Physician*					
	1	2	3	4	Others	Total
Well	16	0	0	0	0	16
Good	0	5	1	3	1	10
Satisfactory	0	0	4	3	6	13
Stable	0	0	0	9	0	9
Total	16	5	5	15	7	48

*A fifth physician always left this line blank.

One physician listed every victim he saw as "well." Another listed almost every victim he saw as "satisfactory."

The physician's conclusion in some rape cases that "nothing happened" is another indication of the focus on the physical condition of the victim. In one case, the gynecologist did an exam of a 14-year-old victim and observed that the hymen was still intact. His attitude was that nothing happened. He expressed surprise when the case went to court.

> I remember her well. Her father brought her in and I talked to him. He was worried that she wasn't still a virgin. So after the exam I talked to him and he was much relieved. I thought that would be the end of it.

The physician did not appreciate the possibility that the assailant had tried as best he could to penetrate the girl against her will. Indeed, follow-up data suggest that that was what happened, and the victim suffered all the emotional symptoms that rape victims usually exhibit. The judge at the trial explained that legally the hymen did not have to be broken for it to be rape—that penetration of the outer lips, of the vulva, was sufficient. The physician, however, was so intent on looking for physical evidence of completed sexual intercourse that he failed to consider the enormous emotional impact that an attempted rape or slight penetration might have on such a young girl. Emotionally, much had happened.

Sometimes even "physical" condition became very narrowly defined. In one rape case, the gynecologist announced that "nothing happened," even though there was a bruise to the perineum and tears of the hymen. Asked why he made this statement, he explained that it was because he did not find any sperm.

Violation of the Body

Medical care requires access to the body and often violates the body boundaries. Hypodermic needles, intravenous procedures, and pelvic exams, for example, are all invasive. Although they are common procedures in our society today, they often cause enormous anxiety.

The rape victim's body has just been violated sexually in a life-threatening, forcible assault. Thus invasive medical procedures may have special significance for her. This is especially likely with the pelvic exam. The assault designed to injure and the medical procedure designed to help both invade the same site on the body.

Whenever possible, victims were specifically asked how they felt about the pelvic exam. Data exist for 45 of the 92 adult rape victims. Of these, slightly more than half indicated some unpleasant emotional and/or physical reaction they had to the exam. Fourteen victims gave dramatic answers about the emotional upset caused by the exam, usually saying it reminded them of the rape. A 21-year-old rape victim spoke as follows:

> The gynecologist was nice and gentle. But it was my first pelvic and I could hardly stand it. What he was doing was so similar to what had just happened. The whole night was scary—the rape and the pelvic. It was too much the same—two times in one night.

Others said things such as, "The pelvic was quite depressing at the time. . . To go through almost the same thing again of something being stuck into you was awful," "It's upsetting that a woman would have to go through such an exam [just because she's been raped]," "It was like here was another male, and I just had a strong negative reaction," "I didn't want anyone to look at me; I didn't want anyone to touch me," "The pelvic felt physically like [the incident itself]." Fifteen victims talked of the physical discomfort of the pelvic exam. They said, "The pelvic bothered me. . . . He hurt when he stuck something up me," and, "The pelvic was painful. I was sore before the exam and felt worse after it." The remaining victims said the pelvic was not a problem. They said, "I've had plenty of pelvics, so that wasn't bad," or "[It didn't bother me], I went through all that [with the baby]." The pattern of response of young victims was similar to that of the adults.

Force, as well as invasion, has special significance for the rape victim. Any procedure imposed upon an unwilling patient may be interpreted as a kind of symbolic rape. Thus, in cases where pelvic exams are forced on the victim, one would predict an especially adverse reaction. It was rare to see an abrasive, coercive manner used during the pelvic, but on a few occasions it did occur. In one or two instances, after trying unsuccessfully to examine a patient, the physician lost his temper. Following is a case in point:

> Sarah, a 15-year-old rape victim, was lying on the exam table. She heard it said that a pelvic would be done. She immediately wanted to know what it meant. The mother said, "You know, they examine you 'down below.' " The victim asked if it hurt. The physician and nurse came in to do the exam. The victim got very upset. She wanted to see what it was that they were going to put into her, and she fought them quite a bit. Neither the physician nor the nurse explained very much to her. They kept ordering her about, telling her briskly what to do. Finally, the physician said, shouting at her, "If you had just stayed still this would already be over. The sooner you just stay put the sooner you'll get this over with." They were not getting anyplace with her. Finally, the mother went in, said something to her, and got her to quiet down enough to go through with the exam.

In a later interview, Sarah's reaction was, "I didn't like the doctor sticking that thing into me. . . . I didn't like a man examining me after what had happened." "Orders to relax" occurred in another case as well. The physician, exasperated at his "uncooperative" patient said, "If you tighten up, I'll really hurt you, I mean it. Let go loose. . . . You've got to relax. It's very important." The physician's directions were similar to those of the rapist. The woman reported that during the rape the assailant said, "If you're calm, I won't hurt you."

Victims also mentioned other medical procedures that bothered them—penicillin shots, blood test, or taking medication with hormones in it. Their comments suggest that under any circumstances they would find these procedures distasteful; they are, for example, always fearful of needles. However, these procedures are connected to the rape, too. The only reason the victims must undergo them is because they were first victimized by the rapist and these procedures are part of the aftermath. Some women explicitly talk about this connection. As one said, with bitterness, referring to the nausea caused by diethylstilbestrol, "It is not fair that he should be running around having a good time while I have to go through this—to have to take medicine that will make me sick."

Victims do not experience the medical aftermath of rape in isolation from their medical histories. On the contrary, being at the hospital triggers memories of such prior situations. Even though victims were not asked systematically about this, 40 percent of the adult rape victims talked about some prior medical experience. Fifteen associated to some prior gynecological or obstetrical procedure they had undergone—a pregnancy, a miscarriage, or the birth of a child. Almost as many (13), associated to some other less obviously related medical problem—allergy tests, tooth extraction, hip operation, bladder trouble. And for smaller numbers, their current experience triggered thoughts of their psychiatric histories or of an exam or injury connected with a prior rape. In a few cases, it was clear that their current experience was colored by their perceptions of prior care they had received at City. One victim laughed and said, in a positive tone, "I've come here a lot—for all five children." And another, who recently had had a month's stay at City, said, "Oh, they're wonderful here. They're wonderful!"

VICTIMS KEPT IN IGNORANCE

Professionals acquire, in their training, esoteric knowledge to which clients do not have access.[30] And professionals have typically been reluctant to share much of this knowledge with clients. The reasons are varied: a desire to maintain their advantaged position vis-à-vis the client, a notion that clients are poorly informed and that there would be tremendous difficulties translating knowledge into language understandable to them,[31] a desire to interact minimally with clients and thereby protect themselves from emotional involvement,[32] or simply the very pragmatic reason of lack of time in a heavy work schedule.

Rape victims complain constantly about not being told anything as they go through "the system." The hospital experience is no exception. As mentioned earlier, one salient issue in victims' views of the hospital is whether they feel they have been given adequate explanations of what is being done to them, of the results, and of the treatment prescribed. On this issue, they want explanations and they tend to be critical of the staff for not providing sufficient information. Of the 14 adult rape victims who mentioned the issue, 10 complained, saying things like, "I didn't know what the doctor meant when he said they might have to stitch me up—stitch what?" "The directions given at the hospital weren't clear," "I didn't know what they were doing [during the exam]; no one explained," or, "[The doctor] was nice, but. . .I felt he could have explained more. I felt I had to ask him what he was doing." A few praised the staff for providing information. As one said, "Everything [at the hospital] was really very good. They explained things to me."

The patients are accurate in their statements that physicians often could have given more adequate explanations. Part of the victim's lack of understanding may be due to the difficulty a person has listening and absorbing information when in a psychological state of crisis. However, observation of actual conversations between physicians and victims revealed a number of cases where explanations were minimal. A few exams were witnessed in which the physician said almost nothing to the victim. More typically, the physician's conversation, even though focused on technical aspects of medical care, consisted of brief explanations and glossed over many of the details.

The explanations given of diethylstilbestrol (the antipregnancy medication prescribed) are a good case in point. The physicians often referred to it as the "morning-after pill"—a term familiar to the public—and said that it would induce the patient's period. Sometimes they said, "It's like a chemical D and C," a phrase that is fairly accurate and also fairly easy to understand. Sometimes they said, "It's nothing like an abortion"—a somewhat misleading explanation since the medication may result in destroying a fertilized egg. Patients typically were not given precise information on how the medicine works: that it makes the uterus slough off its lining and thus prevents the implantation of any fertilized ovum. Patients whose religious convictions are such that destruction of a fertilized ovum would be upsetting thus are not given the information they would need to make a fully informed moral decision. Nor were the risks of diethylstilbestrol discussed, although there has been much public controversy over the drug's effects. Medical opinion at the hospital tends to be that a one-time prescription to prevent pregnancy does not entail the same danger as prolonged usage. But the point is that the issue of risk was seldom mentioned. The few occasions on which it was discussed were at the initiative of the patient. One victim, knowledgeable about the public controversy, criticized the oversight, saying, "[The doctor] didn't explain too much, didn't go into the bad effects of diethylstilbestrol, but just gave it. . . . I felt taken advantage of."

In summary, although the conversation of the physicians did focus on the technical aspects of care, the information they provided was less than what a number of patients hoped for. As we follow the victims through the criminal justice system we shall see this complaint reappear again and again. Victims typically want information and feel that they do not get very much. When they do receive explanations, they are more apt to evaluate the professional's behavior positively. When they do not get explanations, the professional's behavior "doesn't make sense" to them and they are more apt to be critical.

DEPERSONALIZED BY THE SYSTEM

As victims go through the bureaucracies—police, hospital, and court—that deal with crime, they often feel depersonalized, lost, and neglected. Although they may find sympathetic, supportive individuals within these institutions who help them, something about the overall organizational structure contributes to the feeling that the institution does not care very much about them. They may also feel that society at large does not care much about what happens to the victims of violent crime.

Depersonalized and Neglected in the Hospital

Victims arriving at the hospital face a large organization that has many of the characteristics Weber talked about in his ideal-type analysis of bureaucracy. It has, to cite some examples, a highly complex division of labor, governance of operations by a system of abstract rules, officials who carry out their duties in a spirit of formalistic impersonality, and management based on written documents—"the files."[33] Futhermore, as more recent writers have noted, this organization has its own time schedule and routines that are set up more for the convenience of staff than for the public it is to serve.[34] And this is an organization that takes emergencies as a matter of routine. What is of vital and pressing importance for the victim is merely daily activity for the workers in this institution.[35] Structural characteristics of the hospital such as these contribute to the victim's feeling of being lost and neglected.

In addition, economic factors can contribute to a feeling of being neglected. Big urban hospitals, especially municipal ones, often handle a large clientele and do so with very limited funds. Their usually busy emergency wards are the focal point of medical care for victims of major accidents (airport, automobiles, subway)in the city, of the injuries suffered by public employees (police officers, firemen), and of victims of violent crime. They also serve as a substitute "family physician" for a large and poor clientele that does not have access to medical care through the private sector. Their resources are strained and the political efforts required to make even small changes involving resources—to obtain funds for a private examining room or for one additional job slot to hire a victim program coordinator—are staggering.

The Timetable. The tension between the patient's emergency and the hospital's routine was felt by many victims. High on the list of issues important to them was whether they had to wait for care. Of the adult rape victims who mentioned the issue, the majority were critical. There were three types of responses. Slightly more than half complained about waiting. In one case, the victim, dressed in a hospital gown, was pacing the floor in the examining room. She said she felt she had been kept waiting a long time. There was a delay of at least an hour before "GYN" arrived. Her friend, who shared the wait, also commented on the time, saying, "No wonder women don't like to report it." A few said they had to wait, but cited a reason that made it acceptable to them. "I had to wait quite a while because a girl was hemorrhaging and that was OK because she needed the attention more than I did." A few said with praise that they had been seen quickly.

Being emotionally upset or physically in pain makes even a short delay seem long. But, in fact, a number of victims did have to wait a long time—an hour or more. Sometimes the delay was because the existing resources were tied up, and the staff had to play one emergency against another. One victim, for example, arrived when the physician on duty was performing emergency surgery on a woman with an ectopic pregnancy. Occasionally victims were made to wait because staff was not willing to act or move quickly. The most dramatic instance of a delay for no good reason—simply a "so-what attitude"—occurred in a sex-stress case. GYN delayed 1½ hours without any particular reason. This attitude and behavior angered the nurses.

> The police, who brought the victim in, stayed at the hospital the whole time. GYN came 1½ hours after being called. The police even came down to the desk and said that there were only five cars out for the whole district and that they would have to make out a report on why they were so long at the hospital. The head nurse said she was also making out a report on the doctor. They had paged him five times, she told the police.
>
> The nurses were quite angry about the delay. The nurse even called for an administrative decision hoping for additional help in rousing GYN to

action. The administrator, however, did not support her. Instead he said, referring to the victim, "Why shouldn't she wait.?" He refused to call GYN. One of the nurses said, "I bet he wouldn't say that if it were his girl friend or wife." The head nurse then took the initiative and called the gynecologist again. She told him he had to get down here, that the police were waiting.

The Rules.   Whether they were made to wait alone was also important to some adult rape victims. Seven mentioned it, and of these, five were critical. Victims ended up alone for two reasons, or two "rules." One is simply the practice of preparing the woman for examination even if the physician is not ready. The physician's time is defined as more valuable than the victim's, and she is to be ready whenever he gets ready. The result is that if there is no one available and willing to stay with the woman, she gets left alone on the examining table. One victim, who arrived at the hospital accompanied only by police, spoke as follows:

> The only thing I remember is being put in the examining room all by myself and for 20 minutes I sat there on the table. People were walking back and forth, and the longer I had to wait, the more nervous I got. I really wanted someone to be with me. I didn't want to be left alone.

A second reason victims may get left alone is that some hospitals have rules prohibiting friends and family from staying with a patient. The main hospital studied did not have a firm and fast rule on this point. However, a few victims did complain that staff would not let their girl friend or boyfriend stay with them during the wait.

The Official and the Files. Hospitals typically have a "historian"—a person in the admitting office who, as a bureaucratic official, writes down the in- take information from each patient for the files. This historian ascertains the patient's name, address, religion, next of kin, age, race, presenting com- plaint, and medical insurance coverage. A victim arrives, emotionally upset, and finds that the first step in the hospital is to answer questions for the record. These matter-of-fact (and in some cases seemingly irrelevant) questions can contribute to a sense of depersonalization and of being pro- cessed for the record. Although not mentioned by a large number of vic- tims, those who did talk about the practice were critical. One spoke as follows:

> Filling out forms and answering questions really turned me off. I know it is necessary, but I had other people with me who could have answered the questions.

Another complained, "I had to answer the same questions on three forms."

Mortification: A Case Example.   One way of looking at the structure of an institution such as a bureaucracy is in terms of the impact it has on the self. Goffman analyzes what happens when a person comes to be an inmate in a total institution:

> The recruit comes into the establishment with a conception of himself made possible by certain stable social arrangements in his home world. Upon entrance, he is immediately stripped of the support provided by these arrangements. . . . His self is systematically, if often unintentionally, mortified.[36]

The admission procedure is an important part of this process of loss and mortification: taking a life history, undressing, issuing institutional clothes, instructions as to rules, assignment to quarters. "The new arrival allows himself to be shaped and coded into an object that can be fed into the administrative machinery of the establishment, to be worked on smoothly by routine operations."[37] The recruit also gets instruction in the privilege system. Many of the things previously taken for granted—the decision on how you want your coffee, whether to light a cigarette—become part of the rewards held out for obedience to staff.

Among rape victims, this mortification process impinges upon those who obtain care on the emergency ward. But it impinges most heavily on the small minority who must be hospitalized. Having first suffered rape—which Goffman calls the "model for interpersonal contamination in our society"[38]—the self is then subjected to the mortification process involved in becoming an inpatient in a hospital.

One 41-year-old rape victim—hospitalized because of considerable bleeding with lacerations to the vaginal wall—spoke at length of her inpatient experience:

> I've never been in a hospital before except to visit. It makes me nervous. I've had run-ins with people, especially those women dressed in green uniforms. One made me get up on the high bed even though the low bed was available. And one of them came to prep me for the operation. I said, "On, no, you don't. They don't know if they're going to operate or not." I said I wouldn't be prepared until a decision was actually made about the operation. And this woman came to give me three shots— two were penicillin but one was to make me sleep. And she wouldn't tell me really what they were and I wanted to know. . . . And I got up to do some things, like get a drink of water. And one of those women said, "You're supposed to be in bed. I have other patients to take care of."

And I had a run-in over whether they'd let me make a telephone call, too. I had such trouble getting to a telephone to call the friend I live with and get her to call my sister. . . . But I'll have to be very careful now, because some of those women I had run-ins with will be coming back on duty.

This rape victim's sense of self clearly was violated not only by the rape, but by the subsequent process of being institutionalized.

Neglected by Society

Victim counseling and compensation programs are being given increased attention today. But still, by and large, victims of crime are a neglected segment of the population. They are left largely on their own to cope financially, legally, and emotionally with the aftermath of the crime inflicted upon them.

Victims sometimes touched on this issue of neglect by raising the question of who should pay for medical care required by victims of crime. It seemed unfair to some that they should not only suffer the assault, but in addition have to pay for the medical attention needed as a result of it. They said things such as, "I got a bill from [the hospital]. . .and I don't think I should have to pay it." "How do you like that! (looking at the prescription slip) I have to pay for this. One way or another, this guy is costing me money!" "Who pays for this visit to the emergency ward? . . . What a thing! Why doesn't the state pay for it?"

Victims occasionally mentioned the negative image they had had of City Hospital. They implied they could hardly have imagined being taken *there!* This image had nothing to do with the quality of care they received. Indeed, after having been there, some changed their tune. As one such victim said, "I'm interested in City now. I have heard so many stories about this hospital. . . . [But] I'm glad there is City. I hope they find the finances to keep the hospital going."

Lack of Continuity of Care

Large bureaucratic institutions are notorious for lack of continuity of services. In a large organization, the complex division of labor may not be well integrated, the left hand often does not know what the right hand is doing, so to speak. Medical care frequently follows this pattern. Departments, even if well organized internally, often do not have good working relationships with other departments. The emergency wards of hospitals are no exception. As a result, patients often feel lost and neglected when they return to other departments for follow-up care.

In the main hospital studied, follow-up care for rape victims, especially adult victims, was not systematic. This lack of concern for continuity results partly from the outlook of many people who select emergency ward work. They like intervening in acute crises, but perceive follow-up work as difficult and less rewarding. Lack of continuity can also be partly the result of the problem mentioned earlier—that communication between departments often is not well developed. Thus, neither the emergency ward personnel themselves nor the staff in the departments most often used for later care have much interest in following victims through the system. Emergency ward staff give patients instructions on when and where to return. But almost always it is the patient's, rather than the institution's, responsibility to see that the instructions are adhered to. Nor are staff in the other departments to which the referrals are made necessarily prepared for the rape victim's arrival.

Adult victims who returned and went to the outpatient clinic or the emergency ward for follow-up treatment sometimes found their visits very difficult. They found it hard to go back and to be asked again by new people why they needed medical attention. One victim spoke vehemently about her return visit:

> The part I didn't like was the next day when I had to go back to the hospital for [more] penicillin shots. The interviewer who you have to talk to and who has to fill out a sheet was very persistent in why I had to have the penicillin. I finally got mad and said, "I was raped." After that he didn't say a word. The nurse was very inquisitive about it too. . . . I didn't think it was anyone's business. . . . I resented their questioning me, as I do anyone I haven't told.

They complained about the "flip" attitude:

> [Have you checked back?] Yes, that is my only problem. I haven't had a period and they said to call if after I stopped taking the pills my period didn't come. I called the emergency ward and the lady at the desk was really flip. I don't think she understood what I was saying. I tried to tell her what happened. She took it for a joke and said, "You know what no period means. You are pregnant." And she hung up.

Others complained about the limited hours the clinic was open (hard to get off work to get there), being shuffled from department to department, the long wait (also hard for the working victim), and the type of clinician they were referred to.

Seeking follow-up care outside the hospital did not necessarily solve the victim's problem. Here is a quote from one who had trouble both in her attempts to return to the hospital and in her attempts to seek help elsewhere:

I really got a bad infection from the attack. It was just awful. And I got such static from people when I tried to get medical care. . . . I was trying to see a gynecologist and each one I called said I had to go see someone else. I called [the hospital] and they said I had to come during clinic hours and I was working at the time and couldn't make it and couldn't ask for more time off because I had to take time off for court and couldn't say why—just had to keep making up stories. When I called other places for a GYN appointment they would say they couldn't see me because other hospitals had my records.

One victim was so worried about people knowing of the attack that she would not call anybody about follow-up care except us, saying "You already know me and know about it."

Some victims felt more at ease seeking follow-up care with their own physician, whom they said was understanding and who made them more comfortable. In one case, the victim's private physician made a house call to see her.

Lack of continuity of care clearly was a problem for a number of victims. Many victims were uncomfortable seeking medical attention originally. Their discomfort was increased when having to do it a second time with different people. Lack of continuity of services is a theme that we shall encounter again as we follow the victims through the criminal justice system. Not only do victims see different physicians and nurses for follow-up, they may also find when they return to the courthouse that their case has been reassigned to a different district attorney.

LACK OF PRIVACY

Rape often causes the victim great embarrassment. One of the victim's main concerns may be whether people will find out what has happened. Yet the personnel in institutions dealing with rape, as they do their work, may make the situation known to others in the community. The hospital is no exception.

Physical Environment

Hospital a Public Place.   Victims risk exposure simply by arriving at the hospital. Waiting rooms, admitting areas, and corridors are filled with patients. For some victims, it may mean seeing people they know from their own community. For those who are not part of the communities typically using the hospital, it means exposure to strangers. One such victim arrived at the hospital with a badly beaten face. The swelling and discoloration could not help but catch peoples' eyes. As she was leaving the hospital, a woman standing in a doorway saw her and said, "My God, what happened to you?" She replied, "I got beat up." The woman answered, "Wow! You look terrible!" Such encounters can contribute to a feeling that "everybody knows."

Busy Nights and Limited Resources. It was common, in the main hospital studied, for a rape victim to come in at a time when the adult OB/GYN examining room was not in use and thus to have complete privacy during the exam. However, the room did contain two examining tables, each shielded by curtains. There were occasions when two, sometimes three, patients arrived and needed attention at the same time. Under these circumstances, both tables were put into use and victims had far less privacy. In one case, the following scene occurred:

> A rape victim in her teens was brought into the accident floor accompanied by her mother and by the mother of a girl friend who had been with her during the incident. It was difficult to get the girl to go through with the exam, so her mother and the mother of the other girl both went into the examining area to be with her. There were complaints that other people were watching. They were. A woman and her friend were waiting their turn to see a physician about what they thought was a miscarriage. The woman's friend was walking around. Not having anything to do but wait she watched whatever was going on. She watched the scene with the rape victim unfold.

Staff at this hospital are aware of the recent public outcry over the need for better facilities for rape victims. They have discussed whether it would be feasible to get a more private examining area for such victims. However, at present, they regard this very much as a luxury item. To take victims to a more secluded area makes such an impact on staffing needs to cover the main floor that it is not regarded as feasible given the current resources.

The Bulletin Board. Staff are very aware of value placed on privacy for patients. Often they will go out of their way to find a relatively quiet place for a patient to sit. However, there are occasions when they are preoccupied by other goals. One example of interest is the practice of tacking charts on the wall. Occasionally there is some reason why a chart needs attention. In one such case, a young patient was to come back for penicillin shots, but had not come. To remind staff of the need for follow-up in this case, someone thumbtacked the patient's chart to the wall near the reception desk in plain sight for all—including other patients—to see.

Confidentiality

There is a long tradition that the doctor-patient relationship is to be a confidential one. The expectation is that "the doctor will not disclose the information received from the patient to anyone not directly involved in the care and treatment of the patient."[39] This duty of the physician is set forth explicitly in various ethical codes. The Hippocratic Oath states:

> Whatsoever things I see or hear concerning the life of man, in any attendance on the sick or even apart therefrom which ought not to be noised about, I will keep silent thereon, counting such things to be professional secrets.[40]

In a more recent formulation—the AMA's Principles of Ethics—the duty is stated as follows:

> A physician may not reveal the confidences entrusted to him in the course of medical attendance, or the deficiencies he may observe in the character of patients, unless he is required to do so by law or unless it becomes necessary in order to protect the welfare of the individual or the community.[41]

Physicians and other hospital personnel face the dilemma of whether to tell people in the victim's network or people in the criminal justice system the results of the medical exam they conduct on a rape victim. Staff are caught under cross-pressure on this issue. They know that the doctor-patient relationship is thought to be a confidential one. But members of the victim's network and of the criminal justice system put enormous pressure on staff to tell and typically present themselves as having legitimate reasons for needing to know the information.

Victim's Social Network Requests to Know. Staff seem to believe that members of the victim's social network, especially family members, who accompany the victim to the hospital have a right to know the results of the exam. Sometimes the victim agrees either explicitly or implicitly to their being given an explanation. But in other cases the victim's permission is not asked. For example, in one case the rape victim was accompanied to the hospital by her brother and a friend. After the exam, the victim and friend returned to the waiting room, but the brother came up to the administrative desk of the accident floor and insisted on knowing the results of the exam.

The victim's brother very much wanted to know if sex had occurred. He asked us, but we referred him to the physician who had done the exam. He called the physician on the emergency ward house phone. The brother had said over and over that his sister's husband was away, that she hadn't had sex with anyone else, and so if there was anything there it was from this guy. He repeated this statement to the physician on the telephone. He said, "But wouldn't there be tightness there [if nothing had happened]?" As the brother was about to hang up he said, "Unhuh, it could have happened," so apparently the physician was telling him something along those lines.

Staff belief seems to be especially strong that parents have a right to know the results of an examination. This belief seems to be related to a general assumption that parents are responsible for their children, and also fits in with the idea of requiring parental permission for treatment; that is, if parents are required to give permission for treatment, then they have a right to know the medically relevant facts. However, staff belief in *what* parents have a right to know extends beyond such questions as "whether the victim was raped" to more peripheral information obtained from the victim. In the following case, the gynecologist revealed what he learned from the 15-year-old rape victim about her sexual practices to her astonished and unsuspecting mother.

After the exam, the gynecologist spent quite a bit of time talking to the mother in the corridor. The daughter was not present. He and the mother were talking quite loudly. He told the mother that he had to ask each one he examined if they had had intercourse before and that when he asked her daughter she had said yes. The mother was most surprised. He said, "Well, I have to ask that of everyone." And then he added, "That's what she said—you settle that one at home."

When a sexual assault may have happened to a young person there does not seem to be any conflict in the minds of staff about giving information to a parent, especially if the parent and victim are at the hospital together. However, a conflict over telling does arise in their minds if the parent's request for an examination of the child "does not seem quite right." For example, a parent may come in and either use the claim of rape to obtain a virginity check on the daughter or explicitly ask for a virginity check. Staff find such situations difficult to cope with and there does not seem to be a clear-cut policy on how to deal with them. Rather, the issue is decided more on an ad hoc basis. The action taken depends on how the person on duty, especially the physician, reacts. Following is a case in point:

Terry, a 15-year-old girl, was brought to pediatric walk-in by her aunt who had raised her since age three. The aunt took the person at the desk aside and said, "My girl was raped two days ago." She wanted the girl examined. Gradually it became apparent that the aunt was concerned that the girl was having sex and didn't want her to get pregnant and wanted an exam done without explaining it to the girl. The gynecologist, however, said the girl had rights to privacy and that he would not examine her for virginity reasons. The aunt was quite indignant that the doctor did not take her side. The aunt explained her position to us:

Aunt:	I don't feel a 15-year-old girl should be giving her body to these good-for-nothing boys. But the doctor sees nothing wrong with it.
Burgess:	What does your daughter [niece] say about it?
Aunt:	She doesn't talk to me. She knows I'm strictly against it. The boys want just one thing.
Burgess:	What does she understand about being here tonight?
Aunt:	She understands that I want to get her examined to see if anything is wrong and she has a bad cough.
Burgess:	So you want to know if she's pregnant?
Aunt:	But the doctor is on *her* side. Like she's the adult and I'm the child.
Burgess:	What did the doctor say?
Aunt:	He thinks she has her rights.

The aunt's request was not seen as legitimate by staff and hence they supported the girl's right to privacy. The case is interesting also from the point of view of the use of rape. The aunt initially used the claim of rape to try to get some service that she felt she could not ask for directly. Cases such as these increase the staff's tendency to be suspicious of all complaints of rape.

The Criminal Justice System Requests to Know.   Whether to tell members of the criminal justice system the results of the examination is somewhat more problematical. Cordial relationships sometimes exist between police and hospital staff, but more often there is tension. Police officers feel they need to know the results of the exam because the results have a bearing on the decision about whether to pursue a case. Yet often staff are reluctant to talk to them. For example, one night the police called back to the hospital asking to speak to the doctor to get the diagnosis on a victim they had brought in. The gynecologist refused to talk to them and had a nurse take the call. She told them the diagnosis was "alleged rape," a reply that told them nothing. They already knew that much when they brought the victim in.

Physicians may have considerable discretion about whether to talk to individual police officers, district attorneys, or defense lawyers when these people pressure them for information. But they do not have so much choice about whether to reveal information when they are called to court. It is true that in many states, the doctor-patient relationship *legally* is one of "privileged communication" or one with "testimonial privilege." That is, "a doctor may not disclose information he has learned in confidence from his patient in a court of law without the patient's permission."[42] However, 12 states, including Massachusetts, do not presently recognize the physician-patient testimonial privilege. "In these states doctors must answer questions about communications with their patients or be faced with a contempt of court finding."[43] And even in states with testimonial privilege, there are many exceptions to the rule and many circumstances under which physicians do testify in court about confidential medical information without the patient's consent. Thus, whether rape victims realize it or not, the information they give to physicians often has a dual audience: hospital staff and criminal justice system.

Parental Permission. One difficulty rape victims have if they are legally minors is obtaining treatment without the incident being reported to their parents. Many victims do not want their parents to know what has happened, or would like to tell their parents in due time and in their own way. The problem, however, is that "in general, the parent or guardian of a minor is the only person legally capable of giving consent to medical treatment."[44] There are exceptions. Many states have statutes specifying certain diseases or conditions—venereal disease, drug dependency, pregnancy, contraception, contagious diseases—for which a minor can consent to treatment. Another exception is that a physician can treat a minor without parental permission in an emergency situation. However, in general, rape has not been one of the exceptions.[45] It is therefore, not surprising that hospital policy tends to be that parents must be notified in rape cases.

When the parental permission rule is enforced, it leads to a difficult choice for the victim. She is in a double bind: no matter which choice she makes, it seems to be the wrong one. If she chooses to maintain her privacy, she is denied treatment, and runs considerable physical risks. Occasionally a victim did make this choice. For example, one victim came to the hospital and got so upset that her mother would be notified that she simply walked out. If the victim chooses to obtain treatment, she is denied privacy and her parents are told. Depending on the kind of relationship she has with her parents, the emotional risks she runs are considerable. A number of victims did make this choice, with varying results. Some found the notification of their parents extremely upsetting. As one victim reported to us:

> The hospital called my parents. . . . They said, "This is the hospital calling and your daughter is here for suspicion of rape.". . .I had to talk with my mother and we had an argument over the phone. I got so upset I tried to get out a door [which turned out to be an emergency exit] and the sirens went on and everything and I had to come back.

Others had a more neutral reaction or even a sense of relief that their parents knew and didn't react "badly."

Staff members held different opinions on the parental permission requirement. One result of this difference of opinion was an uneven application of the policy. Often there was uncertainty about how to handle a victim's request. Two similar cases coming into the same ward might be handled differently for no apparent reason. Sometimes the adult emergency ward staff treated a minor without calling a parent, sometimes staff insisted on calling. Another result of the difference of opinion was staff conflict. Occasionally the issue of parental permission led to open conflict, as in this case:

> Martha, a 16-year-old rape victim, first arrived at the adult emergency ward. She made it clear she did not want a parent notified. On the EW side, the executive officer gave permission for her to be treated without contacting the mother. But then, because of her age, it was decided she should be seen in pedi walk-in. There the nurse said the mother had to be notified. She held to the rule that executive permission was only if the parent could not be located. The mother was contacted.
>
> The EW nurse and the pedi nurse engaged in open conflict over the management of the case. Later the EW nurse complained to us, "I can't stand nurses who are so rigid—who just say we have to do thus and so, just because it is some administrative rule, and don't even try to do anything else." She singled out for emphasis the fact that the pedi nurse was making no effort to try to get the victim examined without a parent being notified.
>
> The issue of territory compounded the dispute. The pedi nurse clearly resented the "intrusion" of the EW nurse into her affairs. She "settled" the dispute by defining the victim as her responsibility and announced simply, "She's *my* patient."

The parental permission requirement may cause both staff and patient to feel trapped by the system. Legal constraints such as these often lead to the practice of defensive medicine—that is, to decisions being made on the basis of what will prevent a law suit rather than on the basis on one's professional judgment or the patient's request.[46] The following scene with a sex-stress victim is a case in point. After an initial sexual experience (touching, not full intercourse), 14-year-old Ellie became very frightened about getting pregnant. Not feeling she could come right out and ask for the morning after pill for that reason, she came to the hospital instead with a complaint of rape. What followed was a two-hour drama centered around the issue of whether she could get treatment without her parents being notified. She wanted the hospital to treat her without notifying her parents. The hospital staff, although sympathetic to her, leaned toward feeling she probably should call her parents. They definitely took the position that no matter how much they wanted to help the girl, they did not dare go against hospital policy or the law. The scene unfolded as follows:

The head nurse went to see if she could get permission from the executive officer to do an exam and give medication without parental permission. It turned out that the executive officer on duty would not authorize it. The nurse returned.

Head nurse: (to victim) The executive officer reinforced the policy. He feels we should talk to a parent.

Victim: (very emotionally) Oh, God! Why do you have to call my parents? I just want to get help without them knowing about it! (crying)

The gynecologist came in. Ellie stood in the center of the examining room and said, very dramatically, looking right at the gynecologist, "Help me!" The gynecologist hopped up on the examining shelf and sat there, talking in an informal pose:

Gynecologist: A parent would want to know. . . . How are your parents? Are they terribly strict?

Victim: No. I'm on pretty good terms with them. And my mother is fairly liberal.

Gynecologist: If you have a good thing going with them it would be better to tell them rather than just be with strangers.

Staff discussed the case outside the exam room. The gynecologist had assumed that at least he could write a prescription. But the head nurse informed him that that was not so. He said he had not realized that the hospital rule was that he could not prescibe if he had not done an exam.

Gynecologist: (to staff) I hate to back down, but I don't want to go against hospital policy.

Head nurse: I can't really understand the girl's attitude.

Gynecologist: There's the legal aspect. The hospital has had so much bad publicity that I just don't dare go ahead and do anything unless it's legal. (big sigh) Oh, the problems of defensive medicine.

Efforts were made to find other agencies that would treat a minor without parental permission. Several likely centers were called, but, it was the weekend. Either there was no answer, or a recording said, "Please call back during regular weekday hours." Another hospital was called, but its policy was even more strict. They required not only that parents give permission but that the police be notified.

Meanwhile, staff identification with the victim's mother increased when they found out that she was a nurse. Her occupation meant she would know the rules regarding the granting of treatment without parental permission.

For about 10 minutes, staff members were obsessed about what to do. Nothing was very helpful. There was a tremendous stall. Everyone seemed caught. No one knew how to proceed.

The victim was still in the examining room, very upset and at times almost hysterical. She realized that to prevent a possible pregnancy one had to act very fast. She said, with panic in her voice, "I don't have time to think." Finally, after two hours, when in Ellie's mind the choice was one of having a good chance of getting pregnant vs telling her parents, she gave in. She called home. Her parents came to the hospital. They granted permission for examination and treatment and stayed with her.

Later, in a follow-up interview, Ellie's mother was asked about how she would have felt if Ellie had been treated at a clinic in which parental permission was not needed. Her reply shows an understanding of the dilemma that parents, children, and institutions face.

It wouldn't have bothered me if she was treated by people like those at the hospital. I can't say enough for how well we were treated. . . . I would prefer my daughters coming to me first. But children do not want parents to know and they need to be able to go to a clinic where they can be treated.

The unknown factor, of course, is whether the mother would have felt the same way if the daughter had been treated without parental permission and something had gone wrong. It is this unknown that increases clinicians' tendency to practice defensive medicine.

Parental Surveillance of the Body

In addition to the question of whether a victim can get medical care without parental permission, there is the opposite issue. Can a parent demand examination and treatment without the victim's permission? In other words, if a parent does consent, can a child refuse to undergo the treatment? According to Annas, "in answering this question, there is very little law that can be relied on."[47]

In practice, staff believe that if there has been some indication of sexual assault, then a parent has the right to demand examination and treatment, even if this demand is counter to the victim's wishes and counter to staff advice. Parents do sometimes make such a demand. They see it as their duty and their right to keep a watchful eye on the sexual experiences of their offspring. This parental surveillance is one more way in which the victim's privacy may be invaded. Following is a case in point:

Two accessory-to-sex victims, Marta (age 9) and Laura (age 12), were brought to pedi walk-in by their mothers. The story was that a 31-year-old neighbor had driven them around in his car and had taken them to an apartment. Laura told staff, "He said he'd give me five dollars if I'd go into the bedroom with him and her money if she would stay out front. He offered me that many times." However, the girls both maintained that sexual intercourse did not occur. The mothers were very intent on having their daughters examined.

Staff said they hoped "to talk the mothers out of wanting an 'internal'" and described the scene as "a sticky situation." The pediatrician's report states he counseled the parents "that if the story is true and that the girls were not [assaulted], that the diagnostic pelvic exam would be their first sexual encounter and this might be one reason not to do a pelvic exam."

The victims were not keen on being examined. Marta objected to a *man* doing the procedure. Neither Marta nor Laura understood *why* a pelvic was needed.

The mothers remained firm. Marta's mother said, "I have to be sure." Laura's mother indicated she wanted the pelvic done to be sure she could believe Laura. The one thing they wanted was an internal exam and it was obvious that nothing further would happen until they were assured that it would be done. The pediatrician had said it was their right and so if they insisted, he would call GYN. They did. The pediatrician looked resigned. He placed the call.

The gynecologist arrived. His consult sheet states, "Hymen intact. . . . Speculum [internal] exam not done, is not considered necessary and would be invasive." He did a pelvic visual exam instead.

Having the exams done satisfied the mothers. There were, however, repercussions. For example, several days later during a wait at the courthouse, Marta's mother said, "I told a friend about going to the hospital and she said 'Did they break her doing the exam?' Could that have happened? I certainly wouldn't want her broken, I wouldn't stand for that!" She seemed relieved to learn that only a visual exam had been done.

There were also repercussions on Marta. She complained to her mother about the doctor. "I didn't like him, he made me take my pants off. It wasn't nice." Her mother replied, "Doctors are different. They don't think like other men. When he looks at you it's just like he was looking at this," (knocked her hand on the table). Marta then added what was one of her greatest concerns—that her mother did not trust her. She said, "You wouldn't believe that nothing happened."

Staff regard it as the parent's right to insist on certain medical procedures. However, as the above case shows, not only the procedure done, but the parent's insistence upon having it done, may make a strong impression on the child. There is no easy solution to this dilemma. The opposite situation—for example, if a parent requested an exam, the exam was not done, and the child was later found to be injured or pregnant from an assault—obviously would have serious repercussions, too.

Access to Private Information: Burden of Proof

Medical care often requires access to information about the patient's private life. As Parsons has noted, "many facts which are relevant to people's problems of health fall into the realm of the private or confidential."[48] How far can a clinician go in this regard? One way in which limitations on the physician's legitimate claims on the patient are defined is through what Parsons calls "specificity of the scope of concern." He notes:

> The role [of the physician] conforms strictly to the criterion of the burden of proof being on the side of exclusion. If the patient asks why he should answer a question his doctor puts to him, or why he should submit to a given procedure, the answer is in terms of the relevance of his health problem—"if you want to get well, you have to give me the information I need to do my job," etc. If it cannot be justified by the relevance to the health problem it is "none of the doctor's business."[49]

Sexual assault cases are no exception to the general need of physicians for private information for making an assessment. However, physicians in their questioning sometimes went further than patients thought was justified. They sometimes asked questions and sought information that patients perceived as being unrelated to the current issue. Joe is a case in point. Because his physicians did not adequately answer the question of relevance, Joe perceived them as being out of line. Joe was a 13-year-old victim of a homosexual rape. A psychiatric referral was made, partly because staff found out that Joe had a history of emotional difficulties, and partly because staff felt especially uncomfortable with male sexual assault victims. Male victims appeared far less frequently than female victims on the emergency ward. When they did appear, staff seemed even less sure of what to do than with female victims. Joe was told to come back for a return visit and did so. Psychiatrists then interviewed him. They also sought to obtain confidential records on him from other treatment agencies. The patient and his family perceived the psychiatrists' requests as inappropriate and became highly upset, as the following quotes show.

Joe has been feeling badly all day. He had to tell the doctors about his school and he got all upset. They wanted him to have a brain test and he got all upset. He said he had just gone down there for shots. He felt this was all embarrassing to him and didn't understand what his school had to do with this situation. . . . The [doctors] wanted all his records released from the children's unit. That is what is so humiliating to him. I would feel so embarrassed, too.

Victim's mother

Joe has been upset because of my signing the form [to release the record]. He said it was like my selling him down the river. And I won't do it. I am writing to the clinic [to tell them not to send the records]. . . . This [clinic record] has nothing to do with this other incident.

Victim's father

[How did your talk with the two doctors go?] They were jerks. They talked about stuff that was none of their business. And they wanted to look at my record and give me brain tests. They just asked a lot of wild questions. [Like what?] Have I ever been in bed with a girl? When I was in seclusion at the unit did I ever hear weird sounds? Was it difficult for me to get hard in my balls while I was on Mellaril? [What did you do about the questions?] I answered them. I felt I had to. But I was burnt up about it.

Victim

From the patient's point of view, the psychiatrists did not adequately explain why their questions and requests for confidential records were relevant to his health problem. Thus, he experienced the situation as an invasion of privacy. He also felt that his behavior in other settings was being held against him in the present situation.

THE RECORDING OF INFORMATION

Since rape victims who go to a hospital or clinic have their predicament recorded in the institution's files, it is of interest to know what information gets selected for inclusion in the record, and what problems this selection process causes for victims if the record later is subpoenaed. Records at the main hospital studied were looked at from the point of view of what might happen if the case went to court. From the victim's point of view, two relevant questions are what information was omitted that might have helped the victim, and what information was included that might have hurt the victim.

Helpful Information Excluded

Consistent with the general focus of American medicine on physical care, bodily injuries of the victims typically got recorded. If anything was slighted in the record, it tended to be the victim's emotional condition. Physicians did not place much emphasis on recording either the emotional symptoms reported by patients (e.g., a patient's statement 'I'm frightened') or the signs of emotional upset visible to the clinician (e.g., hands shaking). However, questions typically are asked in court about the victim's emotional state after the assault (the expectation is that she should have been upset).

Occasionally, some physical injury also was omitted from the record. For example, one victim interviewed at the hospital was obviously bruised, and yet her medical record stated "no injuries." Such discrepancies were rare. If such a record did go to court, it could have important consequences. If there is a discrepancy between what the victim says on the witness stand and what the medical record says, it does not seem to occur to people that the medical record might be inaccurate. Rather, they assume the victim is in error.

Damning Information Included

From the victim's point of view, the medical record may include too much information. It may contain material that many people today consider irrelevant to the question of whether the person was raped and that will discredit her in the public eye.

Most of the medical records of the rape victims studied did contain reference to some damning issue. When such a reference occurred, almost always the victim came off looking badly; in a few cases, such a reference made her look good (for example, the record stated she was a virgin). However, even these positive statements may hurt victims in general because they, like the negative statements, perpetuate a concern with the issue.

Prior sexual experience was the damning issue most frequently discussed; 53 of the 115 rape victims' records explicitly stated whether the victim had had prior sex. Terms used included: date of "last voluntary intercourse," "hx [history] of coitus" vs "no prior coitus" or "denied any past coitus," "marital introitus" vs "tight introitus," "only inserted one finger," "used small pediatric speculum," "hymen—old tears," "virginal hymen" vs "hymen not intact." In some cases, additional information was included: "had coitus with boyfriend," "slept at her boyfriend's house," "started sexual life at age 17." Prior sex also was implied through other kinds of information—mention of birth control, vaginal infections, and so on. Less frequently, medical records included information on alcohol use, patient's psychiatric history, or designations such as "patient uncooperative."[50]

The material on the records suggests that physicians are put in an awkward position. There may be a conflict between the medical and legal aims of writing the record. There are questions that a physician must ask to do an assessment considered appropriate by medical standards.[51] A gynecologist typically will ask for a gynecological history, including questions about pregnancies, abortions, births, vaginal infections, and birth control. The custom has been to include answers to these questions in the written record. Yet many people today would ask what these pieces of information have to do with the legal question of whether the rape occurred.

The material on the medical records also indicates, however, that physicians feel they have a certain license to label patients. Phrases such as "started sexual life at age 17" and "living with boyfriend" clearly have—in the public eye—connotations of being "promiscuous" or "loose." Likewise, a phrase such as "patient uncooperative" makes a judgmental statement about the patient; more neutral language, such as "patient declined treatment" could be used by physicians if they so chose.

SPECIALIZATION AND PROFESSIONAL ISOLATION

The three main groups of professionals who work with rape victims are the police, health clinicians, and lawyers. The most striking thing about these three groups is their specialization and the lack of communication between them. Each group sticks to its own field and neither learns from others nor teaches others any of its specialized knowledge even though this knowledge is relevant to the duties at hand. Physicians who gather evidence and lawyers (district attorneys who prosecute cases and defense lawyers who represent the accused) who need this evidence for their courtroom arguments do not talk to one another, except perhaps about an individual case. They do not discuss ways in which their joint work might be integrated so as to better protect the rights of both the victim and the defendant.

Physicians are uninformed about legal procedures. Thus, the medical evidence that will be used in court either to acquit a defendant or to prove a defendant guilty is being collected by physicians who do not know the definitions of various crimes and who do not know what types of evidence are needed to make the judgment of guilt or innocence of the defendant. Crime and its definition is not a subject often taught in medical schools. As new doctors begin their work on the emergency ward the only orientation they receive on these matters is informal and consists of advice handed down from senior resident to new resident. A legally trained person does not instruct them, even though these doctors will be called upon to examine alleged victims of such acts as attempted murder, child abuse, assault and battery, and rape.

Physicians, as a result, do not necessarily know the definition of rape, even though the results of their examination will be used in legal proceedings and even though on the witness stand they may be asked whether the victim was raped. According to Massachusetts statutes at the time of our study, rape was defined as carnal knowledge of a female by force and against her will.[52] It should be noted, incidentally, that judges differ in their readings of the law on the issue of penetration; some say penetration of the vulva is sufficient, others say it must be of the vagina. Throughout our project, we asked a number of physicians, "What is the legal definition of rape?" Some gave fairly accurate definitions, like the physician who said:

> It is penetration of the vagina against the patient's will. (pause) Any penetration, [however slight].

Others gave erroneous answers. Three physicians answered as follows:

> The legal [definition of rape] is if there is any evidence of sexual assault whether or not there is penetration.
> I don't know what degree past the hymenal ring needs to be penetrated [for it to be rape].
> I'm not sure, but I think [rape] is when the woman is. . . forced by any reason to have intercourse. It doesn't have to be intercourse, but forced for any sexual activity such as oral or anal [sex].[53]

Emergency ward personnel are trained only very selectively in the techniques that could be used to gather evidence. Physicians, for example, seek evidence of penetration by looking for the presence of tissue damage and by preparing slides to look for sperm. But they seem unaware of the many types of evidence that police manuals and police officers concerned with the subject often recommend—collecting the victim's clothing and carefully folding it to prevent dried stains from brushing off, giving the victim a comb and envelope to gather hair samples that might have been left by the assailant, clipping the victim's fingernails to provide skin scrapings of the assailant.

Lawyers and judges do not know the meaning of medical terms, even though they make judgments based on their reading of medical records. Sometimes medical charts are explained in court by a physician who testifies. At other times records are introduced into court as evidence with no medical person present to interpret them. Consider, for example, the following scene that occurred in district court during a hearing for probable cause for rape.

> The medical record was introduced and became the focus of great attention. The defense lawyer claimed he could understand at least part of it. The prosecutor said he really could not read it. The judge asked to see it, pored over it again and again, complaining, "I can't understand it, why do doctors all write so illegibly!" Someone asked if anyone from the hospital was present to interpret the chart, but no one was.

Thus, the medical record was introduced as evidence and the defense lawyer, the prosecutor, and the judge pored over the record and argued about it, unable to understand it but using it as evidence anyway.

This lack of communication between professional groups is a phenomenon that one sees again and again as one follows victims through the criminal justice system. It has been observed by other researchers, such as Chappell, who notes the absence of effective liaison between police and prosecutor's office and the negative effect this lack has on the prosecution of rape cases.[54]

NOTES

1. Talcott Parsons, "The Professions and Social Structure," in *Essays in Sociological Theory*, 2nd. ed. rev. (Glencoe, Ill.: The Free Press, 1954), p. 41. (First published 1939 in *Social Forces.*)

2. David Sudnow, "Dead on Arrival," in *Where Medicine Fails*, Anselm L. Strauss, ed. (Chicago: Aldine 1970), p. 113.

3. Julius A. Roth, "The Treatment of the Sick," in *Poverty and Health: A Sociological Analysis*, John Kosa, Aaron Antonovsky, and Irving Kenneth Zola, eds. (Cambridge Mass.: Harvard University Press, 1969). p. 237.

4. Everett Cherrington Hughes, "The Making of a Physician," in *Men and Their Work*, (Glencoe, Ill.: Free Press, 1958), pp. 121-22. (First published 1955 in *Human Organization.*)

5. The concept of patient requests was developed in Aaron Lazare, "The Walk-In Patient: A Reformulation" (paper delivered at Grand Rounds, Massachusetts General Hospital, Boston, February 16, 1971).

6. At this hospital, for prevention of VD, two penicillin shots is only the initial dosage. A total of four shots (4.8 million units), given in two sets of two, is typically prescribed.

7. Michael Balint, "The Drug, 'Doctor,'" in *Medical Care: Readings in the Sociology of Medical Institutions,* eds. W. Richard Scott and Edmund H. Volkart, with the assistance of Lynda Lytle Holmstrom (New York: Wiley, 1966), p. 286. Reprinted from Michael Balint, *The Doctor, His Patient and the Illness* (New York: International Universities Press, 1957). (Emphasis in the original.)

8. Julius A. Roth, *Timetables: Structuring the Passage of Time in Hospital Treatment and Other Careers* (Indianapolis: Bobbs-Merrill, 1963), p. 61.

9. Roth, "The Treatment of the Sick," p. 231.

10. Howard S. Becker, Blanche Geer, Everett C. Hughes, and Anselm L. Strauss, *Boys in White: Student Culture in Medical School* (Chicago: University of Chicago Press, 1961), p. 329.

11. Ibid., p. 320.

12. Roth, "The Treatment of the Sick, p. 231.

13. Erving Goffman, "On the Characteristics of Total Institutions," in *Asylums: Essays on the Social Situation of Mental Patients and Other Inmates* (Garden City, N.Y.: Doubleday Anchor Books, 1961), pp. 1-124; Roth *Timetables,* pp. 1-62.

14. Goffman, op. cit., p. 7

15. Ibid., p. 9.

16. Ann Wolbert Burgess and Lynda Lytle Holmstrom, "Accountability: A Right of the Rape Victim," *Journal of Psychiatric Nursing and Mental Health Services* 13 (May-June), pp. 11-16.

17. Priorities were defined in terms of the relative *frequency* with which the issues were mentioned by patients in response to open-ended questions about their hospital experience.

18. LeRoy G. Schultz, ed., *Rape Victimology* (Springfield, Ill.: Charles C. Thomas, 1975), p. 220.

19. Only two victims mentioned the race of the physician. Both were white women who had just been raped by black men. As one woman—who showed no evidence in other interviews of being prejudiced—said, "One of the doctors was black and the [assailant] was black and I started crying."

20. Ann Wolbert Burgess and Lynda Lytle Holmstrom, "Crisis and Counseling Requests of Rape Victims," *Nursing Research* 23 (May-June 1974), pp. 196-202.

21. Eleven of the 92 adult rape victims were having their menstrual period at the time of the rape.

22. Ann Wolbert Burgess and Lynda Lytle Holmstrom, "Sexual Assault: Signs and Symptoms, *The Journal of Emergency Nursing* (March-April 1975), pp. 11-15.

23. Severity of injury was coded as follows:
    1. None: no bruises noted; nothing "abnormal" recorded
    2. Minimal: some bruise noted but no laceration or bleeding
    3. Moderate: laceration(s) noted; treatment necessary
    4. Severe: bruises and lacerations; consults required; consideration of hospitalization

24. W. F. Enos, J. C. Beyer, and G. T. Mann, "The Medical Examination of Cases of Rape," in Schultz, op cit., p. 230. (First published 1972 in *Journal of Forensic Sciences.)*

25. Lynda Lytle Holmstrom and Ann Wolbert Burgess, "Rape Victimology: Past, Present

and Future Research," paper read at the American Association for the Advancement of Science annual meeting, Boston, Mass., February 23, 1976.

26. Schultz, op. cit., p. ix.

27. Enos, Beyer, and Mann, op. cit., p. 221.

28. Lynda Lytle Holmstrom, "Review of Schultz: Rape Victimology," *Sex Roles: A Journal of Research* 1 (December 1975), pp. 398-400.

29. Since the time of the study, however, staff—primarily nurses—have carried on a victim counseling program. Through their efforts, intervention for emotional as well as physical aspects of sexual assault has been provided.

30. Everett C. Hughes, "Professions," *Daedalus* 92 (Fall 1963), pp. 655-57; Eliot Freidson, *Profession of Medicine: A Study of the Sociology of Applied Knowledge* (New York: Dodd, Mead 1970), p. 10.

31. Lois Pratt, Arthur Seligmann, and George Reader, "Physicians' Views on the Level of Medical Information Among Patients," in Scott and Volkart, op cit., pp. 307-08. (First published 1957 in *American Journal of Public Health.*)

32. Fred Davis, "Uncertainty in Medical Prognosis, Clinical and Functional," in Scott and Volkart, op. cit., pp. 315-17. (First published 1960 in *American Journal of Sociology.*) Elisabeth Kübler-Ross, "Reactions to the Seminar on Death and Dying," in *On Death and Dying* (New York: Macmillan, 1969), pp. 218-39.

33. Max Weber, "Bureaucracy," in *From Max Weber: Essays in Sociology,* H. H. Gerth and C. Wright Mills, eds and trans. (New York: Oxford University Press, 1958), pp. 196-244. (Originally published as *Wirtschaft und Gesellschaft,* Part III, Chapter 6, pp. 650-78.) Peter M. Blau, *Bureaucracy in Modern Society* (New York: Random House, 1956), pp. 28-31.

34. Roth, *Timetables,* p. 31.

35. Ibid.; Everett Cherrington Hughes, "Work and the Self," in Hughes, *Men and Their Work,* pp. 42-55. First published 1951 in John H. Rohrer and M. Sherif, eds., *Social Psychology at the Crossroads* (New York: Harper) pp. 313-23.

36. Goffman, op. cit., p. 14.

37. Ibid., p. 16.

38. Ibid., p. 28.

39. George J. Annas, *The Rights of Hospital Patients: The Basic ACLU Guide to a Hospital Patient's Rights* (New York: Avon 1975), p. 121.

40. The Hippocratic Oath quoted from Ibid., p. 125.

41. AMA Principles of Medical Ethics, 1957, quoted from Ibid.

42. Annas, op. cit., p. 122

43. Ibid.

44. Ibid., p. 137.

45. A new law significantly expanding the medical rights of minors went into effect in Massachusetts on October 28, 1975. It permits certain categories of persons below age 18 to consent to their own medical care, including a minor who is pregnant or believes herself to be pregnant and minors who reasonably believe that they are suffering from or have come in contact with diseases defined as dangerous to the public health by statute.

46. Many other occupational groups and institutions operate defensively. For example, decisions in the railroad industry regarding grade-crossing equipment are often made to

minimize litigation costs rather than to minimize accident rates. F. Ross Holmstrom, Private communication.

47. Annas, op. cit., p. 139.

48. Talcott Parsons, *The Social System* (Glencoe, Ill.: Free Press 1951), p. 452.

49. Ibid., p. 456.

50. The comments here refer to damning information written by clinicians. In addition, the form has lines that are to be filled out by the historian (e.g., patient's address, party responsible for payment). If the patient's address is an institution or if the patient is on welfare, then this type of damning information goes on the record also.

51. Some potentially embarrassing questions are asked for legal reasons; that is, with the intent of helping the physician gather and interpret evidence. For example, the question about last voluntary intercourse is asked with the intent of helping to determine whether sperm found is from the assault or possibly from some prior sexual encounter.

52. Massachusetts General Laws Annotated, chap. 265, sec. 22. The 1974 law broadens the definition to include *male* victims, forced *unnatural* acts, and the *threat* of bodily injury.

53. At the time this statement was made, Massachusetts law did not include forced anal or oral sex within the definition of rape.

54. Duncan Chappell, "Forcible Rape and the American System of Criminal Justice," in *Violence and Criminal Justice*, Duncan Chappell and John Monahan, eds. (Lexington, Mass.: D. C. Heath, 1975), p. 94.

CHAPTER 5

■

Getting the Case to Trial

You bitch, you're going to suffer.

RAPIST'S MOTHER TO
VICTIM

*You can't drop the charges.
They can order you to come.
. . . You've got to testify.*

POLICE OFFICER TO
VICTIM

Erving Goffman has emphasized the importance of "cooling the mark out" as a general social process. He explains that "in the argot of the criminal world, the term 'mark' refers to any individual who is a victim or prospective victim of certain forms of planned illegal exploitation. The mark is the sucker—the person who is taken in."[1] In the con game, the "sting" or "blowoff," when the mark's money is taken, may be followed by another phase, called "cooling the mark out." "One of the operators stays with the mark and makes an effort to keep the anger of the mark within manageable and sensible proportions. . . . The mark is given instruction in the philosophy of taking a loss."[2] Moving from the con game example to the larger society, Goffman argues that people who have to be "cooled out" are found in many types of social settings. To identify them, he suggests asking: Where are there persons acting as if they were entitled to the rights of a certain status, and then having to face up to the fact that they do not qualify? To determine the ways in which persons in such a position can be cooled out, he suggests asking how they can be made to accept the immense injury that has been done to them so as to go on without raising a squawk.

By starting the court process at their own or other people's initiative, rape victims are making the claim that a victim is entitled to the rights of a particular status: prosecutrix in a rape case.[3] During the long pretrial process, however, many victims will be made aware of the fact that they do not qualify for this status. They got started in the court process because someone squawked. Things begin to occur that encourage them to not squawk any more. Cross-pressures are exerted on victims—threats and appeals to make them drop charges, other threats and appeals to make them persevere. The process is long and wearing; from rape to trial may take two years. The many stages to go through include arraignment, hearing for probable cause, grand jury, and trial—or plea bargaining—at superior court. Delays are the rule rather than the exception. The district attorney, like police and physician at earlier stages, evaluates the case. The court bureaucracy contributes to a sense of depersonalization. And the courthouse scene may entail not only formal but also informal confrontations between victim and defendant.

There is attrition of cases at each stage. Only a small percentage of cases ever get scheduled in superior court. It is the unusual victim who remains enthusiastic to press charges through this whole time. The process of getting a rape case to trial acts as a way of cooling the prosecutrix out.

CROSS-PRESSURES ON THE VICTIM

Many people have a stake in how a rape case turns out. They often subject the victim to pressure to try to get it resolved to their advantage. They do things either to try to get the victim to drop the case or to continue to prosecute. Pressures from the victim's own network were discussed in Chapter 3, in the section on the decision whether to press charges. In addition, the victim may be subjected to pressure from the assailant, his social network, defense counsel, police, and prosecutor.

Pressures to Drop Charges

The assailant, his social network, and the defense counsel may pressure the victim to drop charges. In our present study, 24 of the 115 rape victims were so pressured. In addition, seven victims reported "mysterious happenings," such as unexplained phone calls, that they thought might be efforts at intimidation.

Assailants and their networks used three main approaches: threats (14 cases), sympathy appeals (5 cases), and bribes (2 cases). In addition, there was harassment from the defense counsel prior to court in 11 cases. Some used several tactics on one victim.

Threats. Some threats made to victims were statements or implications of intent to do physical harm if the case went to court. Victims reported such threats as "The man on the telephone said his name was Cullen and that he'd get me if it was the last thing he did," "[His mother] said there'll be lots of trouble if those boys get sent away," and, "He keeps talking of killing me." In another case, the scene at the courthouse went as follows:

> The rapist's mother, a large, heavyset woman of about 40, came up to one of us and then went over to another female. She said to each, "Are you the one who's trying to frame my son?" After the hearing she knew the victim's identity. She went over, stuck her finger right in the victim's face, and said, menacingly, "You bitch, you're going to suffer." The victim later expressed her fear of being confronted by some such person in the subway or street. She sighed, "Another face to memorize."

Other threats were statements of intent to embarrass the victim if the case went to court. One victim told us, "His girl friend said 'I'll make a liar out of you.'" Another said, "His friend told me he was going to say in court that I made a pass at him."

Sympathy Appeals. Assailants or their families sometimes made appeals for the victim's mercy. Their pleas, often highly emotional, emphasized how much the assailant meant to others, cited religion, or begged forgiveness: "His wife and kids were over here crying and begging not to have me do anything to their father," "A Mary called—she said his baby needed milk and Pampers—he needed to be working, not in jail," "He wrote me [from prison]. He wanted me to come and visit him. He said he was ashamed before me and before God. He wanted forgiveness."

Bribes. Occasionally an assailant or his family offered to pay the victim to not testify. In one case, the assailant called the victim's home repeatedly. "He said he would pay money to keep this quiet." In another case, the victim reported, "My boyfriend Walter told me the boy's mother was paying people to testify [against me] and that she also wanted to pay me for not testifying or pressing charges—but Walter didn't give her my number."

Mysterious Happenings. Victims sometimes reported mysterious events that frightened them. Although there was no proof that these events were related to the rape, victims wondered if there were a connection, especially when they could not find other explanations. In one case, in which threats had been made, for example, someone pushed the victim's father down some stairs. In another, the victim started getting obscene phone calls. The caller asked, "Nancy, is that you? Do you want to fuck?" In another case, the victim would answer the phone and hear only heavy breathing.

Harassment by Defense Counsel. Victims sometimes reported that the defendant's lawyer talked, or tried to talk, to them. Defense counsel sometimes exerted great pressure to get victims to talk, telephoning their homes repeatedly, visiting them at work, contacting members of their family. Following is a case in point:

> The public defender called me and said for me to come to her office—that she wanted to talk with me. I don't think I should.
>
> *Victim, age 18*

> I didn't want to break the law. The defense lawyer said, "You're breaking the law if you don't talk to me." So I was careful to explain that I was not refusing to talk to her, but that I was just going to talk to the police officer first to find out what I should do. . . . I called [the station]. . . . The officer told me that I didn't have to talk to the defense lawyer, so I didn't.
>
> *Victim's mother*

Another victim reported, "[The defense lawyers] call me, my parents, my brothers and sister. They have called my husband's employer. They all ask questions about me." In this case, everyone was instructed to make the same reply: "It's none of your business."

When defense lawyers did speak with victims or their families they gathered information that they later used in court against the victim or they tried to persuade the victim to lower charges or drop the case. They appealed to the victim's sympathy ("How would you like it if . . . it was your first offense?") or suggested the uselessness of going to court ("They'd only get probation"). Victims in general experienced such visits and calls as harassment.

The practice of defense lawyers visiting victims seems to be regarded with ambivalence at best by the legal profession. Defense lawyers justify their behavior saying they are being conscientious in preparing their case ("There's nothing illegal with that; one is supposed to investigate the case"). Prosecutors sometimes tease them ("I hear you've been to see Karen"). And judges sometimes characterize the practice as a bit irregular ("It *is* most unusual").

Pressure to Go Through with Court

Police and prosecutor sometimes pressure the victim not only to press charges, but to persevere in the court process. They may make threats, specifically, the threat of arrest ("If you don't come, I'll have to go down and arrest you".) Like this one, the threat may be made in a humorous context, but still the message is clear: Be at court. They also may appeal to the victim's sympathies ("You can't back out on me after all the work I did to arrest him"). And they may appeal to the victim's sense of civic duty. The following example is especially interesting because the tactics of the officer switched once the victim said she wanted to consult a lawyer.

> *Rose:* I don't want to press charges. I want to drop the rape charges. The sergeant pressed the charges. I didn't have any control over it.
>
> *Officer:* You can't drop the charges. They can order you to come. This is not a crime against you. It's a crime against the Commonwealth, against society, against people in Dorchester and in Springfield. To let them go is a worse crime than the crime they committed against you. You've got to testify. Look, a lot of people went out of their way to help you. Not us—after all we get paid for it. But the guy who helped you. He took a risk—they shot at him.
>
> *Rose:* I'm scared. After people testify, they get them, like the Mafia.
>
> *Officer:* This isn't the Mafia. They're just young punks.
>
> *Rose:* But they're so young.
>
> *Officer:* They didn't show you any respect—no respect for your youth. And if it wasn't you it might have been some other woman.
>
> *Rose:* I know, I know. But I want to talk to my lawyer.
>
> *Officer:* (exhibiting an immediate change in demeanor, tone of voice, and tactics of argument) Now Rose, you've been through a lot. What you need is some rest to take your mind off it. . . . You'll feel better. What you do is talk to your lawyer later today. And this morning at the hearing you just tell your story.[4]

Pressure likewise may be used on witnesses to try to get them to testify. In one case, an assailant had raped several girls in a housing project. Two victims had gone to court. The district attorney thought he needed the testimony of a third girl as a witness. The mother refused to bring her to court. He tried to persuade her:

> We all want to see that guy off the street. I understand that your daughter is under stress and will be under stress in court. But what about when she sees this guy on the street? Fran and Polly have done their part, now it's your turn.

The mother still refused. The district attorney said, "Well, thank you, he'll be on the streets soon."

In summary, the cross-pressures described above play on the initial feelings victims had about whether to press charges. It will be recalled that reasons to not press charges included fear of reprisal, feeling sorry for the guy, and wanting to avoid both the hassle and embarrassment of court. Reasons to testify included the notion of duty to protect other potential victims. The subsequent threats, sympathy pleas, harassment, and appeals to civic duty play into these earlier feelings.

DELAYS

Delay, Barry Schwartz argues, is an important topic for sociological investigation. Delay entails two kinds of obvious costs: losses occasioned by it (value foregone through idleness) and degradation (implications for the self of being kept idle). Schwartz's interest is in exploring how these costs are distributed through the social structure and by what principle. In other words, what is "the relationship between location in a social structure and the expenditure of waiting time"?[5] He looks at server-client relationships and asserts that "the distribution of waiting time coincides with the distribution of power."[6] There is a correlation between the position the individual occupies and the degree to which the individual waits for and is waited for by people in other positions. "The least powerful may almost always be approached at will; the most powerful are seen only 'by appointment.' . . . The powerful tend not to ask for appointments with their own subordinates; rather, the lowly are summoned."[7] Waiting is affected by the client's resources, powerful clients being relatively exempt from waiting. Waiting also is affected by whether there is an opportunity for the client to go elsewhere—is there competition (e.g., many banks in one area) or a monopoly (e.g., the government passport and visa service)? Court, Schwartz suggests, is an informative example of the monopoly situation. In some courts, all parties scheduled for a certain day are told to be there when the judge arrives. "While this tactic guarantees that the judge's valuable time will not be wasted, it also ensures that most parties will be kept waiting for a substantial period of time; some, all day long."[8] Schwartz concludes that control of time is not a coincidental by-product of power, but rather one of its essential properties.

Delay in Rape Cases

Numerous delays are the rule rather than the exception in getting a rape case to trial. Nothing could be more revealing of the lowly position rape victims occupy in the criminal justice system than the waiting time they must endure.

Repeated postponements or continuances are typical. The hearing for probable cause at the district court level may well be postponed three or four times. Often it is postponed at the request of the defense—the defendant has defaulted, he has changed lawyers, the lawyer has not appeared, the lawyer has not had time to prepare the case, or a witness for the defense is not available that day. Sometimes it is postponed at the request of the prosecution—the victim does not appear, the case is not prepared, or a prosecution witness is not available. At the superior court level, postponements again are likely, partly for the reasons discussed already, partly because there is a backlog that makes scheduling cases for trial difficult. The time between date of the rape and final verdict may easily be a year to two years.

Each date that the case is scheduled at district court or at the superior level the victim is to appear at court. The docket is compiled according to the principle of "overscheduling."[9] In other words, typically everyone is told to be at court at 9 or 9:30 A.M., even though their case may not be called until the afternoon. Usually one has to wait for the case to be called even to find out whether it will be heard. Thus, the victim often waits around the courthouse for several hours only to be told that the case is to be postponed. Even if the case is heard, she often waits several hours. She must also wait to be interviewed by the district attorney. The entire process is one of "hurry up and wait."

The victim typically is summoned to court not only in the legal sense, but in the general sense of being told when to appear rather than being consulted about the time of the appointment. Sometimes victims are asked what date would be convenient for them, but by and large their schedules are a minor factor in setting the court dates.

Victims are not the only ones who wait. Victims and defendants have several things in common: they both occupy a lowly position in the criminal justice system and both are relatively powerless. Both are summoned. Both must wait to talk to the lawyer, wait for court sessions, wait for their day in court. Beyond these similarities, however, there are important differences in the situation of victim and defendant. Some defendants wait in jail.[10] Some victims wait because the defense deliberately uses delay as a tactic, thinking that the longer the case can be postponed, the greater the chances that it will be dropped or that it will become weaker, and that the defendant will go free. Another group that does an inordinate amount of waiting is the police; much of the victim's wait is shared by the officer on the case.

Victims' Reactions to Delay: It Costs

As Barry Schwartz suggests, delay entails not only the "queue" itself (a social structural aspect), but also "waiting" (the orientation of the personalities that constitute the elements in that structure.) "The study of delay is therefore a task requiring psychological as well as structural and interactional modes of analysis."[11] That is, one must look not only at the queue but also at the subjective view of the actors—of the client and server.

Court delays are a major focus of rape victims' complaints. The aspects that victims in the present study found most bothersome are shown in Table 1.

Table 1.   Rape Victims' Reactions to Court Delays*

Costs	
Psychic energy: it's wearing	15
Monetary and time cost to family, friends**	14
Monetary and time cost to victim	13
Memory Loss	5
Total	47
Benefits	
Practice helps	2
Total	2

*Tabulated from open-ended questions and spontaneous comments. Some victims mentioned more than one aspect.
**Sometimes leading to decreased network support at court.

As will be recalled, Schwartz mentions two categories of costs: losses (value foregone) and degradation (implications for the self). Most of the rape victims' explicit complaints fall into the category of losses: psychic energy consumed by the delay, financial and time losses, and memory loss. The degradation costs do not tend to be mentioned so explicitly by victims, but come through more between the lines.

Psychic Energy Consumed: Wearing the Victim Down.   Rape victims find the long court process, and especially the many delays, wearisome and discouraging. Victims get emotionally prepared for court—"psyched up"—and then experience a letdown if the case is continued ("I got all worked up for nothing"). The court process seems to last forever ("How much longer will this go on?"). Victims may feel worn down to the point where they no longer care what happens. They say such things as, "I don't feel I want to go to court anymore. . . . I am tired of it. . . . I was ready to testify then, but I'm tired of it now." Some victims found waiting the hardest part of the court experience. One, asked what suggestions she had for other victims, said:

> *Believe* people when they say [court] will take a long time. That was the worst part—waiting. Everybody told me it would take a long time. But I still didn't really know what it would be like [to wait].

Monetary and Time Costs to Family and Friends. Court delays increase the financial and time losses for relatives and friends who accompany the victim to court. Each delay means more lost work or schooltime, lost pay, interrupted days, or expenses (babysitter, lunch, transportation).[12]

A number of family members or friends continued to come to court with the victim despite these costs. They complained at length. As one said:

> I can't keep taking days off. They postponed it and didn't talk with us. . . . I can't keep losing a day's pay going into that court!

In other cases, delays made court sufficiently costly that it diminished network support at court. The family member or friend would come to court, nothing would happen, and the decision would be made to not go through that again. In one case, a parent took two days off from a working-class job, but decided it meant too much lost money to do again. In another case, a parent canceled the day's professional appointments, but when nothing happened at court, he decided he would not do it the next time. One victim who ended up going to court without family or friends summed up the situation, saying, "I guess once was enough for everybody."

Monetary and Time Costs to Victim. Each court delay means more lost work- or schooltime, lost pay, interrupted days or expenses for the victim, too. One victim said, "If I have to go to court for several days, who pays for my missing work?" Another, after a day at court, said, "It's four o'clock—another workday shot." Another said, "My boss is nice about it, but I'm losing pay." Young victims often missed a lot of school:

I haven't been to school much this month with court—I've missed 11 days. Had to go to the clinic too. [How are your grades?] I failed this marking period. I hope to get them up, though—I have two more months.

The cost of missing work or school is compounded by some victims' desire to keep other people from knowing what has happened. Thus they are faced with the additional problem of getting time off without revealing the reason for the absence. One victim reported:

My hardest problem has been getting off from work to go to court. I haven't told them at work [that I was raped] and have to make up excuses.

Younger victims who miss school are also sometimes very reluctant to reveal the reason for the absence.

Memory Loss.   A few victims said that the delays made it hard for them to remember the details of the incident. One said:

I had forgotten most of it until I had to come here [to court] today. I had to put everything out of my mind or I wouldn't be able to do my schoolwork. So much has happened in a year.

Another said, "There is such a long delay to make you forget the details."

Practice Helps.   Almost all comments about delays and waiting were complaints. However, occasionally a victim reported that the delay had positive aspects as well. It meant that they had been to court more than once and that they had grown accustomed to the procedure. As one victim's mother phrased it, "[Court] isn't as bad as it used to be. We have been so many times that we are used to it."

Degradation.   The degradational costs of delay are not mentioned so explicitly by victims. Nevertheless, a sense of loss to the self does come through when one reads between the lines. It seems to come through most in comments having to do with the conditions of waiting. Victims may talk about sitting unnoticed ("We went to court and waited till 2P.M. No one said anything to us"). They may talk about waiting in the courthouse corridor ("It was awful just standing out in the hall that day"), or about a wait that occurs *during* the appointment with the DA, who may interrupt the interview for other business that takes priority:

[At court] I was pushed around and it seemed no one was concerned about me anymore. They just popped me in and started asking me my story and I have to tell it at 40 miles per hour. Then the DA jumped up and ran out. It was awful.

Delay: A Case Example

There is a cumulative effect of the queuing and the waiting that does not come through in these isolated quotes. The cost—indeed, oppression may not be too strong a word—that victims experience through delays may best be shown through a detailed case example.

May 5: The Attack on Gail, age 13, by Mr. Porter, neighbor, age 45.

May 7: District Court, first appearance
We arrived at the courthouse about 9:30. Gail and her father, Mr. Watts, were already there with the police officer, standing in the corridor. The first thing Mr. Watts did was pull the neck of her dress back to show us the bruise on her left shoulder. Mr. Watts took time off from his maintenance job to attend court and Gail was missing school. Court consisted of a long wait. Gail seemed restless. Many cases were called before the Porter case. We sat through "an assault" and "a robbery." Gail was observant. She watched what other people did and wondered where she would have to go when called. Finally the Porter case was called. The court appointed a defense lawyer and ordered the defendant to be examined psychiatrically. A new date was set.

May 21: District Court, second appearance
We arrived at court only to find out that the case had been postponed. Porter was in Bridgewater,[13] presumably for psychiatric tests. Gail and Mr. Watts had already left. Later, Mrs. Watts said, "My husband went to court and they told him it was postponed. He took a day off from work and lost the day's pay because when he went to call [his boss] back they said they had someone to take his place so not to bother to come in. . . . My husband thinks they are doing this to discourage people from pressing charges. . . . We are discouraged over this. My husband was pretty angry he had to go down there—that they didn't tell him not to come."

May 25: District Court, third appearance
We arrived at court at 9:30. Gail and Mr. Watts were there. We stayed until 1:00 or so, at which time we found out that the defense lawyer was nowhere to be found. During the long wait, Mr. Watts was both supportive and cross with his daughter. Gail got restless waiting. She did things to pass the time of day—played with her clothes, took her pulse and counted how many times it beat in a minute, looked at a burn on her hand, took her

coat off and put it on again several times, ate cough drops, went for a walk. Mr. Watts was upset by the waiting. He complained as 11:00 drew near and the judge had not yet appeared. He said, "What the hell are they doing, they tell you to be here at 9:00!" He was concerned about his job. "I think I might lose my job because of missing work." We sat through a marijuana case and others. At 1:00 the Porter case was called. The judge was annoyed that the defense lawyer was not there. A new date was set.

June 1: District Court, fourth appearance, hearing for probable cause

We again arrived early as instructed. The case was called at 11:00. Mr. Watts was very angry waiting. He was afraid the hearing would be delayed. The defense tried for another delay. Mr. Watts said if that happened he would not bring her back. He had come four times and his boss was ready to fire him. He absolutely would not come back again. During the wait for other cases, Gail was quite restless. At one point, Mr. Watts said, "We better not sit here till 1:30 again!" The hearing was held and the court found probable cause.

February 20, the following year: first day of trial, superior court

We arrived at court early as directed. We met Gail and Mr. Watts. Gail seemed subdued. Mr. Watts repeated his concern about losing his job. "But," he added, "I have to come to court with her or I wouldn't be a good father." Jury selection began at 11:00 and took about 45 minutes. The trial began. Gail was the first witness. During lunch recess the issue of when the trial would be over came up. Gail found out there was a possibility that it would not end today and that she would have to come back tomorrow. She got very upset when she heard this news and cried. Mr. Watts put his arms around her and held her. Walking back to the courtroom Gail was still upset. Mr. Watts said, "I know it's tiring but it's just as tiring on me to come to this stinking court!" Gail finished testifying. Then Mr. Watts took the stand. At 4:00 court ended for the day.

February 21: second day of trial

Mr. Watts testified again. Mrs. Watts expected to, but the case did not get that far.

February 22: third day of trial

Mr. and Mrs. Watts came again. Preparing mentally and emotionally for her testimony, she said to us, "Coming to court two days makes me feel more at ease today. I've gotten used to the surroundings." At 2:30, the defense lawyer gave his opening statement. He then called Mrs. Watts to the stand as a witness for the defense.

February 25: fourth day of trial

Verdict from jury: assault with intent to commit rape, not guilty; indecent assault and battery, guilty.

February 26: disposition

Sentence: four to five years at Walpole.[14]

Defense lawyer to defendant Porter (whispering): "You'll be out in 16 months if you're good."

Depersonalization

The courthouse scene as a whole can contribute to a sense of depersonalization. As with the hospital, victims may encounter individuals at the courthouse who are sympathetic. But still, the organizational structure may be oppressive. Because delays are perhaps the most striking of such organizational features at court, they have been discussed at length. However, others deserve at least brief mention. At court, as at the hospital, the tendency is to keep the victim in ignorance. Advice and explanations from the DA are limited, as is discussed later. Indeed, one victim only found out after court was in session that the rape charge had been dropped; the grand jury had only returned indictments of unnatural acts and of assault and battery. Later asked if there were any parts of the court procedure that she had special feelings about, she immediately brought up not being told. She said, "I didn't find out about that till I was in court. . . . I just remember somewhere along the first day in court realizing there was no rape charge . . . . It was a funny way to find out." There is a lack of continuity of service here too. As one victim said, "I've had a different DA every time I've been to court." And even more than at the hospital, there is a lack of privacy. Victims not only often wait in the courthouse corridor, but the court session is open to the public, unless victim or defendant is young. Thus, many of the themes that occur in the hospital experience are repeated in the courthouse scene.

THE DISTRICT ATTORNEY ENCOUNTER

The district attorney is one more official the rape victim encounters if the case goes through the court process.[15] The interview by the district attorney is another important step in the victim's career through the criminal justice system. To evaluate and prepare the case, the DA asks the victim to go over the details of the story. This interview, like previous ones with other authorities, may be unsettling.

The DA—Who's He?

Victims have some notion of what the police officer's role is, but are far less certain of what the district attorney is supposed to do. Rape victims will sometimes ask, "Do I need to get a lawyer?" They do not necessarily understand, until it is explained, that the DA is to represent their side. (A more precise statement would be that the district attorney represents the state, and that the state's interests and the victim's interests do not always coincide.[16])

The Interview

Questions and Style.   The questions district attorneys—all male in the present study—were observed to ask fall into four main categories. First, they almost always ask what happened. They ask many "who-what-when-where" questions. In one case, the questions were:

> How did this all start?
> When was the first time you saw this man?
> OK, then what happened?
> Did you accept the beer?
> Did you have to go by his house to get to your house?
> How did you get into the room?
> You had no conversation with anyone?
> What was in the room?
> Then what happened?
> Did he take all your clothes off?
> He kept his forearm against you the whole time?
> Where were you during this?
> How did you get there?

The "what happened" questions may include considerable attention to the sexual details of the incident. In a few cases, they included intimate questions about the victim's clothes and sexual response. For example, the DA in a matter-of-fact manner asked one victim:

> What clothes were you wearing?
> Was the blouse sexy?

Did you have a bra on?
Did you have an orgasm?

In a few cases at superior court the DA did not ask the victim what happened. He relied instead on a transcript of the grand jury testimony.

Second, district attorneys often focus on force and resistance ("What did
you do to try to stop him? What weapons if any did he use?" "Did you
scream? Why?" "How did you get away?"). Third, they often focus on
reporting the rape ("What time did you call the police?" "Who called?"
"When did you notify the police?" "How did you get to the hospital?").
Fourth, they may ask questions about the relationship between the victim
and offender ("Have you ever had sexual relations with the defendant?"
"Do you know him socially?"). Questions about the victim's background
and earlier behavior also may be asked ("Have you had intercourse before?"
"How much had you had to drink that day?"), but they do not seem to be a
major focus of attention.

As in the police interview, style is just as much a part of the DA's interview as the questions that are asked. Many district attorneys have introductory phrases they use to try to put the victim at ease. These phrases are
similar to ones some police officers use. They explain why the question
must be asked or they acknowledge to the victim that the question may be
embarrassing. Examples are: "I need to know what happened. I haven't
heard [your story] before. There are questions I must ask," "Practice telling
it to me," "Everybody here is old enough [to know about these things]," or,
"I'm going to have to ask you a very personal question." A joke may be used to break the tension. "You can tell us everything here. . . . We'll. . . . de-
fang the defense." Sometimes, however, DAs were abrupt to the point of
eliminating any social pleasantries.

DAs, like police, sometimes "test" victims. They may ask a question to
see what answer the victim is apt to give once she is in the courtroom. In
one case, the test went as follows:

District attorney:	I just want you to know that the defense lawyer will harp on a couple of things: that you drank the beer he gave you and that you went willingly to his apartment. So be prepared to answer. Why did you go to his apartment?
Victim:	I had the beer and I thought he had a refrigerator in his room.
District attorney:	OK. Just answer it that way and remember he will harp on it. Just wanted you to know.

Advice and Explanations Limited. Rape victims by and large are unfamiliar with the workings of the court. Most have not been to court before,
and they do not know what to expect or what is expected of them. Do DAs
give explanations and advice so that victims can prepare mentally for what
is coming? The data suggest that in general they do not.

All case preparations that were observed (the 23 instances with 13 different DAs when we were present during the conversation between DA and
victim to prepare the case) were ranked as to the amount of advice and explanation given by the DA. "Minimal" meant that from none to two
pointers were given. For example, one victim simply was told, "Answer as
you feel you should." Another was told, "If I understand what you told me
. . . you were scared. . . . So get that across in court." Another was told only, "When you have to tell [the sex part] it will go something like this—the
man pulled down my pants and then he took his penis out and placed it in
my private area." "Medium" meant three to four pointers were discussed.
For example, one victim was told these three tips: "Just answer yes or no.
Don't be fresh, no matter what the lawyer says. And tell the truth."
"Detailed" meant that the DA practiced the style of questioning with the
victim or gave an extensive explanation of what to expect or what to do; a
case example is presented later in the chapter.

In most of the preparations observed, the amount of advice and explanation given was minimal (see Table 2). This pattern was especially pronounced at the district court level where almost all preparations fell into that
category. At the superior court level the situation changed somewhat, but
still more cases fell into the "minimal" advice category than into either the
"medium" or the "detailed" categories.

Table 2. Level of Court and Amount of Advice and Explanation DA Gives Victim

		Amount of Advice		
Level of Court	Minimal	Medium	Detailed	Total
District	13	0	1	14
Superior	4	3	2	9
Total	17	3	3	23

From a psychological point of view, it makes sense to prepare mentally
for a stressful experience. Various types of data suggest that when one is

prepared for such an experience, one survives it better emotionally. Janis's research on surgical patients and the recent trend in prepared childbirth are two examples.[17] In our study, victims typically responded better to those encounters with professionals in which explanations were given to them than to encounters where they were not given.

Pressure. DAs occasionally were observed to put victims under considerable pressure, either to strengthen their story (as one victim put it, "to spice it up") or to lower charges to assault and battery. Melba's case provides an example of the former. The DA tried several times to get her to make a statement stronger than what she maintained was true.

> The DA was preparing the case for the hearing for probable cause. He asked Melba, "How did you know it was a knife? Did you see a knife?" Melba said she felt something, she thought it was a knife at her throat and later at her stomach, but that she had never seen it, she just felt something sharp. The DA kept at her on this point, saying perhaps now she could remember seeing something, such as a flashing blade.

Despite his efforts, Melba stuck to her original story. She did, however, experience sufficient stress that at this point in the preparation of the case she began crying.

Emily's case provides an example of pressure in the opposite direction—to reduce the seriousness of the case. The hearing was held. At the end, the suggestion was made by several parties to lower the charge to assault and battery. The conversation between DA and victim went as follows:

> *District attorney:* Don't get me wrong, I'm prepared to go all the way if that's what you want. But downtown [i.e., at superior court] it will be like this, but five times worse. Is this something that's going to affect your life forever?
> *Emily:* Well, what's done with him won't change that.

It was agreed by DA, judge, victim, and defense that the charge should be lowered to assault and battery. The defendant was found guilty, given a two-year suspended sentence, and put on probation for six years. Later the DA reflected on the case:

> *District attorney:* I think justice was served
> *Holmstrom:* Well, it would have been dismissed downtown.
> *District attorney:* Yes. After all, there is a reasonable doubt. She might have gone up [to his place] and, you know—(laugh). I know

what's going on. This wasn't like some rapes I've seen
where I grew up—with the women really upset afterwards.

Holmstrom: Did the defendant have a record?

District attorney: No, not a thing. If he had had a record, then I would have
argued very differently.

In several other cases, the DA made a more neutral inquiry as to how the
victim would feel if the charge was lowered to assault and battery.

Victim Requests. The concept of patient requests was developed by
psychiatrist Aaron Lazare.[18] He and his research staff conceptualized the
patient as a customer whose requests—hopes for treatment or
"help"—always affect the clinical negotiations and even the clinical outcome. For example, in cases where the professional either did not identify or
respond to the patient's request, a regressive step was a potential alternative
that might occur on the part of the patient. Lazare has encouraged professionals to listen carefully to ascertain how the provider can help the patient
and suggests that this approach is one way to encourage greater participation on the part of the patient. Data from our study suggest that it might be
useful to expand this notion to include victim requests[19] or, more generally,
client requests.

DAs differ in the degree to which they take victim requests into account.
Some of the cases described above, for example, show DAs exerting considerable pressure to get victims to make decisions the way the DA wants
them made. In other cases, however, DAs made an attempt to find out what
the victim's needs were. They asked what the *victim* wanted to have happen. For example, in one case there was considerable discussion about
whether to prosecute the case on forcible rape or on statutory rape charges.
The latter charge was a possibility because of the victim's youth. It would
have eliminated the difficult issue of consent from the trial. The DA spent
considerable time trying to ascertain the victim's request. He went ahead on
the more difficult charge of forcible rape only after he found out that the
victim wanted to do so. In another case, the trial led to a hung jury. The
question was whether to go through a second trial on the rape charge or
whether to plea bargain. The defense lawyer wanted to have the charge
reduced to assault and battery and have his client plead guilty to that. A
second rape trial meant the victim would have to testify all over again. Plea
bargaining meant the victim would not have to testify; however, it would
never be determined legally whether the rape occurred. The DA thought
that a big factor in the decision should be the victim's wishes. He said,
"Technically it is not her decision, but I will honor her wishes." These cases
suggest that it would be useful in future studies to gather data more

systematically on the negotiation of requests between DA and victim, and to see whether the course of these negotiations later correlates with the victim's feelings about the way she was treated by the criminal justice system.

The DA's Role: From Interrogator to Counselor. The overt behavior of DAs in their interaction with rape victims varied considerably. Each DA had his own typical way of dealing with victims. The position seems to allow for a fairly wide range of acceptable definitions. At one extreme, a few DAs seemed to view their role mainly as that of interrogator and moral arbiter. At the other extreme, a few seemed to view their role mainly as one of legal counselor for the victim. Most DAs were somewhere in between. Two case studies are presented below of the extremes. District Attorney Gilles, who was observed on several cases, is an example of the former. His approach is illustrated by the way he dealt with Ana.

We were waiting with Ana, age 14, and her mother, Mrs. Alvarez, in the corridor at superior court. DA Gilles arrived. He didn't offer to get anyone a seat. We all stood while he prepared the case in the hallway. He didn't take much time to do it. Mainly he just had Ana read the transcript of the grand jury testimony. He asked, "Do you have any trouble with English—can you read, speak English?" Ana said she had no trouble. Then he asked, "When did you come up from Puerto Rico?" Mrs. Alvarez explained that they were not Puerto Rican.

DA Gilles read the transcript out loud—the questions and answers. He got to the part where it said she had been walking alone at eight o'clock in the evening. He pointed his finger at this sentence and said, "Here's the first mistake—a young girl out alone walking without anybody—that's your fault." He looked at Mrs. Alvarez as he said it, and he spoke in a punitive voice.

The DA went on reading the testimony. When he got to the sex part he no longer read it out loud; instead he had Ana read it to herself. He asked, "Are you sure?" Ana said, "Yes." He said, "This is a serious charge." He told a story about how, when he was a defense lawyer, he had had to defend a father who was accused of raping a girl and fortunately the father was able to make the jury believe him and not the young girl. The DA turned to Mrs. Alvarez and said, "You don't automatically get a verdict of guilty in these cases—these cases are hard ones."

Ana had tears in her eyes after the DA left. She said, "He made it seem like I committed a crime. He made it sound like I was asking for it."

Later the DA came back over, chucked her on the cheek, and said, "Are you mad at me?" Mrs. Alvarez at one point said, "Whose side is he on?" Just before court started the DA told Ana, "Tell the truth." This was the only advice he ever gave her. He did not tell her anything about how to testify. He did not give her any explanation about what was going to happen.

Ana asked us if this was going to be the only time she would take the stand. No one had explained to her that this first session was not the trial. We weren't sure ourselves what was scheduled. But after a while it became apparent that there was to be a hearing on a motion made by the defense. Ana testified. The motion by the defense was denied.

That evening we talked to Ana about how she felt. She said, "I didn't like the DA—the way he was talking to me. . . . He was rude to me. I started crying because he upset me."

The trial started the next day. During one recess the DA said repeatedly to us and to Mrs. Alvarez, "This isn't rape. There is no medical corroboration of what she says. This isn't rape." Indeed, in his closing argument to the jury, the DA referred to the charge as "statutory rape." The defense lawyer rose and corrected him, saying, "The charge is forcible rape."

The proceedings lasted several days. Ana and Mrs. Alvarez came to court for four days. DA Gilles mostly ignored them. He never said hello or good-bye. After court, for example, he would just walk out ahead of them and go right to the elevator. At the end of the trial, he left without saying anything to them. Ana said, "I think the DA was against me."

It is not surprising that Ana felt the DA was against her. Gilles acted as interrogator and moral arbiter. He was openly suspicious of her story, made judgmental comments to her face, did not give advice or explanations, had no thought for privacy, and even dispensed with the social niceties. From Ana's point of view, he constituted an additional source of victimization.

District Attorney Balsam, also observed on several cases, conceived of his role more as legal counselor for the victim. Technically, of course, DAs represent the state, and victims are not clients in the same sense that defendants are clients of defense lawyers; for example, DAs are duty bound to turn over exculpatory evidence to the defense. Nevertheless, some DAs took what might be called "the counselor approach." They acted as counselors in the traditional sense of the word—as one whose profession is to give advice in law and manage cases for clients in court. DA Balsam's approach is illustrated in the way he dealt with Denise.

We arrived at superior court and met Denise, age 23, in DA Balsam's office. We sat in there for about an hour as he prepared the case. He went over the story in detail. He "played it straight." There were no observable indications of suspicion or moral judgment. He simply asked about what happened in a very straightforward way.

DA Balsam prepared meticulously for what he thought would be the big issue in the trial: identification.

He asked how she was able to see the defendant and thereby later identify him: when could she, when did she get a good look—the first time, the second, or what? He said, "Answer truthfully," although it was clear he hoped she could pinpoint the time when she got a good enough look to identify him. He also asked, "How could you tell one from the other?" She replied that it was easy because the defendant "was clearly the biggest of the four."

He explained why he was asking some of the questions: "We better go over all the incidents [all the rapes] even though I hope that in court I'll only have to take you through those done by the defendant." "Why did you do that? I know why, but I want to see what you'll say."

He gave her some advice on how to testify: "We'll have to refer to the men as 'the man on my left' and 'the man on my right' through all the testimony up to the point where you can identify him." "When asked the amount of time or some such thing, be sure to say, 'approximately.'"

He warned her about some of the tactics of the defense: "Of course [the defendant's] wife and friends will provide alibis to cover him." "The defense will try to make a big deal of the fight you and your husband had. It's no big deal, but the defense will try to make it one."

He said some things indicating his general support: "It's perfectly natural that you can't remember all the details—it would look suspicious if you could remember it all, actually." "It will be hard when the defense asks some things, but I'll protect you with objections." "If we don't get a conviction, don't feel bad. It's very hard to get a conviction for rape in [this] county, and so it's no reflection on you."

After the trial began, he spoke with her during recesses and also said good-bye at the end of the day. Later we asked Denise how she felt about court. She said she thought that DA Balsam could have gone into so much more in the courtroom than he did. But, as regards how she herself was treated, she said she felt she was treated OK throughout the whole situation—she had no complaints about that.

It is not surprising that Denise reports she was "treated OK." DA Balsam took seriously her claim of rape, refrained from any moralistic comments, provided explanations and advice, showed concern for privacy, and paid attention to the social niceties. In short, he was at the opposite end of the continuum from DA Gilles on five issues of professional behavior that victims say are of concern to them: indications of suspicion, judgmental comments, explanation and advice, privacy, and general "style."

The data suggest that there is a psychological payoff to victims when DAs conceive of their role more as legal counselor. Whether there is any legal payoff to DAs and victims in terms of higher conviction rates is questionable, at least in the short run. For example, both of the above cases led to verdicts of not guilty. If there were any impact on the conviction rate, it would be in the long run. If more victims were treated like Denise was, then it is at least possible that more rape victims would be willing to go through the court process. Unless they go to court there is not even the possibility of a conviction.

DAs' Evaluation of the Case: The Ideal Rape Victim

DAs, like police and hospital staff, have in their minds an image of what constitutes the "ideal" rape victim or case. Police talk of "strong" and "weak" cases. Hospital staff talk of whether a rape case is "legitimate." DAs talk about whether the victim "will make a good witness." They also talk about the "problems in the case."

The Good Witness. DAs believe that the impression the rape victim creates on the witness stand is one key factor in what will happen in the courtroom. They want a victim who will be good on the witness stand. If the case ends in acquittal, there is a tendency to blame the victim for the outcome. After a not guilty verdict it is common to hear the phrase "she was not a good witness," much like one hears clinicians label certain patients "bad patients."

The criteria DAs use for defining a good witness are the victim's ability to give consistent testimony and the victim's appearance and demeanor. To be "good," a victim above all else must be able to give explicit, consistent testimony. In preparing one case, for example, the DA said positively of the victim:

> She seems quite stable, explicit in her story, there are no discrepancies. . . .
> I have read the grand jury notes and there are no discrepancies. . . . Even
> going over the delicate parts, she seems to do well with that—talks right up.

In a case where the DA did not get a conviction, he said, "She was easily confused and so contradicted herself." In another case that led to a not guilty verdict the DA said, "What can you expect with the girl changing the story so many times?"

"Good witnesses" not only give consistent stories, but they are able to do so within the rules of courtroom procedure; that is, in a very controlling and stressful context. One "bad witness" was a victim who got so upset during the trial that she walked out in the middle of her testimony. Good victims also are expected to cooperate in the preparation of the case—that is, to be helpful as the DA is getting the story—and to not thwart the DA's strategy in court.

DAs' evaluations of witnesses typically are voiced behind the scenes. But like physicians doing examinations of rape victims, they sometimes lose their patience and directly confront the victim with subjective reactions. The scenes with Emma are a case in point.[20]

> During the preparation, the conversation went as follows:
>
> *District attorney:*   Do you want to see this man convicted?
> *Emma:*   Yes.
> *District attorney:*   Then you'll have to be more convincing with the jury than you are being with me.
>
> He then asked for her assistance: "I want you to get your head straight tonight. I have some homework for you. (Gives her a pad of legal paper) My present to you. Write it down—chronologically. That will be a big help to me."
>
> He talked to her again the next day. Afterward he commented to us: "I'd like someone to talk to her about her testimony. . . . The way she tells the story it is not too convincing. . . . Maybe you could tell that I was getting a bit exasperated [yesterday]. . . . She brought in a few things today she had written down for me, but not too much. . . . It's as if she doesn't care."
>
> After two days of the trial he confronted her again: "You shouldn't have answered after the objection was sustained, but you did. That certainly didn't help. Maybe you *wanted* to say [that damning information]!"
>
> He then asked her not to come to the trial anymore: "You're excused tomorrow. You don't have to come. It would be better if you didn't come. If you're here they could call you again and have all sorts of people identify you. I'd rather you stayed home and rested. You can call me to find out the result."

DAs have their requests, too. In this case it is for the victim not to continue to attend the trial. One possible interpretation is that he thought her absence was a better strategy for the case because she was a "bad witness." She did stay away from then on. The verdict was not guilty.

DAs secondarily evaluate the victim as a witness in terms of her appearance and demeanor. They worry about what impression these will create on the jury. In one case, the DA spoke as follows:

> You see, the whole case will really rest on her credibility and her ability to tell her story and convince the jury. Her demeanor and sincerity will lend itself to her credibility as far as the jury is concerned. She seems to be sincere [when she talks] and if she comes across this way at the trial, it will go well.

In another case, the DA said, "She does not make a good witness. She has a habit of smiling when she is upset and that is not good." In still another instance, the DA was assigned two related rape cases. Audrey and Libby had both been raped by the same defendant, but he was being tried separately for the two charges. Audrey's case ended in a not guilty verdict. Afterward the DA said, "I wish I had Audrey's body and Libby's case." Realizing that his comment might be misinterpreted, he hastened to explain. He said Libby's case was stronger (evidence of bruises), but that Audrey looked better (more conservative and less tough).

The Problems of the Case.   DAs evaluate cases in terms of the legal difficulties they present. They speak of the "problems of the case" or of which case is "stronger" or whether the case is a "bad one." The comments of some DAs suggest that they often think of these difficulties as challenges to be attacked by their legal expertise. If the verdict is not guilty, the problems then serve to explain why it was not possible to get a conviction. DAs focus on whether the story is consistent ("The jury would not like to hear a discrepancy"); medical evidence of force and penetration ("No lacerations, contusions, or sperm—it doesn't look good"); victim's behavior ("This case is a bad one—she waited three months to tell anyone who did it"); victim's reputation ("The alcoholism"); and the relationship between the victim and the offender ("It will be a hard case because of the circumstances"—she knew the defendant and let him into her apartment). Occasionally, DAs mention the racial issue. Referring to a case of a black woman raped by black men, a DA said, "That's a typical 'Roxbury rape'[21]—you can't get a conviction [with blacks] even if you have a good case."

In addition to the legal challenges of the case, DAs also talk about whether the victim was really raped. Some victims, they feel, are just inventing the story ("Could she be making up the story?"). Cases of doubt may become matters of conscience for the DA, as discussed later in the chapter.

Behind the Scenes: Perceived Moral Character.   Much of the face-to-face interaction between DA and victim is nonjudgmental. But DAs, like police and clinicians, make numerous judgmental comments behind the scenes. DAs focus especially on the victim's perceived intelligence and sometimes on her reputation.

The most common judgment DAs were heard to make was whether the victim was intelligent. DAs, more than the other professional groups, are quick to label a victim as "not too bright" or as "retarded." They will say things such as, "What's her IQ? . . . Her parents are imbeciles. Just talking to them you can tell that," "She [22-year-old victim] has had 3 grades of school. . . . She really is slow," "I don't think she's [19-year-old victim] too smart—a lot of the words were misspelled.

One can only speculate on why DAs, more than other groups, focus on the attribute of intelligence. It may be because performance in the courtroom requires a high degree of verbal and mental skills. DAs need a witness who can express herself clearly and who can think quickly on her feet. Otherwise, she will not get the story across and she will be tripped up on cross-examination. One DA phrased the issue as follows. He said he didn't understand why victims had difficulty answering questions about facts, adding, "I have a 4-year-old daughter and if you ask her the time of day she can give you an answer." Asked by a listener whether he wasn't being a bit harsh, he admitted that the system really only works for people who can verbalize well. The others are at a disadvantage.

DAs on occasion also were heard to make judgments behind the scenes regarding the victim's reputation. In a few cases they said things such as, "I think she's a pig. She admitted to me she's had sex before with others," and, "She's a donkey." DAs were rarely heard to make judgmental comments openly to the victim's face. The few observed times concerned victims that DAs thought were "asking for it." In one case the following judgment was made.

District attorney: Any girl that hitchhikes is asking for it.
Victim: I don't hitch any more, but at the time, everyone was doing it.
District attorney: If my daughter ever did it, I'd slap her face.

Another example is the case of Ana, described earlier, in which the DA said it was a mistake for her to be walking alone at 8 P.M.[22]

The District Attorney's Concerns

There has been much discussion recently about how victims feel they are on trial in the courtroom. This theme is explored in later chapters. Less attention has been given to the DA's concerns about prosecuting such cases. Their spontaneous comments suggest that they focus on their image as competent professionals, matters of conscience, and their allocation of time and effort.

The DA on Trial: Professional Competence.[23] The police officer's competence is on the line when evaluating rape cases. The DA's competence also is on the line when evaluating cases and especially when stepping into the courtroom.[24] As one DA, speaking quite emotionally, phrased it:

When I have a case I want to do the best job I can for my own professional pride. When I have a case, *I'm* on trial. I'm going to try to win because I *like* to win.

Their worst fear seems to be of not looking well in court. As one DA, preparing a case, said, "I don't want to get up there and look like a fool." Later, after everything went wrong for him in the case—the victim gave inconsistent testimony, the gynecologist got tripped up by the defense lawyer—the DA burst out, "This was my worst day in court!"

The courthouse community—judges, other lawyers, court officers, policemen—keep track of how the various lawyers are doing. In one case, without a conviction, a veteran police officer commented, "I hoped [the DA] would win. He's so young and it was his first rape case." In another case, the DA was subjected to considerable teasing by a colleague about not getting a conviction. His fellow DA laughed and said, "Weren't you decisive in your final argument? Didn't you say, 'this is the guy!'" In still another case without a conviction, the DA reported, "The judge called me in to say . . . that my closing argument was really good."

It is in this context of career image and professional competence that victims who change their stories, or who do not tell all of the story during the preparation of the case, are most upsetting to the DA. DAs do not like surprises once they are in the courtroom. Changes and surprises make them look bad. In one case, for example, the victim's girl friend suddenly admitted on the witness stand that the two girls had telephoned the defendants prior to going over to see them. The DA asked a few more questions and then quickly called for a recess. Later the DA revealed how upset he was by this new information. He talked repeatedly of the "bombshell" the girl friend had dropped, and exclaimed, "Imagine having to call a recess because of testimony given by a state witness—it's unheard of!"

Matters of Conscience.   DAs sometimes get assigned cases where they find it very hard to make a judgment. DAs have a legal obligation to turn over exculpatory evidence. But perhaps of more interest is how they feel about cases they regard as borderline—where the evidence is not clear cut.

Cases regarded as borderline often get resolved by "foot dragging." Things move very slowly and somehow the case never gets scheduled for trial. In such cases, DAs may express a concern for the defendant. In one such case, the DA requested that the only defendant still in custody be let go on personal recognizance. "It wasn't fair to have him in jail all summer." In another case, the DA was trying to decide what to do. "I don't want to see an innocent man's reputation discredited."

Occasionally a case goes to trial and the evidence comes out in such a way that the DA's opinion shifts dramatically during the proceedings. Only one such case occurred in our sample. It is the case mentioned above where a prosecution witness revealed information on the stand that the DA had not known before and that made the victim "look bad." Not only did the

DA complain about being made to look bad in court himself, he also became very worried for the defendant. The case became a matter of conscience for him. His reaction, as well as that of the DA in district court, is described below:

We met Leona, age 15, and her family at district court. We went to the hearings for probable cause for the two defendants, Ned and Ron. During one hearing we happened to stand right next to a group of the defendant's friends and heard their conversation. Regarding Ron, they whispered, "And he's the one who *didn't* do anything!"—implying that one or several others among them *had done* something to her. (Ron was later charged with being an accessory before the fact.)

The DA, after preparing the case, said, "I believe she was raped. But there's not enough for rape. It should be lowered to assault and battery. The least involved, Ron, may get the heaviest penalty just because [he's older]." After the hearings, the DA made derogatory comments about her sexual behavior and said, "You have to read between the lines. . . . I think she went along with the first and got mad after *several* did it. I [prosecute] because it's my job."

We met Leona and her family at superior court. A different DA handled the case. Ned pleaded guilty to abuse of a female child. Ron pleaded innocent to being an accessory before the fact. Testimony was taken. It came out that the girls had not just happened to meet the defendants. They had made arrangements ahead of time to meet them. The DA reacted strongly to the *change* in the story. He reacted equally strongly to the *information itself.* He said, "It's an out-and-out case of fornication."

Ron's case was dismissed. But Ned had pleaded guilty. Sentencing still had to be done.

The DA was very upset. He said, "The judge wants to send this Ned to the can and I don't think this is rape. I think he should go back on the streets . . . . There is rape and there is rape. . . . I heard a big bombshell. . . . I don't think the guy is guilty and I can't see him going to Concord.[25] He needs to be back in school. After all, the girls said they planned to meet the boys that evening. . . . I'd rather have a robbery or a murder than these rape cases."

The next day the DA said, "I'm really torn." His hands were shaking a little bit. He said, "The more I think about it, the more I'm convinced that Ned shouldn't be sent to prison . . . especially since he has no record. . . . If he goes to Concord, he'll never finish school. . . . I would feel differently about the case if the guy had been much older than she . . . or if she had been a virgin before. . . . And she lied to me—one time she said she hadn't talked of going there, later she admitted she had. . . . This is not a real rape."

The DA seemed very upset. He said, "I'm going to do my best to try to get him probation. . . . I called up the school to see how he is as a student. He's an average student—but, so what, weren't most of us just average students?" The DA went over more and more to the side of the defendant, both in his feelings and his actions. He argued in court on behalf of Ned and recommended probation. The judge announced immediately that he accepted the recommendation. He said there would be three years probation, with two conditions attached: that Ned finish school as long as that was financially possible for his family, and that Ned and his family be respectful to the girl's family.

Leona's case is of interest in that it shows differing ways in which DAs may resolve their feelings about victims who do not match their image of the ideal case. The DA in district court believed she was raped, but responded very negatively to her and distanced himself, saying he only prosecuted because it was his job. The DA at superior court decided it was not a real rape. He responded to the human drama, became conscience-stricken and emotionally involved, and then worked actively on behalf of the defendant.

The Harried Prosecutor: Allocation of Time and Effort.   One hears often of harried public defenders who receive many cases at the last moment and who have little time to prepare. One hears less often about harried public prosecutors. Yet often they, too, receive cases at the last moment and are faced with the task of preparing several cases simultaneously. In one instance, the DA received his assignment an hour before the hearing started; later he revealed that it had been his first rape case. In another instance, the DA was having a bad week. He had had three murders already, was on a case of student demonstrators that meant facing 11 defense lawyers, and the defense lawyer on the rape case "was driving him crazy." This workload and how to handle it is a focus of the DAs' concerns. As one of them put it, while talking of the problems they have prosecuting rape cases, "The DA usually has two or three other felony cases that he must prepare that [same] day." Occasionally a DA made an explicit connection between the hectic schedule and the selection of which cases to spend time on. One DA, evaluating the merits of a case, said, "I don't want to waste a lot of time on this and have the jury come back in two minutes with a not guilty verdict." DAs sometimes talk of the pressure of the job, saying things like, "I obviously can't be two places at once," or, "I'm tired when I get home."

THE CORRIDOR SCENE

Not only does the rape victim face the defendant and his network in the courtroom. She also often must face him or his network in the courthouse corridor. These different settings lead to different kinds of scenes.

The courtroom itself has all the trappings—high bench, judicial robes, official protocol—required for a highly structured and ceremonial confrontation between defendant and the state, or, as victims experience it, between defendant and victim. Here the interaction by and large proceeds within the rules of official protocol. Victim and defendant both are told what to do—where to walk, where to sit or stand, when to speak. Outbursts are the exception rather than the rule.

The "corridor scene" is a vivid contrast. The general setting, especially in the busier district courthouses, is pandemonium. Often a crowd—prosecutors, defense lawyers, policemen, defendants, victims, relatives, friends, and onlookers—either sit waiting or scurry about their business. The victim's side and the defendant's side often both wait in the halls. There are fewer restraints here on the interaction between defendant and victim, and the confrontation is more freewheeling.

Hostility

The corridor confrontation typically is hostile. Victim and defendant and their family and friends may participate in outright threats, bravado, or taunting. In the following case, the defendant simulated bravery, while the victim's side ridiculed him.

> We met Leslie at court and waited in the corridor for the hearing to begin.
>
> Mulhern, his girl friend, and his lawyer were standing together in the hallway talking. Mulhern and the lawyer were joking and laughing. The lawyer was laughing about the details of another rape case—details he later used to support his position in court that his client was innocent.
>
> We stood with Leslie and several friends (three young women and three young men) in another group. They stared over at Mulhern and said things in loud voices, like, "I wonder what it feels like to be a sex pervert."

In some cases, relatives get more involved in confrontations between the two sides than do the victims or defendants themselves.

> The case had been continued. We were standing around in the corridor with Betty; her mother, Mrs. Roberts; and a police officer. We formed a little circle. The defense lawyer came up and asked the officer, "What's the doctor's name?" The officer had a slip of paper in his hand with the physician's name on it. He started to show it to the defense lawyer.
>
> Mrs. Roberts grabbed the paper and blew up at the defense lawyer saying, "Oh, no, you don't. Get your own information." The defense lawyer snapped back, "I have a right to do what I'm doing and you have a right to do what you're doing, so shut up." Mrs. Roberts touched the defense lawyer's arm

Table 3. Attrition of 109 Reported Rape Cases in the Criminal Justice System by Age of Victim

Last Stage the Case Reached	Age of Victim		
	Preadult (16 and under)	Adult (17 and older)	Total
Reported; victim could not identify assailant.	5	36	41
Reported, assailant identified; victim did not press charges	1	12	13
Reported, assailant identified; police handled as a "station matter" (police discouraged formal charges, but gave severe warnings to the boys in presence of their parents).	1	0	1
Reported, identified, charges pressed; no arrest made	2	5	7
Charges dropped at victim's request prior to hearing for probable cause	0	4	4
Dropping charges requested by victim prior to hearing for probable cause; instead, case continued for 2 years—could be heard if defendants got into other trouble	1	0	1
Defendant disappeared and defaulted at district court level.	1	0	1
Hearing for probable cause at district court or juvenile hearing settled the case	1	3	4
Defense appealed, after hearing for probable cause, on procedural grounds to state supreme court. Case returned to district court for second hearing. Victim disappeared prior to second hearing.	0	1	1
Charges dropped at victim's request prior to grand jury	0	1	1
Grand jury settled the case; no indictment on any charge	0	0	0

Victim disappeared at superior court level	0	1	1
Victim formally requested dropping charges prior to superior court trial.	1	3	4
Defendant disappeared and defaulted prior to superior court trial	1	2	3
Defense obtained dismissal prior to superior court trial	0	2	2
Indictment placed on file by mutual agreement of the parties prior to superior court trial	0	1	1
Defendant declared incompetent to stand trial; confined to state psychiatric facility	0	1	1
Plea bargained at superior court level prior to trial	2	4	6*
Tried in superior court	8	10	18
Total	24**	86	110**

*There are a total of 7 plea cases in the sample, 6 at superior and 1 at district court.
**The totals are 24 and 110 respectively (rather than 23 and 109) because one young victim's case with multiple assailants led both to a plea bargain and to a trial.

and said, "I hope it happens to you [i.e., I hope your daughter is raped]. I put a hex on you." He left.

The police officer explained, "He has a right to know." Mrs. Roberts, exploding at the officer, shouted, "I hope it happens to you. I hope something like this happens in every household—to every man—so you'll know what I've suffered."

Pathos

Sometimes the corridor confrontations have more of an awkward, painfully embarrassing, even pathetic quality. Lois's situation is a case in point. Both victim and defendant had waited in and about the corridors for several hours. Lois, the victim, sat much of the time in a small interviewing room off the main corridor. The door was open and twice the defendant Carlos wandered in.

The first time Carlos came over and touched Lois and said, "You believe in God, I believe in God, and everything will be OK." Then he held out his hand to me, we shook hands, and he said, "Carlos," introducing himself.

The second time Carlos came in he said, "Oh, Lois, Lois, soon fini, soon fini, since eight o'clock, since eight o'clock." He was visibly upset.

After the hearing—which resulted in a suspended sentence for assault and battery—Carlos kept muttering to everyone, "Thank you, oh, thank you, thank you, thank you." Carlos thanked everybody. He came over and shook Lois's hand and shook my hand.

People at the courthouse kept saying, "He's pathetic."

ATTRITION AT EACH STAGE

Most rape cases fall by the wayside long before they ever reach plea bargaining or trial. Looking at where and why cases drop out, the main finding is that they do not drop out at any one stage. They drop out at many stages along the way and for many different reasons (see Table 3).

The victim's inability to identify the assailant is the most frequent reason for a reported rape case to not progress very far in the criminal justice system. If the rapist is not known to the victim, attention in the early stages of the case is focused on trying to make an identification. Police typically have victims look at photographs (files of mug shots) at the station. They also may drive victims around the neighborhood where the rape occurred to look for faces. Despite such efforts, in the present sample, 41 of the 109 rape victims whose victimization was reported to the police were unable to identify their assailants.

The next biggest drop-off came from victims' unwillingness to press charges in the early stages of the court process. Nineteen victims initially did not press charges or soon dropped charges. Thirteen of these did not press charges, one was persuaded by the police that the incident should be handled as a station matter, and five requested to drop charges prior to the hearing for probable cause (permission was granted in four cases). As this chapter indicates, such decisions by victims should not be viewed in isolation, but rather in the context of the cross-pressures brought to bear upon them.

In a modest number of cases (seven) the police failed to make an arrest even though the victim made an identification and pressed charges. Sometimes the police could not locate the assailant. Sometimes they knew where he was, but were reluctant to make the arrest.

A few cases (four) ended at the district court hearing for probable cause or at a juvenile hearing. Three adult victims had their cases end at hearings. The decisions were no probable cause, conviction on lesser charges only, and plea bargaining right after the hearing—guilty on a lesser charge. One young victim's case ended at the boys' juvenile court hearing. The two youths were declared to be delinquents and then released in the custody of their parents.

Not a single case was dropped completely by the grand jury. In each case that the grand jury heard, an indictment was returned on some charge. In two cases, however, it did not return an indictment for rape, but for other offenses (kidnapping, unnatural act).

At superior court, attrition occurred for a variety of reasons. Four more victims requested that charges be dropped. All four were cases in which much foot-dragging had occurred—the cases had gone on and on without much happening. In three cases, the defendant defaulted. In two other cases, the defense obtained a dismissal. These two are especially interesting. In each of these, the victims had been conscientious and had showed up on the various scheduled court dates. They then each missed just one time—one said she got mixed up on the date, the other said she was never notified. In each case, on the day of the absence, the defense was successful in obtaining a dismissal.

A minority of cases made it through the criminal justice system. Only 24 cases made it sufficiently far to be plea bargained or tried. Seven were plea bargained, one at district court and six at superior court. Eighteen cases went to trial. (One case led both to a plea and a trial.)

Age of victim seems to be important in how far the case goes. Young victims' cases were more likely to go further. Young victims were more able to identify their assailants, charges were more likely to be pressed and less likely to be dropped, and the case was more likely to go far enough through the system to be plea bargained or to go to trial. For example, 8 of the 23 young, but only 10 of the 86 adult reported rape cases eventually went to trial. (see Table 3).

It is clear that the attrition rate is high in rape cases and that only a minority ever get to plea bargaining or to trial. Is the attrition rate in rape higher than for other types of major crimes? Recent comparative research by Williams suggests that it is. Her conclusions are based on her analysis of cases of sexual assault—forcible sexual assaults of adults and sexual assaults of children whether or not they were forcible—in the District of Columbia.[26] She compared these cases to murder and manslaughter, aggravated assault, robbery, and burglary.

Williams looked at where cases dropped out and why. One particularly interesting stage is the "papering of a case."[27] The "papering rate" is the percent of arrests police made that in turn are filed by the prosecutor when the case is initially screened. The sexual assault papering rate was only 74 percent, and the only lower rate was for aggravated assault (murder and manslaughter, 97%; robbery, 88%, burglary, 88%; sexual assaults, 74%; aggravated assault, 70%). The reasons for "no papering" in the four crimes with considerable attrition are of interest. Sexual assault and burglary cases were the least likely to be dropped because the victim declined to prosecute (aggravated assault, 61%; robbery, 34%; burglary, 22%; and sexual assault, 22%). Sexual assault cases were the most likely to suffer attrition because there was a question about the witness's personal credibility (sexual assault, 15%; robbery, 7%; aggravated assault, 2%; burglary, 2%). Sexual assault cases were the second most apt to be dropped for insufficient evidence (burglary, 47%; sexual assault, 38%; robbery, 34%; aggravated assault, 12%).

Williams's data thus do not support the stereotype that rape victims are more reluctant than other victims to prosecute. However, they do support the idea that rape victims have a harder time having their claim of victimization believed.

SWEPT ALONG AND COOLED OUT

It should be clear by now that for a victim to take a rape case to court is no easy task. It is the unusual victim who unequivocally wants to press charges and maintains that position from start to finish. Many victims change their minds. Many victims are, or become, ambivalent.

Victims are subjected to cross-pressures. Two general processes are at work. Once the court process is started, victims tend to be swept along at least a certain distance by the perseverance of other people and by the workings of the system. Once the button is pushed, so to speak, the machinery of the system begins to move victims through it. At the same time, many factors contribute to cooling the prosecutrix out. The pretrial route is a long one, and costly in many senses of the word. It is stressful, wearing, expensive, and degrading. As long as it hangs over the victim's head, it is a disruption to the victim's life, a piece of unfinished business. As a result, many victims are cooled out.

The victim goes through the long pretrial process with only minimal support. Some are fortunate to have a very understanding friend or relative. Police officers typically follow cases start to finish, and some officers go out of their way to help victims. But in general, no one, as part of his or her role, is assigned the responsibility of seeing what happens to victims and supporting them as they go through these many steps.

NOTES

1. Erving Goffman, "On Cooling the Mark Out: Some Aspects of Adaptation to Failure," *Psychiatry*, 15 (November 1952), p. 451.

2. Ibid., p. 452.

3. The victim/witness in a rape case may be called the prosecutrix, Pamela Lakes Wood, "The Victim In A Forcible Rape Case: A Feminist View," *American Criminal Law Review* 11 (Winter, 1973), p. 341.

4. At the time of this scene, the officer believed Rose to be a rape victim and presumably was treating her as he would treat a rape victim. She is counted in the present study as a sex-stress victim since she subsequently testified in court that she had been soliciting and that the boys, after having sex, robbed her of her earnings.

5. Barry Schwartz, "Introduction," in *Queuing and Waiting: Studies in the Social Organization of Access and Delay*, (Chicago: University of Chicago Press, 1975), p. 4.

6. Barry Schwartz, "Waiting, Exchange, and Power: The Distribution of Time in Social Systems," *American Journal of Sociology* 79 (January 1974), p. 867.

7. Ibid., p. 847.

8. Ibid., p. 853.

9. Ibid., pp. 845, 853.

10. Schwartz notes that even when resourceful persons must wait, they suffer less than the less resourceful. For example, defendants who can afford bail wait in the community; the others wait in jail. Ibid., p. 850. For an analysis of the impact of delay on the defendant see Lewis Katz, Lawrence Litwin, and Richard Bamberger, *Justice Is The Crime: Pretrial Delay In Felony Cases*, (Cleveland: Case Western Reserve University Press, 1972).

11. Schwartz, *Queuing and Waiting*, p. 7.

12. Reimbursement for travel expenses is a cloudy issue. Some victims were reimbursed and some were not. With some victims the issue was explicitly discussed, with some it was ambiguously discussed, and with some victims the issue was not even mentioned by anyone in the system.

13. Bridgewater is a state institution under the department of mental health to which defendants are sent for psychiatric observation and evaluation.

14. Walpole is a Massachusetts correctional institution typically used for defendants with longer sentences and who are found guilty of the more dangerous crimes.

15. In the Boston area, rape cases usually are prosecuted by district attorneys (actually, assistant district attorneys) even at the hearing for probable cause. Occasionally a police prosecutor takes up this task.

16. In two cases, the rape victims had their own lawyers in addition to the DA. These lawyers came to court but had no appreciable impact on the way the case was handled at the courthouse.

17. Grantly Dick Read, *Childbirth Without Fear*, (New York: Harper, 1944); Richard I. Feinbloom, "Natural Childbirth," in *Pregnancy, Birth and the Newborn Baby*, prepared by Boston Children's Medical Center (Delacorte Press, 1971), pp. 189-200; Irving L. Janis, "Psychological Preparation," in *Psychological Stress: Psychoanalytic and Behavioral Studies of Surgical Patients* (New York: Academic Press, 1974), pp. 352-94. (First published 1958, Wiley).

18. Aaron Lazare, "The Walk-In Patient: A Reformulation," (paper delivered at Grand Rounds, Massachusetts General Hospital, Boston, February 16, 1971); Aaron Lazare et al., "The Walk-In Patient as a 'Customer': A Key Dimension in Evaluation and Treatment," *American Journal of Orthopsychiatry* 42 (October 1972), pp. 872-83.

19. Ann Wolbert Burgess and Lynda Lytle Holmstrom, "Crisis and Counseling Requests of Rape Victims," *Nursing Research* 23 (May-June 1974), pp. 196-202.

20. As should be clear from the following account, DAs may work diligently on cases with "bad witnesses."

21. Roxbury is a predominantly black neighborhood. The expression "Roxbury rape" is used by whites (as in this particular case) and by blacks alike.

22. Although we have no systematic data on it, defense lawyers also were heard to make behind-the-scenes judgments of their clients.

23. Both police and DAs talk about their professional image as regards work with rape victims. Hospital staff do not seem to pick up on this issue—possibly because most rape victims have injuries that are seen as medically routine rather than medically difficult. Such injuries are seen as easy to treat and as not challenging one's professional competence.

24. DAs talk about the issue primarily as regards superior court, possibly because it is relatively easy for them to obtain probable cause at the district level, but very difficult to obtain a conviction for rape at the superior level.

25. Concord is a Massachusetts correctional institution typically used for defendants receiving sentences of five years or less.

26. Kristen M. Williams, "Sexual Assaults and the Law: The Problem of Prosecution," revised version of paper presented at the American Sociological Association annual meeting, New York, September 1976.

27. Ibid, p. 11.

CHAPTER 6

■

In the Courtroom

I think her extracurricular ac-
tivities are a very important
bit of evidence. Her reputation
has a great deal of bearing on
this case.

> DEFENSE LAWYER TO
> JUDGE

The girl's reputation is not the
point here in this hearing
today.

> DISTRICT ATTORNEY TO
> JUDGE

The district hearing for probable cause and the rape trial often become occasions of drama. Both the institution of the court and the individual actors employ "presentational strategies." The court has several audiences, including defendant, victim, jurors, and the public. It presents itself to them as the embodiment of the legal order. The prosecution and defense's various audiences include the judge and jurors. Prosecution and defense create their own definitions of reality and try to convince others that their version of the truth is the more plausible. The rape victim is treated by many as though she is the offender. Technically, only the defendant is accused of a crime. But as the theatricals in the courtroom unfold, it becomes clear that in people's minds the victim is as much on trial as the defendant. The lawyers pit the defendant's reputation against the victim's. They place his word in opposition to hers. She says he raped her. He says—either by his testimony or through pleading not guilty—that he did not. The court must select which of these mutually exclusive statements to believe. It is not an easy task. The stories contradict each other. The evidence, even when corroborated, always is subject to multiple interpretations. And the stakes are high for the various parties. For the defendant, a verdict of guilty may deprive him of his liberty. For the victim, a verdict of not guilty means that her suffering as a victim[1] and as a witness[2] has been in vain. For defense and prosecution lawyers, professional competence and reputation are at stake, as seen in Chapter 5.

FRONT, ORGANIZATION, AND RULES OF THE GAME

"Front": Courtroom Ceremony

Goffman has called our attention to "performance" and to the ways individuals marshal their activities to convey certain impressions to others.[3] An important part of performance is the "front," or expressive equipment employed, which includes the "setting" (furniture, decor, scenery, and stage props), appearance (indicators of social status), and manner (indicators of the part to be played in the interaction, such as initiator or follower).[4] As Ball has pointed out, this notion can be extended to the presentational strategies of institutions.[5] Studying an illegal abortion clinic, for example, Ball asked how "the setting and actions *qua* impressions [are] manipulated to maximize the clinic's image over and above successful performance of its task and contradict the stereotypic stigma of deviance?"[6] His observations suggest that by highlighting luxury and cost (expensively furnished waiting room) and by medicalizing the situation (use of surgical language, white uniforms, pseudosterility procedures), such a clinic is able to encourage a legitimate rather than deviant definition of the situation.

"Front" can be seen to be an important part of any institution's functioning. Speaking of the juvenile court, Emerson states:

> While the juvenile court hearing serves a variety of purely instrumental ends, court staff invest it with much more than mere administrative character. The courtroom proceeding is perceived and constructed as a ceremonial confrontation between the legal order and one who has violated that order.[7]

Emerson's focus is on juvenile court and its effects (intended and unintended) on delinquents. Nevertheless, many of his observations—especially those regarding the *authoritative* and *intimidating* features of the courtroom—are applicable to district court hearings and criminal trials as well.

The court's presentational strategy is to highlight its own authority and to subordinate all who come before it. It does so vis-à-vis the accused, as Emerson has documented. What our study makes very clear is that it subordinates the victim-witness and others as well.

The authoritative and intimidating features of the courtroom are many.[8] A formal, authoritative, solemn atmosphere is fostered by the furniture, the costumes, and the rules of interaction. As Hazard says, "Walk into an empty courtroom and look around. The furniture arrangement will tell you at a glance who has what authority."[9] From the courtrooms we observed in this study, the following picture emerges. The judge's bench is on a raised platform, sometimes with a high-back leather chair visible to those below. The rest of the furniture is positioned so that the attention of other persons is directed toward the judge. In private hearings, the judge may be seated on the bench or may sit at the head of a long and imposing table. The judge is flanked by flags, symbols of the power and authority of the state.

The costumes increase the ceremonial atmosphere of the occasion. The judge wears the traditional black robe, which Kessler suggests has mystical significance. "The robe is a symbol of the role to be played by all persons involved in the situation. . . . [It] is a convenient shorthand symbol for the institution of justice as a whole."[10] At superior court, officers are dressed in blue and gold-trimmed uniforms. Others—persons escorting defendants in custody, some policemen, some witnesses—also may be in special uniform.[11]

The physical layout is such that, in Goffman's terms, the "frontstage" and "backstage" clearly are separated.[12] There are special passageways that facilitate peoples' movement in the wings. The judge, once robed, enters the courtroom through a special door, rather than mingle with the crowd in the public corridor.

Machinery for recording the proceedings makes the performance irrevocable. At superior court, sessions do not start unless the court stenographer is present to record every person's every word.[13] In district court, defense counsel often tape-records the testimony.

Linguistically, the occasion is separated from the realm of the everyday. Archaic language is used for announcing the beginning of court, for stating some of the charges, and in some of the statutes that are mentioned—all in a manner reminiscent of using Latin in a religious ceremony.

Deferential behavior is expected, especially vis-à-vis the judge. When the judge enters or exits, an officer cries out, "Court rise!" Those present in the courtroom are expected to stand. Court officers frown on talking; silence is expected. In one case, expression of deference by such means was especially dramatic:

> At the conclusion of the testimony, the judge asked one of the officers for the statutes on rape. The officer went out and was gone for at least 10 minutes. Everyone in the courtroom sat in silence. When he returned with the law books, the judge took them and began turning the pages very slowly, reading each one. This continued for a full 20 minutes (timed by observer) while everyone sat in utter silence. At the end of the 20 minutes, the judge announced his decision.

The movements of defendants and witnesses are carefully controlled. The defendant, especially if in custody, is escorted to his place. The victim may be escorted up to the witness stand. Both defendant and victim are isolated from their support networks. The defendant sits in a special box or in a special area enclosed by a railing. When testifying, the victim is alone on the witness stand. She is further isolated if witnesses are sequestered. In such cases, she goes in to testify first, and her friends and family if they are to testify are left outside the courtroom. Since almost all participants are male, female victims face a further form of isolation—being separated from members of their own sex. In one case in which the witnesses were sequestered, the victim, age 16, was the only female in the courtroom when she testified, except for Holmstrom as the sociological observer.

Some judges adopt a patrician image, doing things that indicate they are above the fray. They may indicate an understanding of the difficulties that all parties face in the courtroom. They may do things to put those unaccustomed to court at ease: for example, comment sympathetically on the difficulty of being a witness. In one case, the judge said to a very upset victim, "We are grateful that you are willing to come to court." But judges may rebuke those who come before them, and some adopt the image of the outspoken "moral arbiter," even on matters not part of the crime under consideration. In one such case, the judge lectured the accused for being "involved in such debauchery." In another, the judge—although he said it was wrong to rape the victim—also publicly denounced her. In a voice that all could hear he said, "She's an alcoholic. She's no good." What both approaches—patrician and moral arbiter—have in common is to emphasize the lack of power of the defendant and victim and highlight the authority of the judge.

While the above analysis has emphasized how the court subordinates defendant and victim, it should be noted that other actors are not immune. Lawyers, as they argue cases, may be put down by the judge. In one case, for example, the defense argued that the incident was a harmless escapade and that "one perhaps might look to his own youth to remember such." The judge interrupted and in quite a severe tone said, "I don't know what kind of a childhood *you* had!" Police may be criticized for the way in which they give their testimony. In one case, the judge lectured the veteran officer on how he was wrong to include certain information in his testimony before the jury. And physicians, who are accustomed to being in control when on their own stage, the hospital, suddenly find that in their role as expert witness they are subjected to control. In one case at a competency hearing, a psychiatrist testified that the defendant was incompetent to stand trial, and was questioned at length by the judge. At recess, on his way out the door, the psychiatrist sighed and said, "The judge is questioning me more than the DA is!"

THE ADVERSARY SYSTEM OF LAW

The Adversary Ideal

The ideology surrounding the American legal system is that the United States should have and does have an adversary system of law—a system "for conducting trials under strict rules of evidence with the right of cross-examination and argument, one party with his witnesses striving to prove the facts essential to his case and the other party striving to disprove those facts or to establish an affirmative defense."[14]

The rape hearing for probable cause and the rape trial are adversary proceedings. Each is an institutionalized conflict with opposing sides.[15] Analysts and critics argue about the amount of adversariness that still exists in the system, a point that is discussed below. The point here, however, is that the hearings for probable cause and trials observed in this study were adversary in the very basic sense that both sides of the story were argued in the courtroom.[16]

The role of the lawyers, whether defense or DA, during the hearing for probable cause and trial is to represent their respective sides. Neither defense nor DA is expected to be impartial during the hearing or the trial. Rather, they are expected to present their side well. Reference to these expectations is sometimes made by participants in the system. For example, one of the more competitive DAs said:

> I used to be a defense counsel and now I'm a DA. . . . When I was a defense attorney I was for hire. It was my function to do everything I could to get the client off. I didn't care whether he was guilty or not. Most of the people

I defended *were* guilty. I would do anything I could. If I had to make the victim look like a bum I made her look like a bum. I did everything I could to win fairly and ethically. I did that as a defense counsel and I do that as a DA. . . . A defense lawyer has a primary loyalty to his client. He has no other except to the oath he took. As long as he does that, he is doing his job. The blade on the other side is supposed to be as sharp.

Judges may make reference to the lawyer's partisan duties, for example, explaining them to the jury at the end of the trial. In one case observed, the judge's instructions on this point were:

Your verdict must rest on a solid foundation, and that is the evidence and the exhibits. The arguments that both counsel made are not evidence. Their arguments are important, but they are partisan. The first obligation of any lawyer is to represent the best interests of his client.

In another case, the judge publicly complimented both defense attorneys and DA saying "what a good job" they did presenting each side and that "the case was well tried."

The essential point here, regarding the victim's career, is that rape victims whose cases go to court become participants in an institutionalized conflict. They must present their own version of the story. Furthermore, they must endure listening to presentation of a version that is diametrically opposed to what they maintain is true.[17]

The Rules of the Game: Conflict Within a Normative Order

Conflict, including warfare, typically occurs within a set of norms.[18] Speaking of antagonistic games, Simmel states, "One *unites* in order to fight, and one fights under the mutually recognized control of norms and rules."[19] Furthermore, he argues, "Legal conflict rests on a broad basis of unities and agreements between the enemies"[20]—both sides are subordinated to the law. Schelling says, "Pure conflict, in which the interests of two antagonists are completely opposed, is a special case; it would arise in a war of complete extermination, otherwise not even in war."[21]

The adversary proceedings between defense and prosecution in the contemporary United States courtroom, like conflict in general, occur within a set of norms. A social definition as to what are the conditions that set the groundwork for a fair criminal trial has been developed. The rules are many, including the presumption of the defendant's innocence, the defendant's right to counsel, the right to have a trial by jury, the right of the defendant to not testify, placing the burden of proof on the state, and the standard of proof beyond reasonable doubt. Three rules are highlighted here because they create such difficult circumstances for the rape victim: the defendant's right to a public trial, to see his accuser, and to cross-examination of the state's witnesses.

Public Setting of Hearing or Trial. Unless she or the accused is quite young, the rape victim must give her testimony in a hearing or trial open to the public. Spectators usually are present. Family and friends may accompany either side. Lawyers may stop by for a while to see how the case is going. There may be members of the general public. Some are there on official business, merely waiting their turn in court. Some are there just for the show, voyeurs in search of sex and violence. In one case, for example, four people walked up to the courtroom door; one said to the others, "Hey, this is where the rape case is going to be tried. That ought to be really good; let's not miss it." At superior court one finds a group of court-watchers—"court bums" as they are sometimes called—who regularly pass the time of day watching cases.

The victim will be questioned in front of these strangers. She will be asked identifying information, such as her name, address, or where she works. She will be asked about intimate aspects of the rape as well as about her personal life. The questioning often concerns minute details of the sexual aspects of the incident. No item is left to the imagination. Everyone in the courtroom is given the chance to participate vicariously in the rape.

Seeing One's Accuser. The right of the defendant to see his accuser means that both defendant and victim are present in the courtroom. Thus, the victim comes face to face again with the person with whom she has had one of the most distasteful experiences in her life. She must testify in his presence. In most courtrooms observed, there was considerable distance between victim and defendant. However, the physical layout of a few district courtrooms left little distance between the two parties. In one instance, the victim stood to testify, and seated slightly below within inches of her was the assailant. In another instance, the victims when testifying were only a few feet from the enclosed area where the defendants were; the defendants jeered at the women throughout their testimony.

Cross-Examination. Prosecution and defense have the right to question each other's witnesses. From the victim's point of view, cross-examination by the defense lawyer is salient. The defense attorney—typically male, occasionally female—becomes the assailant in this new arena. The cross-examination recapitulates, on a psychological and verbal level, the original rape. The victim was controlled physically by the assailant during the rape.

Now in court during cross-examination she is controlled verbally by the defense lawyer. Previously, her attempts at self-defense[22] were limited by the assailant's force or threat of force. In the courtroom, they are limited by the skills of the defense lawyer. It is he, not she, who understands the workings of the courtroom. The rapist's force rendered her physically helpless. The defense lawyer's inquiries may render her verbally helpless. His questions become weapons. His way of wording questions may make her say the opposite of what she wants to say. Rape and cross-examination both constitute attacks. Both are controlling situations in which the victim is made to do or to say things against her will.

Amount of Adversariness: Cooperation Between Defense and DA

Since the adversary nature of rape hearings and trials to which victims are subjected was emphasized above, brief mention should be made of a prominent theme in the literature: namely, that although ideologically our legal system is supposed to be adversary, in practice it is not. Analysts and critics are not referring to restrictions on conflict imposed by defendant's right to a fair trial. Rather, they mean that the defendant's right to an adversary proceeding may not in practice be honored. They state that adversariness is muted by the organizational structure of the court and by long-term relationships of cooperation between defense attorneys, both public and private, and DAs.[23] Thus, in fact, defense attorneys and DAs negotiate cases. The result is a very high percentage of cases settled through plea bargaining rather than by combative trial.[24] Sudnow, focusing on the public defender, states that "both P.D. and D.A. are concerned to obtain a guilty plea wherever possible and thereby avoid a trial."[25] He points out that the public defender and the district attorney are co-workers in the same courts.[26] Carlin, Howard, and Messinger note a "weakening of the adversary system" and cite as contributing factors the large volume of cases, pressures for efficiency, and increasing emphasis on diagnosis and treatment by nonlegal personnel.[27] Skolnick points out that DAs must concern themselves not only with prosecution but with administrative matters such as keeping the calendar moving. "Administrative requirements . . . make for a reciprocal relationship between prosecutor and defense attorney that strains toward cooperation."[28] Blumberg maintains that all court personnel, including defense lawyers, tend to direct the accused toward a plea of guilty. Defense lawyers, whether public defender or privately retained, have long-term relationships with the prosecutor's office. "Accused persons come and go in the court system schema, but the structure and its occupational incumbents remain to carry on their respective career, occupational and organizational enterprises. . . . In short, the court is a closed community."[29]

Clearly there is a concern in the literature with whether sufficient adversariness exists to protect defendants. Thus it might be worthwhile to look at whether cases in the present study were plea bargained or tried. In most cases, neither happened—the cases simply suffered attrition long before there were any concrete plans for trial (see Chapter 5). However, 24 of the 115 rape victims' cases in our study eventually reached a point where a decision was made to go forward to trial or to plea bargain. In most (75%) of the 24 cases that got this far, one or more defendants went to trial. These trials, with one exception, were trials by jury. In a minority (29%) of these cases, the defendant pleaded guilty. In absolute figures, 18 victims' cases were settled by trial,[30] and only 7 were settled by pleas. (One case with 2 defendants led to both a trial and a plea.)

Plea bargaining typically is discussed from the point of view of the defendant's rights, the role of lawyers, and principles of the legal system. However, our study suggests that there are implications for victims as well. In cases where the defendant pleaded guilty to rape, the main effect on victims was that they did not have to testify in superior court. They thus were spared this very traumatic experience. In cases where the defendant pleaded guilty to a lesser charge (such as assault and battery), it also meant that it was never officially determined whether the rape occurred. A conviction was obtained, but there was no official recognition of the accused and the complainant as rapist and rape victim. Instead, it was decreed that a lesser crime had been committed.

MULTIPLE REALITIES: CONSTRUCTING A CASE

As victims go through the system, it becomes clear that the key issue is not whether a rape occurred, but whether people believe a rape occurred. As in any type of behavior, it is not the act per se that is significant, but the meaning given to it by various actors.[31] "If men define situations as real," the Thomases write, "they are real in their consequences."[32] And Schutz states, "It is the meaning of our experiences and not the ontological structure of the objects which constitutes reality."[33] To understand the social world means to understand the way people define their situations. "It is idle for the neutral observer to point out to committed actors the 'objective' situation."[34] Furthermore, as Dreitzel notes, definitions are not left to individual preferences, but instead result from negotiations of interacting partners. Cicourel, in his work on the social organization of juvenile justice, finds that the labeling and punishment of juvenile delinquents are determined through a bargaining process in which there is a redefinition of the acts committed according to certain pragmatic rules.[35] "The object (the delinquent) or delinquent act can be transformed by invoking an ideology to reread the 'facts,' character structure, family structure, mental stability and the like. The rereading highlights theoretical issues inherent in all decision-making."[36] Daniels, in her work on the social construction of military psychiatric diagnoses, finds that psychiatric diagnoses "will not 'hold still' but waver, change, and adjust to circumstances."[37]

As our study makes clear, the label *rape* does not "hold still" either, but wavers, changes, and adjusts to circumstances. The definition is problematic at all stages of the victim's career—during the incident, at the police station, at the hospital, at the DA's office. It is especially problematic in the courtroom. It is here that one sees concerted and dramatic efforts made by the various parties to create different definitions of rape and different definitions of what has occurred in the incident under consideration.

Definitions of Rape

Multiple definitions of rape surface in the courtroom. There is what is written in the lawbooks. There is the judge's interpretation of rape and the instructions given to the jury as to the meaning of the statutes and precedent cases. There are the common-sense layperson's views that jurors bring from their everyday lives. There are the ideas that defense attorney and prosecutor have about what lies in the minds and emotions of judges and jurors, and of how they are most subject to persuasion.

Legal Definition of Rape.[38]   The laws of Massachusetts at the time of the study state that rape is the carnal knowledge of a woman by force and against her will.[39] Stated in more familiar language, rape is the penetration by the male by force, the female being unwilling, not consenting. Another statement of definition, after referring to forcible and statutory rape respectively, notes its essence: Rape is the carnal knowledge of a woman against her will or of a female child with or against her will, its essence being the felonious and violent penetration of the person of the female.[40] The law refers only to acts committed outside the context of a marriage.

The Judge's Instructions.   The judge, at the conclusion of a trial, instructs the jury as to the meaning of the law. Regarding rape, most often judges were observed to emphasize the meaning of carnal knowledge or penetration and willingness or consent.

Judges vary in the way they instruct juries on the issue of consent. In one case, the judge explained, "If she consented, then there was no rape. If she yields out of fear of death or harm, this yielding does not mean consent.

The law does not require heroic effort on the part of the woman." In another case, another judge said:

> The key is, was she willing? . . . The degree of resistance is often crucial for the jury to consider. The man should not be convicted if the woman just puts up a little bit. If the contact is sufficiently arousing to her so that she yields before penetration, then there is no rape. . . . [However,] if the woman's consent is brought about by immediate fear of bodily injury and being afraid because of it, the law says that is not consent.

Judges also vary in the way they explain the issue of penetration. In one case, the judge said, "The law is the male has to penetrate. He doesn't have to place his entire penis in. He doesn't have to ejaculate." In one case, a second judge said, "There must be penetration. Penetration of the outer lips, or as I believe the doctor put it [in his testimony], vulva, is sufficient to be rape. It does not have to break the hymen." In still another case, a third judge said the question is, "Did the defendant's male organ penetrate the vagina of [the victim]? Penetration, however slight, must occur. . . . Emission or ejaculation need not be proved by the Commonwealth."

Force may also be explained, again in varying ways. In one case, the judge said simply, "Force is used like we usually use the word." In another case, a different judge explained that "the man must use sufficient force to accomplish his purpose. There do not have to be bruises."

The issue of fresh complaint—reporting the rape—received prominent attention in judges' instructions in two trials. The judges' instructions were slanted in opposite directions and had different imagery in the examples. In one case, the testimony was that the victim had not reported the rape promptly. The judge emphasized the significance of not making a prompt report.

> The law presumes if a woman is raped, she'll say something. In olden times, the language was "hue and cry." Today it is, "Did she make a fresh complaint?" For example, if a woman says to her husband casually much later, "Oh, by the way, the milkman raped me," then one wonders why [she says it this way]. Such testimony is to show her consistency. To fail to say something [about having been raped] is significant.

In another case before a different judge, the testimony was that the victim did report the rape promptly. This judge emphasized the significance of making the report.

> The statement outside of court that the girl ran in and told of having been raped—that is called fresh complaint. And in alleging of rape it is admitted

[as evidence]. Rape is not committed in Harvard Stadium in the afternoon. It's committed by two people. But right after when she is in a position of safety and she forthwith tells about it, the law considers that worthy of consideration—to help you determine credibility.

The variation observed in judges' instructions on rape laws raises interesting questions. The above analysis is based on detailed notes of judges' instructions taken by one of the co-authors[41] at seven jury trials for rape. Six different judges presided at the seven trials, and the features of the seven cases being heard differed. Therefore, it cannot be determined whether the noticeable variation in instructions correlates more with the particular judge or with features of the case being heard. This question and the question of the impact of instructions on the jury seem worthy of investigation in the future. One court official chatting with us about verdicts insisted that "it all depends on how the judge instructs the jury." It would be interesting to know if there is empirical support for this statement.[42]

The Jury.[43] Jurors not only have definitions of rape presented to them in court, but they bring with them common-sense notions from their everyday lives. Various studies suggest that there are discrepancies between the legal code definition of rape and definitions that exist in the normative standards of the community. A study by Klemmack and Klemmack, for example, reveals considerable discrepancy in the definitions. The people they studied were females obtained from a random sampling of dwelling units listed in a city directory. They presented seven situations, each meeting the legal definition of rape, to these women and asked them if the event constituted rape. An especially striking result was the importance of the degree of interpersonal relationship between assailant and victim. "If any relationship is known to exist between the victim and the accused, no matter how casual, the proportion of those who consider the event rape drops to less than 50 percent."[44] In addition, attitudes of the women studied (the definers) toward family life and toward premarital sex proved to be important.

A recent study by Harrell and Sagan of "simulated jurors" looked at relationships between definer's characteristics, victim's characteristics, and consequences of the act (whether it caused a pregnancy). The people studied were college students, and each person was presented with a written case account of a rape. "Male subjects were . . . significantly more lenient in sanctioning rape without pregnancy than were female subjects. . . . The major sex difference in perceptions of seriousness and suffering is that males minimize the seriousness and suffering of rape when pregnancy does not occur."[45] Other studies that give us information on definitions of rape have looked at attackers' characteristics in relation to those of the victim (such as inter- and intra-racial rape)[46] and victims' characteristics (such as degree of respectability).[47] Still others are looking at attitudes toward femininity and masculinity that are "rape supportive" on the part of the general public[48] and at how rape is portrayed favorably and as an almost normal part of male-female sexual relations in certain types of mass media.[49]

Still another research approach has been to compare jurors' decisions and judges' decisions. Kalven and Zeisel's work on "the performance of the jury measured against the performance of the judge as a baseline"[50] is especially revealing. Their study, analyzing many types of crimes, utilized 3576 actual criminal jury trials in the United States. For each trial they had data on the decision of the jury. They also had communications from the trial judges on how they would have disposed of the cases if they had come before them without a jury. In this sense, the study was like a "grand experiment" with matched verdicts that let one see how often jury and judge disagree and the direction of the disagreement. To analyze whether juries take into consideration the contributory fault of the victim, the authors created two categories of rape: aggravated rape (extrinsic violence used, or several assailants, or defendant and victim complete strangers), and simple rape (all other cases). The amount of jury disagreement regarding verdict correlated with type of rape case. In aggravated rape cases, it was 12 percent; in simple rape it went up to 60 percent. They also looked at the response to the major charge of rape. "The result is startling. The jury convicts of rape in just 3 of 42 cases of simple rape; further, the percentage of disagreement with the judge on the major charge is virtually 100 percent (20½ out of 22)."[51] These figures, in conjunction with other data, permit "the conclusion that the jury chooses to redefine the crime of rape in terms of its notions of assumption of risk."[52]

The implication of these various studies is that members of the general public and members of juries use extralegal considerations in arriving at their definitions of rape. And, of course, as other studies show, so do judges.[53]

Lawyers' Views of What Will Persuade.   As lawyers prepare for the hearing for probable cause or the rape trial, the focus of attention becomes how to put together a good case.[54] Their energies typically seem directed at how to marshal the evidence to create a definition of the situation favorable to their side. Lawyers have developed a set of notions about what they think the judge and jurors think. District attorneys try to put together the pieces of a particular case so that it will fall within definitions of rape held by judge and jury. Defense attorneys try to put the pieces together differently so that the case under consideration will fall outside those definitions.

Lawyers' conscious awareness of this image-building process is reflected in their informal comments at the courthouse. In one case, for example, the two defense lawyers were chatting in the courtroom prior to the opening of court for the day. One said to the other, "My argument is that she's beginning the oldest profession in the world. . . . I'm talking about the psychology of the people *there* (pointing to jury box)." In another case, the defense lawyer volunteered to us that he had found out that the victim had several aliases and that she previously had been charged and convicted of prostitution. He seemed excited about this news and said he planned to use it in court. The focus of his comments was on how he could use the victim's background against her and for his client.

After a case was closed, defense lawyers sometimes chatted with us about what they thought really happened and why they argued a certain way. In one case, after the defendant was acquitted, the defense lawyer said:

> I think what really happened is that there was a consensual thing. . . . I think she lived with the story for so long that she came in her own mind to believe that she was raped. I think this is what really happened. But I couldn't use this as a line of defense because the jury would have convicted if I'd argued it as such.

A similar process of constructing a case occurs with DAs too. In one case, the DA mentioned in passing that he believed the victim. But he spent his energies worrying about how to phrase the closing argument. His problem was that in court it had come out that the victim, who was white, had a good friend who was black. The DA said:

> I want to tie it together at the end, argue that she couldn't get help in a black neighborhood, that she complied out of fear but that's not consent. But I can't do that if her best friend is black!

The focus on building a case also is revealed in lawyers' comments when certain precedents or evidence matching their definition of the situation are ruled irrelevant or inadmissible. In one instance, the DA was upset that the judge ruled against him.

> The judge was against me right from the start—like the judge saying that hiding in the closet when arrested is not relevant. That is not so. There have been many cases, many precedents, where if a person is a fugitive, that can be used. One *can* infer from this.

And in another case, the DA said he was "very mad" when photographs helpful to his side were not admitted as evidence. These comments are from behind-the-scenes conversation about strategy. Below is an analysis of the finished product as seen from the vantage point of an observer in the courtroom. The attempt is to analyze the hearings and trials especially from the point of view of what happens to the rape victim. Hence disproportionate emphasis is placed on the analysis of defense strategies—on what is said about the victim and on cross-examination of the victim.

Defense Thematic Strategies: Blame the Victim[55] and Misidentification

The main strategy that defense lawyers of both sexes use in rape cases is to blame the victim. They argue that the victim consented to the sex or that she fabricated the sexual activity. Sometimes they use the issue of misidentification. They may also talk of technicalities and police procedures. The approaches described are used in juvenile hearings, in hearings for probable cause, and in trials.

Blame-the-victim strategy is similar to what Emerson calls counterdenunciation in his study of many types of cases seen in juvenile court. Counterdenunciation "seeks to undermine the discrediting implications of the accusation by attacking the actions, motives, and/or character of one's accusers."[56] The important point is that to denounce a person—to accuse a person of a crime, for example—means that one is opening up oneself to examination. "If the denouncer's character and involvement in the situation are not impeccable, misconduct cannot be presented as unmitigatedly wrong."[57] The accuser may in turn get accused. Emerson, referring to a case history from his study, shows how the counterattack can apply in a case of rape.

> The situation of the rape "victim" dramatically illustrates the risks of denunciation for the victim-complainant. . . . Successful denunciation requires evidence of the girl's own morality and purity. . . . She risks counterdenunciation from the boys, who could well have defended themselves by claiming that she made the first advances and consented to the acts. A girl denouncing others for rape, therefore, may ultimately suffer greater discrediting than those she accuses.[58]

In the rape cases observed in our study, the defense lawyer and the DA focused on eleven issues in building their opposing definitions of what occurred:

1. Did the female consent to sex or did she not consent?
2. Did the female struggle or did she not struggle?
3. Did the female know the defendant or not know him?

4. What is the female's sexual reputation?
5. What is the female's general character?
6. What was the female's emotional state at the time of the incident?
7. Did the female promptly report the rape to someone?
8. Is the female spiteful?
9. Is the female claiming rape to avoid punishment?
10. Is her statement that sex occurred accurate?
11. Does the female's statement describe rapists' behavior?

The following tables show the frequency of these issues in the 28 hearings (juvenile hearings and hearings for probable cause) and 12 trials that the researchers observed firsthand.

Table 1. Blame-the-Rape-Victim Issues in 28 Hearings*

Did the female consent?		22
Can consent be implied?		28
Did the female struggle?	28	
Did the female know the defendant?	21	
What is the female's sexual reputation?	21	
What is the female's general character?	20	
What was the female's emotional state?	18	
Did the female report the rape promptly?	18	
Is the female spiteful?	6	
Is the female claiming rape to avoid punishment?	5	
Is the female's statement that sex occurred accurate?		6
Does the female's statement describe rapists' behavior?		0

*Of the 115 rape cases in our study, 39 went to hearing for probable cause or juvenile hearing. This table is based on the 28 hearings observed firsthand by the co-author(s) or research assistants. Specifically, 22 hearings were observed by the co-author(s), sometimes with an assistant also present; 6 hearings were observed by research assistants only; and at 11 hearings there was no observer present. In 13 hearings, verbatim notes were taken while court was in session. In the other 15 hearings, notes were written by memory immediately afterward.

The prosecution presents the victim in as favorable a light as possible regarding the above issues, thereby trying to thwart a successful counter-denunciation. The defense presents the victim in the worst possible light. In the strategy of blaming the victim, defense lawyers trade on current normative expectations for sex roles. They trade on the tendency of the public at large and apparently also many jurors to blame the victim. Rape is not seen by the public as the result of social expectations in which females are defined as the appropriate objects of male violence. Rather, certain girls or women are seen as "asking for it," "fantasizing about it," or "just plain lying." Ryan has called attention to the general process of blaming the victim.[59] His reasoning can be applied to the issue of rape as well. If one comes to believe that rape is the female's fault, then who can find any fault with the rapist or with the male-dominated society?

Table 2. Blame-the-Rape-Victim Issues in 12 Trials *

Did the female consent?		10
Can consent be implied?		12
Did the female struggle?	12	
Did the female report the rape promptly?	11	
Did the female know the defendant?	10	
What was the female's emotional state?	10	
What is the female's general character?	10	
What is the female's sexual reputation?	8	
Is the female spiteful?	5	
Is the female claiming rape to avoid punishment?	5	
Is the female's statement that sex occurred accurate?		6
Does the female's statement describe rapists' behavior?		4

*Of the 115 rape cases in the present study, 18 went to trial. This table is based on the 12 trials observed firsthand by the co-author(s) or research assistants. Specifically, 10 trials were observed in their entirety or major portions thereof by the co-author(s), with additional observations made by research assistants; 2 trials were observed by research assistants only; and in the remaining 5 trials (which settled 6 cases) there was no observer present. In 9 trials, the observer took verbatim notes while court was in session. In the remaining 3 trials, notes were written by memory immediately after the court sessions.

Consent. When a victim states that a male has raped her, a possible counterdenunciation is that she consented to sex. Defense lawyers may inquire about this issue directly and explicitly. They may ask simply, "Did you consent?" or they may use other language, such as asking if the act was "voluntary." The prosecution, in contrast, tries to show the reason for the victim's behavior—namely, the defendant's use of force, threat of force, and inducement of fear, since "consent" under such conditions legally does not constitute consent at all. In one case, the defense lawyer blamed the victim, saying she consented. The DA's opposing approach was:

District attorney:	Did you consent?
Victim:	(pause) Yes (said tentatively and with a nervous smile).
District attorney:	What was the basis of your consent?
Victim:	That he would strangle me.

If the defendant takes the stand, another approach can be used as well. The defendant then can testify that the victim had sex voluntarily. In one such case, the defendant, asked if he forced himself on the victim, replied, "No, she went freely." In another, the defendant testified, "We had relations, but she did it willingly." There also may be testimony about statements the defendant has made. In one case, there was testimony that after the incident the defendant said, "I sexed her, but I didn't use force."

A picture of the victim's consent to, or initiation of, preliminary sexual activities is sometimes emphasized, since jurors may interpret that to mean consent to sexual intercourse. In one case, various friends of the defendant came to court and testified on this issue. One of them, Mrs. Davies, testified as follows:

Mrs. Davies:	[They were on] the studio couch.
Defense:	Talking—what about?
Mrs. Davies:	Just general things.
Defense:	At some time did they do anything?
Mrs. Davies:	They started hugging and kissing.
Defense:	What did you do?
Mrs. Davies:	I told them they had to get out because I had a little baby.

Another defense witness testified, "She grabbed him by the neck and started kissing him. . . . Mrs. Davies told them to leave." Another defense witness testified, "Mr. Terban and Della were sitting in the long chair. They was kissing. Mrs. Davies said, 'You all have to go, I won't have that.'" The defendant was acquitted.

Sometimes, moving even further away from sexual intercourse itself, consent to being in the situation is emphasized by the defense. The argument is that since the victim went to the place willingly, she knew what would happen. "That appears to be an agreed-upon rendezvous," "You knew what his intentions were," "You willingly went to that house," "You went [there] voluntarily. . . . You knew it would be deserted and you could fool around."

Defense lawyers get at the issue of consent in any way they can, no matter how indirectly. They use anything they can about the victim's behavior, emotional state, or character that increases the plausibility in the judge's or the jurors' minds of the female having consented. To accomplish this, defense lawyers trade on current normative expectations for sex roles. They know that anything the female does that deviates from the norms of "appropriate female behavior" can be used to attack her in court. Certain stereotypes, such as the vindictive female, can be used against her as well. Thus defense lawyers trade on the issues discussed below to *imply* consent.

Struggle and Force: Woman As Defender of Her Honor.   There is a myth that a woman cannot be raped against her will, that if she really wants to prevent a rape she can. In professional circles this view may be stated as "It's really not possible to rape a woman unless she's willing—physiologically possible, I mean—is it?"[60] An example of this view as expressed in more vernacular conversation was given earlier—"you can't put a peg in a moving hole." Most women at present are socialized so that they do not know how to fight. The irony is that females who are not supposed to know how to fight suddenly are expected to struggle, fight and resist to a high degree, try to run away, and call for help when they are attacked and their lives are threatened. And they are to prove in court that they did so.

The prosecution typically tries to show either that the victim did struggle or that she had no real opportunity to do so. The standard defense is to try to show that the woman did not struggle, that there must have been many people around to whom she could have run or called out, that she passed up innumerable opportunities to escape. For example, in one case, the defense repeatedly asked the victim questions about the layout of the area she and the defendant passed by: How many people were there in front of each of the places they passed, how many by the restaurant, how many in the laundromat, how many by the university, weren't they students, weren't many of them big and strong, why didn't she call out to them for help, why didn't she scream, why didn't she run to them for help? The victim testified that at one point she did call out, but the people paid no attention so she thought calling out might not do any good and she did not do it again. The defense also emphasized that there had been no bruises.[61] The defendant was acquitted. Another defense, if bruises do exist, is to argue that they have a cause other than the assault. "All the marks were consistent with [her playing] soccer."

The expectation that a woman should always attempt to prevent the rape through struggle leaves women in a double bind. If they do not struggle, they have a very hard time in court. If they do struggle, they run the risk of incurring even worse injuries at the hands of the rapist.[62] What the general public, and hence one would assume many jurors, does not know is that struggle on the part of the victim increases the violence perpetrated by certain types of rapists. Clinical psychologists A. Nicholas Groth and Murray L. Cohen summarized the matter well when they reported on interviews with patients who were convicted rapists. "One rapist answered, 'When my victim screamed, I ran;' another said, 'When my victim screamed, I cut her throat.'"[63]

Knowing the Defendant: The Rapist As a Stranger.   There is a myth that rapists are strangers who leap out of bushes to attack their victims. In fact, as various studies show, rapists may be strangers attacking by surprise or they may be well known to the victim.[64] Nevertheless, the view that interaction between friends or between relatives does not result in rape is prevalent. The issue of the relationship between victim and defendant is used in court to blame the victim. The defense tries to establish that there is a relationship between the two parties and tries to portray this relationship as an intimate one. The defense thereby tries to imply that the female consented to whatever sexual activity occurred. In one juvenile court hearing, the defense lawyer cross-examined the 13-year-old victim as follows:

Defense:	You knew him?
Victim:	Yes. He went to my school.
Defense:	What school do you go to?
Victim:	Central.
Defense:	You were friends?
Victim:	Yes.
Defense:	You visited his home?
Victim:	Yes, [my girl friend] and I had gone there—but to see his sister.
Defense:	You liked him?
Victim:	Yes.
Defense:	You had even telephoned his house?
Victim:	Yes, I had telephoned there three times, once to . . .
Judge:	Skip it.

In another case, the defense lawyer asked the victim, "Did you know him?" "Had you been to his house before?" "Didn't you like him?" The father of the two defendants testified, "She was at my house several times socializing." In still another case, the victim testified that the defendant was an acquaintance of her husband, and the defense insisted he was a friend of her husband.

If the relationship of the defendant to the victim is that of former boyfriend, the victim is especially subject to counterdenunciation. In one case, the defense lawyer shouted in court, "It's outrageous that a girl friend should bring such charges." It is easy for the defense to portray such victims as "out to get the guy" and—as is discussed later—to present them as "spite cases."

Sexual Reputation: The Madonna—Whore Complex. Individual women are seldom thought of as having integrated personalities that encompass both maternal love and erotic desires. Instead, they are categorized into one-dimensional types. They are maternal or they are sexy. They are good or they are bad. They are madonnas or they are whores. The split view of woman has been noted by many writers. The historian Vern Bullough, discussing the formation of Western attitudes, describes the "two faces of woman"—"the dutiful housewife and loving mother on the one hand; the erotic lover, temptress of man, on the other."[65] Chafetz, a sociologist, has reported on a study of the words people think most Americans use to describe masculinity and femininity. "A basic dualism is . . . displayed toward the female, who is simultaneously held to be 'sexually passive, uninterested' (the Virgin Mary image) and 'seductive, flirtatious' (the wicked Eve tempting poor, innocent Adam). This theme runs throughout the history of Western civilization, and our mores concerning 'good' and 'bad' females have no parallels for males"[66] Research by Clifton, McGrath, and Wick found "strong evidence for distinctive stereotypes of housewife and bunny."[67]

The split view of woman is used against her in court. On the books, the legal definition of rape makes no distinction between "good" and "bad" victims. However, the rules of evidence do.[68] The jury does, too. Jurors tend to be "over 30"—raised during a time when normative expectations for sexual behavior of females were more conservative than among certain groups of young people today. Defense lawyers know their bias. They trade on it and do all they can to discredit the sexual reputation of the victim—to portray her as a bad woman. Furthermore, defense lawyers know that many jurors still think in terms of the double standard. The defendant's past sexual behavior, if it gets mentioned at all, will be judged in different terms than the woman's. A sexually active man will be perceived as a sexually normal man. A sexually active woman will be perceived as a bad woman. If she consented to sex before, so the argument goes, the chances are high that she consented to sex this time, too. Although this view may be out of keeping with the sexual practices of a large proportion of women today, this line of defense is persuasive with juries.

It takes very little to discredit the victim's sexual reputation. It is easily done through indirect evidence and through innuendo, implication, and suggestion. First, defense lawyers will ask questions or make comments suggesting that the rape victim is "worldly" or "experienced." Their cross-examination of her may include questions such as, "Haven't you been downtown before?" "[You had] no orgasm at that time—you've had enough experience to know?" "You seem quite familiar with these [sexual] terms," or, "You've had experience." They may make similar comments about the victim to the judge, although that does not always go over so well. In one case, the defense lawyer said, "Your honor, this young lady is obviously a woman of the world." His statement angered the judge. In another case, the defense lawyer's statement and the DA's counter went as follows:

Defense lawyer:	(to judge) This is a serious offense and punishable by severe sentences. I think her extracurricular activities are a very important bit of evidence. Her reputation has a great deal of bearing on this case.
District attorney:	(to judge, sternly and emphatically) The girl's reputation is not the point here in this hearing today.

The judge sustained the objection.

A variation of the above is for the defense to imply the existence of a boyfriend or boyfriends when there has been no evidence that any exist. For example, in one case a pubic hair was found during the gynecological examination of a prepuberty victim. The prosecution argued that it had come from the defendant and that it corroborated the victim's account. There was no evidence during the trial that the victim had any boyfriends. But the defense lawyer proposed the following alternate explanation for the hair during his closing argument: "Did she pick it up from one of her boyfriends? These things happen."

Second, defense lawyers use the victim's clothes and appearance to discredit her sexual reputation. They argue that her attire was sexy and provocative. The victim thus can be discredited for behavior that our society expects: looking attractive. It is a normative expectation in our society that women are to dress and walk and talk in a way that is sexually provocative to men. Yet if they look this way and happen to become rape victims, their appearance is held against them. Furthermore, the defense lawyer implies that their sexual appearance is an indication of what their sexual behavior must be. In one case, the defense lawyer asked, "Your clothing left your midriff exposed, did it not?" In another case, he said, "Weren't these underwear too small for you, and didn't some of your pubic hair show above them?" In still another case, the defense lawyer asked the victim questions to establish that her "short shorts" were "skintight," that her weight was 139 and her shorts were only size 12.

Victims can be defamed merely through gossip about their clothes. Consider the following exchange concerning a 13-year-old rape victim:

Defense: Do you know Jackie King?
Witness: Yes.
Defense: Do you know Jackie King's reputation for chastity?
Witness: Yes.
Defense: What is it?
Witness: She is loose with her body. I have heard people say that.

As the testimony went on, it became clear that Jackie's reputation for lack of chastity was based mainly on chatter about the big afro wig and the tight pants she often wore. The DA, in his closing argument, tried to counter the innuendos by pointing out the defense's strategy:

They've portrayed her as something less than to be admired. . . . And [the testimony about] the wig—it's to make her look trashy.

But the victim remained defamed. The two defendants were found guilty of statutory rape but not of forcible rape.[69]

Third, defense lawyers will use vaginal infections to imply sexual experience and loose behavior. It is true that venereal diseases, such as gonorrhea or syphilis, are spread almost entirely through sexual contact. But other infections, such as vaginitis, in fact may occur at any time from childhood to old age and have other causes. However, this is not well known by the general public. For many people, any vaginal infection has connotations of being "dirty" and "unclean." In one hearing for probable cause, this line of defense was used dramatically:

The defense lawyer announced, "I don't want to say it out loud," thereby heightening interest in whatever topic was so taboo. He walked over to the judge and talked in a very low voice, pointing all the while to the medical record. It was hard to hear him. It sounded like he was talking about some kind of discharge. The prosecutor went over, listened, and walked away, saying loudly, "Well, I know a lot of gynecologists, too, and that isn't any different from what every woman in America has."

There followed a very flamboyant exchange between the defense lawyer and the DA. The prosecutor boomed out, "Well, you can put *this* in the record. I'm going to have [the defense counsel] indicted if he insists on playing doctor!"

Fourth, if there is any concrete evidence about the victim's prior sexual activity, defense lawyers also will try to use that. They may cite a document: "the hospital record shows she was not a virgin." Or they may question the victim herself. Following is a case in point. It was a difficult one to prosecute because the victim, age 16, had had sex voluntarily just prior to the rapes and also voluntarily with the first of the several males involved in raping her. The defense lawyer asked about prior sexual activity on the day of the rape.

Defense:	What were you doing with Michael?
District attorney:	Objection.
Judge:	No, he can have that.
Victim:	He just wanted to show us the apartment. I've *known* these kids for four years.
Defense:	Did you have any sex while there?
District attorney:	Objection.
Judge:	I permit it.
Victim:	Yes, I did.
Defense:	With *who*?
District attorney:	Objection. The witness is not on trial here.
Judge:	Sustained.

Later the defense asked about the sexual activities of the victim's girl friend at the beginning of the incident.

Defense:	Did you overhear their conversation?
Victim:	Yes.
Defense:	They were making out?
Victim:	Ya, that's Sally.
Defense:	They were getting quite involved?
District attorney:	Objection.
Judge:	Sustained.
Defense:	Sally was petting, manually touching?
District attorney:	Objection.
Judge:	Sustained.

There were questions about the route taken to get to the apartment. Then the defense returned to the sexual activities of the girl friend during the ride.

Defense:	Relations were friendly [during that time]?
Victim:	Yes.
Defense:	More than friendly, at least with respect to Sally petting?
District attorney:	Objection. He has an obsession with—
Judge:	(interrupting) Mr. Neale, please! Sustained.

There were questions on marijuana use, going willingly to the apartment, the layout of the apartment, clothes, and so on. Then the defense returned again to questions on sex—this time, the victim's own sexual activities at the beginning of the incident:

Defense:	You willingly went into the bedroom?
Victim:	Yes.
Defense:	Willingly had sex with Bruce?
Victim:	Yes.
Defense:	Did you enjoy sex with Bruce?
District attorney:	Objection.
Judge:	Excluded.
Defense:	I believe that relates to the witness's state of mind and I think state of mind is critical for consent.
Judge:	(to victim) Did you want to have sex with another person?
Victim:	No, I did not.
Defense:	During the course of this time with Bruce did you tell him you previously had had sex?
District attorney:	Objection.
Judge:	She may answer.
Victim:	I don't want to answer.
Judge:	I want you to.
Victim:	Yes, I did tell him.

The case was difficult for the DA. He tried to show that her relations were not merely casual. On re-direct exam he asked:

District attorney:	Before arriving [at the apartment] you had sex—you had known him some time?
Defense:	Objection.
Judge:	(to defense) *You* went into it.
Victim:	Yes, three years.

The court found probable cause. But later, after trial at superior court, the verdict was not guilty.

Fifth, defense lawyers may ask if the victim had previously had sex with the defendant. They may ask the victim this question, or they may put the defendant on the stand and ask him if the victim had previously had sex with him.

Sixth, even when questions on sexual reputation and activities are excluded by the judge, defense lawyers may find alternate ways of getting at the same information. In one trial, the first defense lawyer's question about a boyfriend was excluded:

First
defense lawyer: Do you have a boyfriend?
Victim: I was told I didn't have to say that if I didn't want to.
Judge: Is there an objection?
District attorney: I don't see its relevance.
Judge: I sustain that.

Later, another defense lawyer representing the second defendant asked a variation of the question and got the answer. He asked, "What's the age of your boyfriend?" The victim replied, "Seventeen." In another case, a defense lawyer at the juvenile hearing eventually got the information he wanted on former sex between the victim and one of the defendants. First he asked the question directly and the following scene unfolded:

Defense: Have you had sex with Ray Manney before?
District attorney: Objection.
Judge: Objection sustained.
Defense: I would like to submit a case—a precedent—in which it was ruled that one can ask the witness in a rape case if she has had intercourse before with one of the defendants if the question is limited to having had it with one *particular* defendant.
District attorney: I still object. This case is an old one—from 1881. Maybe a hundred years ago this fit the times. But customs have changed in the last hundred years and now even if a woman has had sex with a particular person before, has consented, that has nothing to do with a later time when she might not want to have intercourse with him again and might not consent. I still object.
Defense: (to judge) May I remind you that we still have a precedent system of law and that even though the case may be a hundred years old, it still has not been overruled and so it still stands.
District attorney: I still object.
Judge: Objection sustained.

Later the defense asked, "What did you do the night before [the incident]?" The judge allowed the question. The victim, during her reply, stated that she had had sex willingly with this particular defendant the night before. In this case, the court had the juvenile complaints against all three defendants dismissed, and adult complaints filed in their place. The hearing for probable cause was waived and the court found probable cause in all three cases. However, at superior court the case dragged on and on, somehow never getting scheduled for trial. After months of delay, the charges were dropped at the request of the victim.

General Character: Anything Not 100 Percent Proper and Respectable.   There is an attempt by each side to discredit the other by reference to general character. The prosecution tries to bring certain facts, such as the man's criminal record, to the attention of the jury.[70] The defense tries to bring out information thought to discredit the female—that she is on welfare, or drinks, or uses drugs, for example. Being on welfare or drinking or drug use could be used to discredit anyone, but where women are involved, these issues are used to imply that the woman consented to sex with the defendant or that she contracted to have sex for money. This, incidentally, is one way in which the criminal justice system works a hardship on less affluent rape victims. When a woman is affluent, it is harder to make the argument that she prostituted herself. When she is obviously in need of money, prostitution is easy to allege.

The poverty and drinking arguments against rape victims work well with juries. Consider, for example, the following case in which the Commonwealth had a strong case against the defendant. The testimony was that the woman, in her thirties, was accosted on the street by a man to whom she recently had been introduced at a bar she frequented. He forced her into an alley, pushed her into a filthy, deserted room, and raped her. She screamed for help. A police officer arrived on the scene. He corroborated the fact that she screamed for help. He also testified that when he arrived the man was still on top of her. She was bruised, as corroborated by the medical record.

The defense lawyer, however, was able to successfully counter-denounce the victim. He argued that the woman had prostituted herself; she had contracted with the defendant to have sex for money and she had gone willingly to the room to consummate the contract. He mentioned her drinking. Her socioeconomic background also came up during the trial. In the closing argument, the defense lawyer explained why she called out and why the police got called:

> I suggest to you that an inference can be drawn in that there was a double cruel joke played on Miss Robins and Mr. Wilson. A cruel joke. These fellows saw Miss Robins and Mr. Wilson go in and their joke was to say, "We're going to get you.". . . The second joke was to go to the telephone and call the police and have them run down the alley. And the woman was tense and she called out. There was no rape. There was a consensual going there. And the double joke.

The defendant stated he paid her $20. This was disputed by the woman and by the police officer who, arriving on the scene, had searched her and found only $7.

The prosecutor, in his closing argument, tried to show that despite her background, she had suffered as much as other victims:

> Miss Robins, and to some extent the defendant, were in an environment that is often not understood by the typical middle-class juror. . . . Her demeanor on the stand—Miss Robins is not the most accomplished witness. She was easily confused and was upset. I ask you to give her some latitude. She's not a secretary or a college student. But, this does not mean that she hasn't suffered as much.

He tried to show how the practical joke theory did not make sense and also went on to talk of how she, despite the difference in her life-style from that of the jurors, had the same rights as any woman. Nevertheless, the victim remained defamed. The defense lawyer's interpretation of the testimony must have made sense to at least some members of the jury. The outcome was a hung jury. A mistrial was declared, and eventually the case was dismissed.

A multitude of things can be used to discredit the rape victim's general character. Indeed, almost anything other than completely proper and respectable behavior can be used: food stamps, criminal record, mental problems, psychiatric history, alcohol use, drug use, absence from school, religious views, and vague innuendos. Here are statements made by defense lawyers. "You did not have much food in the refrigerator. . . . And you were going to get your food stamps?" "Where did you meet the defendant's sister?" (Lawyer knew they met at a reform school.) "Are you aware that she has been given psychiatric tests?" "In addition to learning disabilities does she have any other behavior problems?" "Are you the same Janet Falk who appeared before this court and was found drunk?" "Do you pop pills?" "This is her complete medical record (holding up a thick manilla folder for everyone to see), but I will not introduce that." "I'd like to know, why isn't she in school?" (Absence from school had not been an issue during the testimony.) "Isn't it true that it had to do with a truancy problem?" "Is [that religion] a belief in God?" "Did you bring all of her other hospital records?" (The physician replied he could find no others.) "Why did you have your name changed?" "Are you into witchcraft?"

Accusations of mischievousness were used to counterdenounce a 13-year-old victim, Gail, whose case was discussed in Chapter 5 in the section on delay. The defense painted a picture of her annoying behavior—she had pulled up the defendant's tomatoes, painted his windows, thrown garbage in his yard. She was a pest. The defendant also testified that on the day of the incident he opened the door and the following occurred:

> Gail popped in. She said she came in to get a cigarette. I said, "I don't have any." She said, "But I want to stay all night." I said, "No." She said she wanted to sit a while. [So] I went upstairs.

Thus, the defense painted a picture of her importunities. The DA, in his closing argument, gave a different interpretation to the defendant's testimony, using the defense's portrayal of the victim's character to show a logical contradiction:

> [The defendant] said he had drinks, he went upstairs to get straightened out. He said later he's awakened by the doorbell and outside is Gail. Consider the background. This is the same little girl who tears up his tomatoes, same little girl who throws garbage in his yard, the same little girl who pesters him for money and cigarettes, and this little girl who awakens him out of a drunken sleep comes into his house. She's a mischievous girl, and he has a lot of [valuable] things in his shop. He'd like you to believe that, "No, I didn't give her a cigarette, but you can sit a while," and that then he goes up to bed [leaving her alone downstairs].

This was not the only argument he used, as is discussed below.

DAs have a difficult task ahead of them once the victim's character has been defamed by the defense. Arguments they use under such circumstances may include that this victim has the same rights as any other victim ("She has the same rights as a debutante from Beacon Hill," "Your job perhaps would be easier if it was a Radcliffe student or a nun. . . . But all three are protected by the same law"); that she or her family has suffered as much as a more respectable victim; and that she has a harder time expressing herself on the witness stand than a more educated or intelligent victim ("On the stand she was no genius—a factory worker, a high school dropout; she was no match for a skilled defense attorney, and she was no match for the defendant"). To these themes the DA may add more general arguments—statements suggesting a link between the victim's situation and the jury ("She may be a poor, unfortunate girl. But she was someone's daughter. She could have been your daughter") and statements about the horrors of the crime of rape ("She was used as a white sex-object to satisfy this man. . . . To punch a girl and to rape her four or five or six times, that's beyond comprehension").

The DA in Gail's case used these five themes. His closing argument is worth quoting at some length because it shows the humiliating things that may be said by a person who is attempting to help the victim. The rape victim's character is not only stripped by the defense, but by the prosecution. She is described in derogatory terms not only by the opposition, but by her "own side":

This little girl from [this poor neighborhood] has as much right as your daughter or mine to not be dragged up to the second floor and have a 45-year-old man try to insert his penis in her vagina and then turn her over and try to act with her like a dog. . . .

What would your reaction have been in [her father's] place? How would you like to have been on that [witness] stand? . . . Even a man who comes from a slum and works two jobs has feelings. . . .

Gail took the stand. She couldn't tell you what clothes she was wearing. She couldn't define the word "oath." [The defense counsel] brought out that her two brothers are retarded and that she is in a special class—probably closer to age 10 mentally and physically. If this victim were more mature, a college graduate with an IQ of 180, I wonder how accurate she would be. She could no doubt define "vagina" and "oath.". . . But how accurate would she be about how her clothes were taken off? But we're not dealing with a mature woman. We're dealing with a child and a child that is slow. And her slowness was no doubt apparent to the defendant and she's an attractive girl and maybe she appeals to people who like little girls. . . .

He isn't charged with the completed act of rape. She never told anybody he had full intercourse. If he had done it she would have been ripped to pieces. . . .

You represent all the people of [this] County. That includes the defendant. But he's not the only one in [this] County who has rights. The fathers who have daughters have rights, too. If you [do not convict], the perverts in our society will come to believe you can rape, and the lives and safety of our female population will be endangered. . . .

We can't go into his brain to determine intent. But I would suggest that he didn't take off her clothes to play doctor, and he didn't put her on the bed to read her a story. What was his intent when he lubricated her vagina? When he said he went into that bedroom to get straightened out, what do you think he really meant? I ask you for justice.

Despite these arguments, plus an emphasis on the considerable physical and medical evidence of sexual assault, the DA was only partially successful in persuading the jury. On the charge of assault with intent to commit rape, the verdict was not guilty. On the lesser charge of indecent assault and battery, the verdict was guilty.

Emotionality of Females. Females are assumed to be "more emotional" than males. The expectation is that if a woman is raped, she will get hysterical during the event and she will be visibly upset afterward. If she is able to "retain her cool," then people assume that "nothing happened"—that she was not raped. In actuality, our data show that many victims, through a conscious act of will, do retain control over their emotions in order to survive the assault. And even afterward, many, although upset, present themselves to others in a composed manner.

The normative expectations about emotionality put women in a double bind. If the women live up to the expectation and become so upset during the rape that they cannot remember details, they are blamed for not being able to testify about the details, or some other reason is advanced for their being upset. If, however, they retain their cool and remember details, it is assumed that nothing happened.

The following case illustrates the plight of the victim in court if she remains calm, cool, and collected during the attack. It is the case of Lauren, 14 years old, who testified at the trial that she was accosted by a stranger on her way home from a girl friend's house. He grabbed her and made her walk to an abandoned building where he raped her. Afterward, he walked her home, gave her a costume jewelry ring, told her his telephone number, said his name was Calvin, and told her not to tell what had happened. She went right into her apartment, told her parents what had happened, and gave them the telephone number. The police called the phone number, Calvin's mother answered, and this led to the identification of Calvin and his subsequent arrest.

Much ado was made by the defense lawyer about the victim's calmness. He said during his closing argument:

> Remember how calm she was. She was so calm that she could remember a telephone number without writing it down. She was so calm that she could wave hi to a boyfriend. That's not the behavior of someone who has just been raped.

The defendant was found not guilty.[71]

If the testimony shows that the victim was upset, the defense lawyer tries other approaches. In one case, the rape victim stated that she was "petrified" and also answered questions about details. The defense lawyer argued that that was inconsistent—that a person cannot be upset and also have a good memory. In another case, many people testified that the victim "was in a hysterical state" and "was crying." The defense argued that therefore the description she gave of the assailant must have been inaccurate. In another case, there was testimony that the victim was upset. The police officer who testified blamed her emotional state on the rape, but the defense lawyer argued that it was caused by alcohol. Whether the victim is upset or not upset, the defense lawyer will think of ways to use her state against her.

Reporting Rape.   Two conflicting expectations exist concerning the reporting of rape. One is that if a woman is raped she will be too upset and ashamed to report it, and hence most of the time this crime goes unreported. The other is that if a woman is raped she will be so upset that she will report it. Both expectations exist simultaneously. It is the latter one, however, that is written into law. As previously discussed, the legal principle is that if a woman wishes to pursue the matter through the courts, she must "make a hue and cry." In more modern language, this is called "making a fresh complaint." The assumption is that if she really has been raped, she will make this known to others immediately and will not lose any time before contacting the police. Any delay is held against the woman. Of course, many women do report rape right away. Others, for psychological or social reasons, procrastinate. A minority of women in our sample waited before reporting the rape. They said they had never been raped before, that they didn't know what to do, that it took them a while to decide how to respond. When such a case reaches court, the delay is held against the woman. The following is an example. The woman was exhausted after the incident and took a while before deciding to go to the police. The defense lawyer used this against her in his closing argument:

> What does she do now that she's free? Go to the police? No, she goes back to [where she is living]. *She* said she talked to someone, but did she bring someone in here to corroborate that? She said she talked to a girl and to Bob, but neither were brought in [to testify]. She went to sleep. Is this credible or incredible? She's back by 8 A.M., she goes to bed, wakes up for brunch. Only then is there a question of going to the police. I don't know why a girl complains of rape when it isn't true. She calls Bob. He asks, "What were you doing in that section of town?" She says, "Well, I had to stay." I don't know the reason. She finally goes to the police.

The defendant was found not guilty.[72]

The expectation that the female will report the rape promptly includes the notion that she also will name the accused promptly if she knows who did it. If she delays in identifying the rapist, it will be held against her. This issue was a major one in the case of Mia, age 14 at the time of the incident. The prosecution emphasized the prompt report of the rape and the reason for the delay in naming who did it.

District Attorney:	Then what happened?
Victim:	[He] got off me.
District Attorney:	Then what did you do?
Victim:	I was crying. I came home.
District Attorney:	Who did you see first?
Victim:	My mother.
District Attorney:	Then what did you do?
Victim:	She called the police and they took us to [the] hospital.
District Attorney:	When did you tell your mother who did it?
Victim:	I didn't want to tell. I was scared to tell.
District Attorney:	When did you tell?
Victim:	When it happened to my girl friend. She told me the same thing happened to her and [the defendant] did it and told her he attacked me, too. He told my girl friend he'd kill her if she told anyone.

Similar information came out in response to a question by the defense attorney. He asked, "What happened with [your girl friend]?" Mia replied, "She told me the same thing and the same people did it to her and [the defendant] said he had attacked me." At this point there was a visible reaction by people in the courtroom. The clerk who was sitting off to the side made a face showing obvious disgust at the defendant. It seemed to be a turning point in the hearing. In his summary statement, however, the defense lawyer emphasized "the lateness of the reporting of the incident." Probable cause was found. However, at superior court the question of what pieces of information she reported when, again became an issue. The defendant was acquitted. Regarding a separate incident—the case of Jackie King discussed previously—this same defendant was found guilty only of statutory rape, not of forcible rape.

The expectations regarding the reporting of rape leave victims in a double bind. If a female does report a rape, defense lawyers often argue that she did so for some other reason, such as to get back in the good graces of her husband or her parents. If she delays, the defense holds this delay against her, saying a raped female would have reported it right away.

Woman as Fickle and Full of Spite. Another stereotype is that the feminine character is especially filled with malice.[73] Woman is seen as fickle[74] and as seeking revenge on past lovers. This stereotype is used against the rape victim, and is especially effective when the assailant is a former boyfriend. The prosecution may emphasize that force and violence were involved. But the defense argues that the rape charge is merely the result of a lovers' quarrel. She consented to sex with her lover, something went wrong, and the rape charge is her revenge. The situation of Thelma, age 18, provides an example. Both sides agreed that Thelma and the accused had been lovers, but differed in their portrayal of the incident in question. At the hearing for probable cause, the prosecution tried to emphasize the issue of force:

District Attorney:	Did you leave?
Victim:	I left. But then he came and grabbed me and said, "Get in this fucking house." He used foul language.
District Attorney:	What was your state of mind when you went back in?
Victim:	I didn't have time to think about anything—he was beating me, punching me then.
District Attorney:	He's beaten you up before?
Judge:	Excluded.

Parts of the medical record were read out loud stating she had bruises on her face. The defense lawyer emphasized the issue of spite, and spoke as follows in her concluding remarks:

Defense:	I make a motion to dismiss the charge of rape—there's no probable cause.
Judge:	You're not going to present any witnesses on that charge?
Defense:	No. Rape is serious. It means intimidation, and by someone you don't know. . . .
Judge:	That's a wrong definition you're giving me. If drunk, a woman can be raped.
Defense:	This is not rape. He had intercourse with his girl friend. He had had intercourse with her on many prior occasions. They were boyfriend and girl friend. They were lovers for a long time. She was pregnant by him. . . .
Judge:	(interrupting) I remember the testimony. He got her pregnant. She had an abortion.
Defense:	It's the classic case of the jilted lover. . . . This is different from ordinary rape. There is no evidence of vaginal bruises. She had it out with the defendant.

Judge: Do you have any doubt that there was assault and battery?

Defense: There probably was a fight.

The DA, in his summary, emphasized that "fear and intimidation *were* a part of it." The judge was not satisfied that a rape had occurred. The defendant was given a one-year suspended sentence on the charges of assault and battery and of unnatural act.

The defense lawyer may denounce the victim as spiteful even if she testifies that she and the defendant were not lovers. She can be blamed for spitefulness if there is merely a good chance of portraying them as lovers. The case of Ann, a 17-year-old virgin prior to the rape, provides an example. At the hearing for probable cause, she first gave her testimony. The defense attorney did not cross-examine her to any great extent. Instead he put the defendant and a male friend on the stand. They contradicted her story point by point, portraying her as the defendant's lover, and turning it into a spite case. Contrary to what she had said, the defense maintained that she and the defendant had had relations several times over the summer, that they were going to get married and were going to get the blood test, that the night of the alleged rape they had had a quarrel and relations were a way of making up after the quarrel, and that the friend of the defendant had seen her leaving the man's apartment several times at 6:00 A.M. The defense lawyer suggested that restitution would be the appropriate solution and asked, "What would you settle for—how much money?"

The reactions of men who listened to the hearing show how the defense's definition of the situation made more sense to them than did the prosecution's. During a court recess, several men who were involved as officials with the case made these remarks in the corridor:

First man: (trying to predict what the judge would decide) The judge feels that it is not a legitimate rape. That's the way the evidence seems to be coming in. It looks like a lover's quarrel—a spite case. (looking over at a young male who had accompanied the victim to court) Who's that? Must be her new boyfriend! (laughter)

Second man: (to third) Watch out—that's what might happen to you. (much laughter by all three men)

Second man: She should pay him!

Court reconvened. Probable cause was found. However, the case never went to trial.[75]

The Female Under Surveillance: Is the Victim Trying to Escape Punishment? Females in our society are more tightly restricted in their sexual activities than are males. Their sexual behavior is more subject to surveillance. Before marriage, they are expected to abstain from sex. After marriage, they are to be the sexual property of their husbands. Even though in practice it is common for females to have premarital or extramarital sex, the norm still exists that they should not. This norm is used against them in rape trials. It is assumed that the female's sexual behavior, depending on her age, is under the surveillance of her parents or her husband, and also more generally of the community. Thus, the defense argues, if a woman says she was raped it must be because she consented to sex that she was not supposed to have. She got caught, and now she wants to get back in the good graces of whomever's surveillance she is under. A variation is to argue that she was out later than she was supposed to be, got caught, and needed an excuse for her tardiness.

For victims of junior high school age, a common tactic of the defense is to try to show that the girl is afraid of her parents, has stayed out later than curfew, experiences discipline problems in the home, and is afraid of her parents and the community finding out about her sexual activities. In one case, the defense and prosecution argued over the relevance of information on discipline. The defense lawyer called the girl's mother to the stand. The following scene occurred:

Defense:	How do you treat Shelby at home?
District Attorney:	Objection.
Defense:	Your honor, there is a great deal of fear involved with this girl and it is indicative of some sources. I want to know what forces were playing on her for her to have such fear.
Judge:	The questions have been objected to.
Defense:	I want to know how the girl is disciplined in her home.
District Attorney:	Objection.

The question was not allowed. Probable cause was found, but at superior court the defendant was acquitted. In another case, the defense and prosecution tried to give different portrayals—strict versus flexible—of the discipline that was used. The defense attorney called to the stand the supervisor of the Halfway House where the victim lived. He questioned her as follows:

Defense:	What is the penalty for a member of the Halfway House if they do not meet the curfew?
Supervisor:	No general rule. The restrictions are based on the particular girl.
Defense:	Would Evelyn have faced a penalty if she had not had a good excuse June 14?
District Attorney:	Objection.
Judge:	OK.
Supervisor:	Some degree.
Defense:	Would it have been particularly severe in Evelyn's case because of prior—
Judge:	(interrupting) I will not permit it. She may respond regarding severity, but not the reason for the severity.

The DA, cross-examining this defense witness, asked, "Are the penalties highly discretionary?" The supervisor indicated that discretion did exist. Probable cause was found, but after trial the defendant was found not guilty. For an older married woman, the comparable tactic the defense uses is to say, "Isn't it true you concocted that story to get back in the good graces of your husband?"

Disputing That Sex Occurred. That females fantasize rape is another common stereotype. Females are assumed to make up stories that sex occurred when in fact nothing happened. According to the stereotype, the sexual details they report are imaginary, part of a fantasy world. Similarly, women are thought to fabricate the sexual activity not as part of a fantasy life, but out of spite. Thus another way to blame the victim is to say that she invented all the sexual activity.[76]

This line of defense may be especially effective if there is little concrete evidence of intercourse. Physical evidence of penetration is hard to come by. There may not be vaginal bruises if the victim is penetrated only slightly or if she is sexually experienced. No sperm may be found. Many gynecological exams of rape victims show "no sperm,"[77] research on rapists shows that many suffer sexual dysfunction at the time of the assault,[78] some rapists use condoms, and emission is not part of the legal definition of rape. Nevertheless, the comments of some judges and the decisions of juries suggest that they want definitive clinical evidence.

Defense lawyers can use a lack of clinical evidence of intercourse to their advantage, as Ivy Johnson's case shows so well. Ivy, age 14, testified that the defendant's private part was in her and that it hurt.[79] The medical evidence, or rather the lack of it, became the central issue in the trial. The defense spoke as follows in his closing argument:

> The medical report is the most crucial piece of evidence in this case. The medical report is very clear. There were no bruises, no lacerations, no abrasions. And when I asked the doctor if there was leukorrhea, [a white vaginal discharge], he said there was no leukorrhea. . . . Her vagina was clean. And the doctor testified that he could not do an exam of the uterus; he could only insert one finger and that is not sufficient [to do an exam].

The DA countered:

> The significant part of the doctor's testimony and medical record is the *history*. In every significant aspect, she said the same thing to the doctor at [the] hospital that she said here in the courtroom. . . . Penetration, however slight, constitutes rape, and she testified that she felt it and that it *hurt*. . . . Do you really believe that the Johnson girl has such a twisted mind as to invent this story? To say not guilty you would have to believe she lied to her parents, to the doctor, and to the police, and that she perjured herself for several days here in this courtroom.

The jury chose to believe she lied. The man was acquitted. Regarding a separate incident, a case against this same defendant became inactive; after the defendant appealed the district court hearing to the state supreme court on a technicality, the victim could not be located.

In other cases in which the defense questions the occurrence of sex, the focus is more on sperm and seminal fluid as physical evidence of intercourse. In the case of a 23-year-old victim, the defense and prosecution gave alternate explanations for the absence of sperm. The defense attorney, in his closing argument, asked how all four assailants could comment on how "good" she was, but not have an orgasm, how the doctor's exam could fail to disclose one drop of sperm. The DA countered:

District Attorney:	The doctor's report said no semen, but I suggest the tampax absorbed it.
Defense:	Objection.
Judge:	Overruled. It's a fair assumption.

The defendant, the only one of the four assailants on trial, was found not guilty. In the case of a 19-year-old victim, the defense and prosecution gave alternate explanations for the presence of evidence of seminal fluid. The prosecutor tried to establish that sex had occurred between the defendant and the victim by calling a chemist to testify about his examination of the victim's clothing:

District Attorney: What else [did you find]?
Witness: The blouse had dirt smears. The "hot pants" were dirty. There was nothing remarkable about the bra except one black hair in one cup. The pants were stained in the crotch. The acid test was positive.
District Attorney: Explain.
Witness: The test for acid phosphatase was positive—was present. It's produced by the prostate gland and normally is found in seminal fluid.

The defense countered by suggesting that the source could have been someone other than the defendant. His cross-examination went as follows:

Defense: When you find [acid phosphatase], once it appears, until laundered, it will stay?
Witness: Yes.
Defense: You can't estimate time?
Witness: No, I cannot.
Defense: It could have been days or months?
Witness: Yes.

The defendant was acquitted.

A second approach the defense lawyer may use to dispute that sex occurred is to give an alternate explanation for some act; for example, for the act of getting up from between a woman's legs. This line of argument was used in the case of an 80-year-old victim who, by the time of the trial, was too senile to testify.[80] The two sides presented different interpretations of the behavior that had been observed:

The defense lawyer in her closing argument stressed that even though there had been testimony about seeing the defendant get up from the legs of the victim, that that alone really did not warrant the conclusion that something sexual had occurred. It might indicate that something was amiss, that he had attacked her to rob her, that she had attacked

him to rob him. But it did not necessarily indicate something sexual
had occurred.

The prosecutor, in his closing argument, stressed his interpretation of
what that almost vanishing breed, namely the concerned citizen—by the
name of Mr. Kemp—had observed. Mr. Kemp saw something in the
bushes, heard something, went to help, and saw the defendant get up
from the legs of the woman. The defendant had no idea of how much
or what Mr. Kemp had observed. Yet when he was trying to persuade
Mr. Kemp to stop and not go after him, he kept saying things like,
"She's a tramp," "She got what she deserved," and, "I was with her all
afternoon." There is, the DA insisted, only one reasonable way to interpret these statements. They all indicate that the defendant was referring to something sexual. He wasn't discussing a picnic.

The DA's definition of the situation was not persuasive enough. The
defense view prevailed. The defendant was found not guilty of rape.
He was found guilty of assault and battery, and got probation and
continued treatment at a state hospital.

A third approach for questioning the sexual activity is to say that
the sexual acts described by the rape victim are not possible for any
male to perform. This image was created in the case of a 20-year-
old victim (age 21 at the time of the trial). The defense lawyer first
cross-examined the victim.

Defense:	Then you were taken and stood up, is that correct?
Victim:	Yes.
Defense:	The other person approached you from the front?
Victim:	Yes.
Defense:	You were standing in nude position and he approached you from the front and inserted his penis into your vagina and the other man came from behind and put his penis in your vagina?
Victim:	Yes.

He then cross-examined the gynecologist to create the image that the
acts the victim said occurred are anatomically impossible.

Defense:	Do you have any opinion as to whether two peo-ple can penetrate a woman standing up?
District Attorney:	Objection.
Judge:	Sustained. Rephrase.
Defense:	Now, doctor, assuming, if you will, a female standing up. Oh, was Miss Goldberg's vagina nor-mal?

Gynecologist:	Yes.
Defense:	Assuming a woman normal in size and standing straight up, is it possible to enter standing—just like this (lawyer posed in a standing position)?
District Attorney:	Objection.
Judge:	Assuming the anatomy of a female, can she be entered?
Gynecologist:	I'd say it was almost impossible. You'd have to slant to go through the vagina, and to the rectum.

The defendant, the one assailant of the two who was on trial,[81] was found not guilty. In separate proceedings, however, he was found guilty and given concurrent sentences on several of 64 counts of armed robbery.

A fourth approach is to argue that the defendant was incapable of performing the sexual acts reported by the victim. In the case of a 33-year-old victim, the defense implied that the accused could no longer perform sexually.

Defense:	Is it true you have a disc injury and that it gives you considerable pain?
Defendant:	Yes, when I stand on my feet too long, I can't walk.
Defense:	Does this injury prevent giving you an erection?
Judge:	No, that is not relevant.

Probable cause was found. But when the case reached superior court, the defendant defaulted and the victim died from other causes. The case is no longer active. In the case of a 13-year-old victim, one defense lawyer and the DA paid considerable attention to whether one of the two defendants could have performed sexually the particular night of the incident. The defense argued:

Any girl can claim rape. . . . Whose story makes more sense? She says both [the defendants] were taking heroin. But she says they had sex. But [there was testimony] he had trouble having an erection. Now that has to be some kind of a record [to take so much dope and then to have sex].

The DA countered:

Mr. Dodd said he had intercourse and that he saw Bennett have intercourse. . . . [Defense counsel] talks about the effects of heroin. . . . But they are competent attorneys and I know that if there was any medical evidence to prove [one can't have sex after taking heroin], they'd have had it here in court.

The DA apparently was convincing on the point that sex occurred. The two defendants were found not guilty of forcible rape. However, they were found guilty of statutory rape.

Stereotype of the Rapist. One stereotype of the rapist is that of a stranger who leaps out of the bushes to attack his victim and later abruptly leaves her. Or the image may be even more extreme—"the rapist as a hideous creature with fangs at full moon, not even human."[82] Research on rapists, however, shows that their behavior may differ considerably from the stereotypes. Rapists may be well known to their victims. The "compensatory rapist" often has the fantasy that the woman will invite him to come back and rape her again, and makes plans to meet her somewhere. This is how some rapists are arrested—the woman agrees to meet him again, the rapist returns, and the woman has two policemen there to arrest him.[83] Because this information is not well known to the public, stereotypes of the rapist can be used to blame the victim. She tells what he did. And because it often does not match what jurors *think* rapists do, his behavior is held against her. The jurors conclude that she made up the story or that it was not rape. In the case of Ivy Johnson described above, for example, the victim testified that the defendant walked her home, gave her a ring, gave her his phone number, and told her his name. The defense lawyer kept saying, incredulously, "Would a rapist do such a thing?" In the closing argument, he said:

> If he had just raped her, why would he give her the ring, his name, the number where he could be reached, and walk her home? Is *that* the behavior of a *rapist?*

Apparently the jury believed the defense lawyer. The man was found not guilty.

In other cases, defense lawyers will use the kinds of sex performed to blame the victim. They will suggest that a rapist would not do such things. In one case, the victim testified about the various types of sex that occurred, including both sexual intercourse and masturbation. But the defense argued, "Is it reasonable that these men go out of their way 52 miles to masturbate? That they would drive all that way, torture her as she says, just to masturbate!" The DA tried to make masturbation sound so terrible that a rapist would do it. He talked about the penetration and "all the other sordid filth like masturbation." The defense may also cite the defendant's character as not being like a rapist. In one case, the defense attorney had the accused testify about his military awards—a Purple Heart, three bronze campaign stars, and a Korean medal. He then argued, "He fought for his country. That doesn't sound like a child molester." DAs also are aware of the stereotypes. They may try to make the defendant fit the image. As one DA said, "Another disgusting term was used . . . . 'You're going to f. whether you like it or not.' Are those the words of a Rudolph Valentino at a party, or are those the words of a rapist?"

Misidentification. Misidentification as a defense strategy may be used either in conjunction with or instead of blame-the-victim themes. It was used in four of the trials observed. In one of these—the case of Hilary Evans discussed below—the main line of defense was that of misidentification. We can only speculate on why the defense lawyer chose this tack. Perhaps it is because Hilary met all the criteria, to be discussed in Chapter 8, of "the ideal victim." She would have been almost unassailable through counterdenunciation.

At both court levels, the major focus of attention in this case was on identification. The prosecution tried to paint a picture of an identification made very carefully and properly. The defense lawyer tried to paint the opposite image of the identification process. At the probable cause hearing, the defense lawyer tried to shake the prosecution witnesses, but he could not. He cross-examined Hilary as follows:

Defense: How long did you take to look [at the photos]?
Victim: I ran through them twice.
Defense: You ran through them twice! (said incredulously—implying that she did it fast and carelessly).
Victim: I had to make sure.

Later he concluded the cross-examination as follows:

Defense: This is a serious charge.
Victim: Yes.
Defense: Look at that boy. Any doubt as to that young man? It's important.
Victim: (shakes her head—she has no doubt.)

Defense:	Have you contemplated this?
Victim:	Yes, a million times (said with slight sigh and in a tone of voice implying she had really agonized over it).
Defense:	Any doubt?
Victim:	No.

The defense lawyer also tried unsuccessfully to shake the testimony of one of the firemen to whom the victim had run for help and who had seen the assailant.

Defense:	You say he looks like the man?
Fireman:	I didn't say he looks like, I say he *is* the man.

At this point it was announced that probable cause was found.

At superior court, the prosecution and defense again tried to build up opposing definitions of the identification process. The prosecution presented a series of identifying witnesses—not only the victim, but also a person who was a member of the community, and four firemen, each of whom testified they had seen the defendant when he followed the victim into the fire station. The defendant, Lewis Reuben, testified that he was never with Hilary Evans. "I don't know her. The only place I seen her was at [district] court." To support this claim, the defense lawyer used several approaches. For one, he argued that the defendant stuttered and the victim had testified that the assailant did not stutter. For another, he used alibi witnesses, including Lewis's mother. Unfortunately from the defendant's point of view, both he and his mother gave bad performances. On the stand, the defendant failed to stutter (he stuttered only a few times during his entire testimony) and his mother failed to give the correct date when she was supposed to have been with him. She said, "I can't remember exactly the date, but he was there at my house." And in response to another question, she replied, "I don't pay no attention to dates." Here is the defense summary argument:

I in no way mean the circumstances happening to Hilary Evans didn't happen. [Rather], he said he wasn't the man. You've heard many say he was with them. . . . I submit to you this is a case where they picked out the photo of a man who looks most like the man involved in this case. . . . It is a case of mistaken identity. A case of identification of a young black man. . . . You heard Miss Evans was struck on the face and the physician reported a broken bone. She was very upset then and gave a description of the man at that time of stress. Was it a good or detailed description? . . . And there is the missing element —no stab wound was found on Mr. Reuben's back. . . . This man who assaulted this poor girl isn't in this courtroom. He's out wandering around with a stab wound in his back. . . . Did the police use suggestive means? . . . Do you recall the testimony of the firemen? . . . I question if they would be looking at her or at the door with the man.

The prosecutor, in his closing argument, countered:

A phony story in a court of law is just as phony [as one] in the street. Defense counsel says he is very sorry for what happened to Hilary Evans and then says his client isn't the right man—that another man is running around with a knife [wound] in his back! But look closely at the evidence. There is evidence that she *tried* to stab him— no evidence his back was bleeding, no evidence of a tear in his shirt, no blood on his shirt or on the knife. . . .

The defense had witnesses who placed Reuben at different places at this time. I ask you to use your common sense. Does the fact that the defense witnesses were either family or friends affect their credibility? . . . And one defense witness has a criminal record. You have the right to use that record when you judge his credibility. . . .

There was an occasional stutter—on the witness stand he was nervous, shaking, crying—and he stuttered a bit at least in the beginning. But during the six hours that he was with Hilary Evans, he was violently acting out and he was in control. . . .

The ordinary and commonplace doesn't get our attention. People remember the spectacular, the unusual, the vivid. Hilary Evans's experience was certainly not ordinary or commonplace. . . .

Hilary Evans was on the stand for only three hours. Is there anyone here who couldn't pick out her picture from 11 photos? She was with him six hours—not three, but *six* hours. . . .

There were six identifying witnesses. [As for the issue of identifying blacks], at the fire station several firemen have been there 20 years—in an all-black neighborhood. Do you feel all black men look alike to them? . . . And she has identified five nonwhite people who she saw for only 5 to 10 minutes, not the six hours that she was with the assailant. She went through hundreds of photos and she said, "When I got to the defendant's photo, it jumped out at me."

The prosecutor's view of the identification prevailed. The jury found Lewis Reuben guilty on all three counts: rape, kidnapping, and robbery. The sentence was life for the rape, plus 25 years for kidnapping and 25 for robbery, to be served consecutively after the life sentence.

Defense Linguistic Strategy: Terms, Sentence Structure, Style

As the lawyer Mellinkoff has noted, "law is a profession of words."[84] And Philbrick, who is interested in semantics, states:

> Lawyers are students of language by profession. Since the language they use is the principal means by which they achieve their successes, they understand as well as anyone the truth of Coleridge's dictum that an inconceivably large portion of human knowledge and human power is involved in the science and management of words. They exercise their power in court by manipulating the thoughts and opinions of others, whether by making speeches or by questioning witnesses.[85]

The hearings and trials observed in the present study were battles of verbal, as well as nonverbal, communication. Linguistic skills loomed large as one of the resources available to defense and prosecution attorneys. Defense lawyers focused on specific content themes, especially those that blamed the victim. In addition, they adopted linguistic strategies that either helped to create an image of reality consistent with the theme of blame-the-victim or that helped to fluster, frustrate, or wear the witness down. The linguistic strategies of defense lawyers included their choice of terms, sentence structure of cross-examination questions, and style of delivery.

The Choice of Terms. Prosecution and defense engage in battles over terms in many types of cases. A recent example occurred in the highly publicized trial of the Boston physician charged with manslaughter after performing a legal abortion. In this case, the prosecution kept referring to "baby boy" and "child," while the defense spoke of a "fetus" and the "products of conception."[86]

In rape cases, the defense lawyer uses words that suggest sexuality; the prosecution uses those that suggest violence. Thus, partly through choice of terms, the defense paints a picture of romance and sexiness, the prosecution one of force and aggression. Inquiring about consent, defense lawyers say, "You liked him. . . . You knew it would be deserted and you could fool around?" "Isn't it true he called you up to cop some fun?" "Didn't the defendant 'sweet-talk' you? . . . And you voluntarily went to bed with him?" The defense, in contrast to the prosecution, uses verbs that suggest desire and choice by victims: "You wanted to take [your pants] off," "So you decided to have your legs apart." "Did the man take you by the arm when you wanted to spend the night?"

Physical acts, such as the placement of an arm or walking, are described in different terms by the two sides. For example, at a hearing for probable cause, a victim (whose face was badly bruised when we saw her at the hospital) testified that the defendant had robbed her, raped her, and then, holding her, forced her to walk around with him without her shoes in an unfamiliar neighborhood. The cross-examination regarding this forced walk included the following:

Defense: Did he have you by the hand or—
Victim: He had his arm around me.
Defense: In other words, a gesture of affection.

The defense lawyer also referred to the walking as "sauntering along." In another case, the victim testified that the defendant "held onto my throat," and that during intercourse "he still had his arm stuck in my neck." The cross-examination went like this:

Defense: Did he threaten you with a weapon?
Victim: His arm.
Defense: But when you let a man kiss you, don't you let him hold you?

The defense lawyer also said things such as, "Then you made love," "Isn't it true you consented to his advances?"

Defense lawyers use words implying closeness in the relationship between victim and defendant, thus trading on the stereotype that what happens sexually between friends does not constitute rape. In contrast, the prosecution, also aware of the stereotype, uses words that imply distance in the relationship. For example, in a hearing for probable cause, the 14-year-old victim testified that she knew the defendant and that he lived in the neighborhood. In the cross-examination, the defense lawyer suddenly began talking about friendship.

Defense: How did you know the defendant?
Victim: He lives in the neighborhood.
Defense: When did you talk on a friendship basis?
Victim: He asked me for money once.
Defense: What else did you do in friendship?
Victim: I told him I had no money.
Defense: So you see him.

The judge said the victim was talking about money and not answering the questions the lawyer had asked; she told the lawyer not to confuse the girl. Later the cross-examination shifted to parties. The victim had testified that she had been to a party, but she had not yet been asked whether she went to this or any other party with the defendant. The defense, however, implied that she had.

Defense:	You'd been to parties with him?
District Attorney:	Objection. This is irrelevant.
Judge:	Sustained.
Defense:	You saw this man on a social basis?
District Attorney:	Objection.
Judge:	Sustained.

Later the cross-examination continued, with a dispute over "when" versus "if":

Defense:	When did you know him well?
Victim:	(No answer.)
Judge:	You might ask her if she knew him well.
Defense:	Did you know him well?
Victim:	Not too well.
Defense:	Did you date him?
Victim:	No.

Finally the victim was able to state that she did not date the defendant, but only after the defense lawyer's repeated use of words implying a close relationship between victim and defendant.

The Phrasing of the Question. In addition to choice of terms, the sentence structure of the question is important. Defense lawyers were observed to use a variety of types of sentences when cross-examining, including ones that might be called accusatory, declarative, and forced-choice. These three types are especially interesting since they are controlling, and therefore difficult for victims. As Scheff has noted, lawyers question "friendly" and "unfriendly" witnesses in a different fashion. With friendly witnesses—ones who will support the definition of the situation the lawyers wish to convey to the jury—they ask open questions and allow the witness considerable freedom. But with unfriendly witnesses they frame the questions differently and try to force the witness to answer in the manner desired.[87]

The accusatory form ("Isn't it a fact that. . . ?") "has been held permissible even though counsel did not have a foundation in fact for asking the question."[88] In the accusatory form, the lawyer paints an image and then asks the victim to agree with that image. Even if she gives a negative reply, he has had the opportunity of painting that picture for the judge or jury. Such questions were heard frequently in the hearings and trials observed. In the following excerpt from a juvenile hearing quoted previously, a series of accusatory questions was used:

Defense: (in accusing tone) Now isn't it true he "felt you up"?

Victim: He *tried* to.

Defense: (in needling, patronizing tone) Now isn't this the way it happened? You and Joey were on the floor and Donald came in and caught you and said he'd tell everybody what he'd seen. And that's when you decided to say you were attacked.

Victim: No sir, it was not! When I got up here I swore I'd tell the truth and I am!

Defense: But isn't that the way it happened and isn't that when you said you'd get them?

Victim: I said I'd take them to court.

This 13-year-old victim had the spunk to give a spirited reply, but not until the defense lawyer had created a picture of consent and romance. The two defendants were declared juvenile delinquents and released in the custody of their parents. Defense lawyers in other cases asked questions such as, "Isn't it true you have a hard time telling one black person from another?" "Isn't it true you smoke cigarettes?" "Isn't it true you were the first to talk?" "Isn't it true that your husband was critical of your behavior?" And in still another case the cross-examination ended as follows:

Defense: Isn't it true that now it's too late to tell the truth?

District Attorney: Objection.

Judge: Sustained.

Declarative sentences also are used by the defense lawyer when cross-examining. Here the defense makes a statement in the guise of asking a question. It really does not matter if the victim answers or not. The defense lawyer uses the statement as a way of presenting an image or of sneaking in information that is not allowed. After

the "question" is asked, the judge may rule that it should be excluded. By then, however, the statement already has been made. In one
case, for example, cross-examination included the following:

Defense: (to victim) So you changed your testimony.
Judge: (obviously displeased) That is for the jury to decide.

In another case it went:

Defense: You have been under regular treatment at the hospital
                        for alcoholism.
District attorney: Object.
Defense: I withdraw.

In still other cases, defense lawyers "asked questions" by making statements
such as, "There was a lot of drinking at this party," "Oh, so you had a
history of fights throughout your entire relationship," and, "You had been
drinking."

Forced-choice questions also are asked. In this type, the defense lawyer
tags onto the end of the question the answers—yes or no—from which the
rape victim must choose. Strong pressure is placed on the victim to answer
only with one of the alternatives provided. A typical question is "Did you
attempt to run, yes or no?" The dilemma for the rape victim is that often
neither answer is meaningful to her. If she did not try to run, for example,
then to say yes would be to lie. But to say no means that she is not allowed
to put it in context. She is not permitted to give the reason for her behavior.
Sometimes the DA will later try to counter such questions by giving the victim the opportunity to state reasons. For example, in a case where the last
question the defense lawyer asked the victim was "Did you attempt to run,
yes or no?" the DA chose to question the victim again:

District attorney: Did you attempt to run?
Victim: No.
District attorney: Did you have an opportunity to run?
Victim: No.

Delivery Style.   The term "style" refers to the co-occurrence of various
linguistic features.[89] Previously, choice of terms and choice of sentence
structure were discussed as isolated items. Delivery style, in contrast, refers
to how various linguistic features interrelate and fit together. It includes, for
example, intonation (often suggestive of different emotions) and speed of
speech (rapid-fire as opposed to protracted). It also includes what Thorne

and Henley call "the structuring of speech events."[90] Here, interrupting the rape victim's testimony and, above all, the sequencing of the cross-examination questions are important. Three delivery styles defense lawyers were observed to use are of special interest because of the difficulties they present for rape victims: rapid-fire attack, needling, and tedious monotony.

In rapid-fire attack, defense lawyers quickly and aggressively fire cross-examination questions at the victim. The following scene from Thelma's case (discussed previously) is a case in point. The scene was especially dramatic; both the rape victim and defense attorney were black females, the former of limited educational and financial resources, the latter highly educated, articulate and trained in a lucrative profession. The defense lawyer shot the following questions at the victim in rapid succession:

Defense:	Did you call out?
Victim:	I was afr—
Defense:	(snapping at her) I didn't ask that. I asked, did you call out?
Victim:	No.
Defense:	Did you struggle, push his hands away?
Victim:	(reply inaudible)
Defense:	Did you close your legs? (There was some confusion in the minds of the judge and others over what was being asked).
Defense:	(repeating, snapping at victim) Did you close your legs when he tried to rape you?
Victim:	(reply inaudible)
Defense:	Now you had intercourse with this man a hundred times—
District attorney:	(standing up and shouting) I object!

A big fight followed between the DA and defense attorney:

District attorney:	(walking back and forth shouting at her) That's an accusation, not a question!
Defense:	(shouting back) That's the kind of intimidation people are talking about against women in the legal profession!
District attorney:	Don't come in here and complain about being a woman. Learn how to practice law if you're going to be a member of the bar.
Defense:	(to victim) You've been treated at [the] State Hospital for—
District attorney:	I object!

Another big fight between DA and defense.

District attorney:	(shouting) She knows better than to do that, she knows better!

This case, even though the victim was quite bruised, ended in district court. The judge announced that he was "not satisfied that there was rape." The court officer then read out the decision: "On the charge of rape, the court finds no probable cause. On the charges of assault and battery and of un-natural act, guilty." The defendant was given a one-year suspended sentence.

Needling is a style in which defense lawyers make sharp prods and gibes at the victim. They make fun of the victim's behavior during the incident (e.g., degree of resistance), a peripheral item (e.g., hairdo), or the victim's "faulty" memory (especially about minor details). In one case, there were questions about why the victim, age 20, screamed or did not scream at various points during the incident. The defense lawyer then asked, "Why didn't you scream. . . . Do you turn being scared and not scared off and on like a light bulb?" In another case, the victim, age 13, made a considerable effort to look especially nice the day she testified at superior court. The cross-examination included the following gibes at her appearance:

Defense:	That's a new hairdo you have.
District attorney:	Objection.
Judge:	Excluded.
Defense:	Did someone in the courtroom fix your hair that way?
District attorney:	Objection.
Victim:	No.
Defense:	Remember the white boots?
Victim:	Yes.
District attorney:	Objection.
Judge:	It's not relevant.

A few questions more, and the victim was in tears on the witness stand. In another case, at the hearing for probable cause, the needling was aimed at the 15-year-old (14 years old at the time of the rape) victim's inability to answer questions about clothing and lighting details ("Were the lights 25, 60, or 150 watts?"). The defense lawyer kept saying, "You mean you do not remember anything?" None of the three cases from which these examples were taken resulted in a conviction for rape. The outcomes were, respectively, guilty of assault and battery, two-year suspended sentence; guilty of indecent assault and battery, four-to five-year sentence; and not guilty.

Tedious monotony is a third important style. It is less dramatic, although devastatingly effective. In this type of delivery the questioning by the defense lawyer is in a low-key tone, but very long and drawn out. The questions are tedious and may focus on peripheral or small details. Most important, the questions seem to go on forever. The rape victim is subjected to a marathon contest. The following questioning sequence—an excerpt from a rape trial at superior court—provides an example. It is from the case of Miss Robbins and Mr. Wilson, discussed previously.

How long were you at the [Prince Cafe]?
Did anyone go with you to the [Prince Cafe]?
Any customers in there?
Was there a bartender or barmaid?
What time was this?
What is your best recollection?
About 6:45 you went to the [Prince Cafe]?
Would it be correct to say you left the [Prince Cafe] at 6:30?
When did you see the defendant?
You were with the defendant when, on Friday, Saturday, Sunday?
You didn't come in Saturday or Sunday?
Mr. Wilson sent Seagrams to your table?
I apologize, he sent C and C.
Was the owner there?
This [person], did you talk with him before or after?
Did you see Mr. Wilson leave?
You were in the [Prince Cafe] from 3 to 7 P.M.?
How long?
Did you recognize the barmaid?
Did she have any conversation with you?
No conversation?
Where did you sit?
What did you order?
When did you see Mr. Wilson?
You had no conversation?
Go back to the night before. Where were you?
Who did you talk to?
Where was Mr. Wilson?
Did you talk with him?
What happened?
Did he tell you his name?
What name did he call you?
What was the extent of the conversation?

Did you sit with them?

What did you have to drink?

Sometime after that you left the [Prince Cafe], what time was it?

What time?

What is your best guess?

You testified at [district] court that—

At this point, the victim jumped up from her chair and shouted, "I'm not going to talk to you anymore, no sir, I'm leaving here. I don't have to talk with you." She marched down past the jury and out of the courtroom.

The judge announced that court would recess. The trial resumed the next day, and resulted in a hung jury. The case eventually was dismissed.

A variation of tedious monotony is tedious repetition of the same material. The defense lawyer asks questions on the same or similar topics over and over. The topic repeated may be relatively nonsensitive (many questions on time) or sensitive (many questions on sex). The following excerpt is from a hearing for probable cause in which innumerable questions were asked about what happened sexually and about resistance. Only one of the several assailants was a defendant in the hearing.

Defense:	A third person entered?
Victim:	Yes.
Defense:	Was that person the defendant or someone else? [Or was] the fourth person the defendant?
District attorney:	Objection.
Judge:	Sustained. Place the order.
Victim:	I'm *almost* positive he was the third. I *am positive* I had sex with the defendant and it was against my will.
Defense:	Describe what the third person did.
Victim:	I'll describe what the *defendant* did. I didn't count.
Defense:	The third person as I understand entered the room and said, "I'm not going to hurt you"?
Victim:	Correct.
District attorney:	Identify the third person.
Judge:	The third person is the defendant.
Victim:	He sat down. He said he wasn't going to hurt. I couldn't stop crying because of what the second had said. I can't remember it all, kissing—
Defense:	You had the sheet on when he entered?
Victim:	Yes.
Defense:	The sheet still on?
Victim:	Yes.
Defense:	He got on top of you?

Victim:	Yes.
Defense:	What efforts did you make to resist?
Victim:	I was pushing him away.
Defense:	Was that all you did?
Victim:	I was crying. I was telling him to leave me alone and I was pushing. What else did you expect me to do?
Defense:	Did you scream?
Victim:	No. I was scared after what the second one told me.
Defense:	Did you cross your legs?
District attorney:	Objection.
Judge:	She may answer.
Victim:	I remember crossing them many times but I don't remember if I did with him.
Defense:	Did you make any other efforts?
Victim:	I tried to talk to them. I kept saying I was only 15. I had just turned 16.
Defense:	What happened when he was on you?
Judge:	I won't permit it. She's been over that twice already.

At this point, the DA interrupted the questioning and insisted that it was appropriate for the victim to have a chair. There was a pause while a chair was obtained. The cross-examination resumed with a few questions on force, and then these inquiries:

Defense:	Did he use his hand to pry your legs?
Victim:	I remember it being done, but I don't know if the defendant did it.
Defense:	Did the defendant penetrate you?
Victim:	Yes.
Defense:	What was the position of your legs?
Victim:	(answer inaudible)
Defense:	So you decided to have your legs apart.
Victim:	I didn't decide anything.
Defense:	Were your legs apart?
Victim:	Yes.
Defense:	Did you make any attempt then to prevent—
District attorney:	The phrasing of the question should be specific.
Defense:	At the point of time at which the defendant penetrated you, did you make any effort to resist?
Victim:	I was making efforts the whole time. I was doing everything I could to prevent it.

There were some questions on types of sex and whether any of the boys asked for a "hand job." Then the questioning went as follows:

Defense:	One asked and you refused?
District attorney:	Objection. The witness has answered once. He's trying to rattle the witness.
Defense:	I'm trying to revive her memory. Did you attempt [a hand job]?
Victim:	No.

In this case the court found probable cause. But at superior court after trial by jury, the defendant was found not guilty.

Effectiveness of Blame-the-Rape-Victim Strategy

Today, the bias in our society is such that it favors the defendant and is against the rape victim. The defense lawyer's definition of the situation, not the prosecutor's tends to prevail in rape trials. This pattern may not have been the case at all periods in our history or in all geographic regions,[91] but it does seem to be generally the case today.

The main strategy defense lawyers use in rape cases is to counter-denounce the denouncer—that is, to blame the rape victim. If they can convince judges and/or jurors that the incident was the victim's fault, then these people will not find fault with the defendant. This strategy is devastatingly effective, as the conviction rate in our study shows. One hundred fifteen rape victims were admitted to the hospital. Twenty-four cases were settled by plea bargaining or by trial. In the eighteen cases that were tried, there were only two convictions for rape (adult victims) and only two convictions for carnal knowledge and abuse of a female child (victims under age 16).

The strategy of counterdenunciation is not limited to rape but is used in other types of cases as well. Emerson has noted that it is more successful when used against a private party (e.g., a victim) than against an official (e.g., a police officer or expert who is a "licensed denouncer").[92] This difference also seems to occur in other arenas. A study of the legal commitment to a state mental hospital by Miller and Schwartz found that persons who successfully resisted their own commitment did so by attacking the private party who denounced them, not by challenging the professional physician who examined them. "All those who attacked the decision or recommendations of the professionals were committed. . . . However, the defendant who turned on his complainants had the best of it and, in such cases, the tables were turned."[93]

One also can speculate whether the tendency to see the defendant's version as more plausible than the rape victim's is related to the relative power of men and women in our society today. Males as a group have more power than females as a group. Schultz and others have argued that male definitions of rape are prevalent.[94] Berger and Luckmann have talked in general about the relationship between power and the social construction of reality. "The success of particular conceptual machineries is related to the power possessed by those who operate them. The confrontation of alternative symbolic universes implies a problem of power—which of the conflicting definitions of reality will be 'made to stick' in the society."[95] They speak both of inter- and intrasocietal conflicts of this type, noting that "he who has the bigger stick has the better chance of imposing his definitions of reality."[96]

NOTES

1. Sandra Sutherland and Donald J. Scherl, "Patterns of Response Among Victims of Rape," *American Journal of Orthopsychiatry* 40 (April 1970), pp. 503-11; Arnold Werner, "Rape: Interruption of the Therapeutic Process by External Stress," *Psychotherapy: Theory, Research and Practice* 9 (Winter 1972), pp. 349-51; Ann Wolbert Burgess and Lynda Lytle Holmstrom, "The Rape Victim in the Emergency Ward," *American Journal of Nursing* 73 (October 1973), pp. 1740-45; Ann Wolbert Burgess and Lynda Lytle Holmstrom, "Rape Trauma Syndrome," *American Journal of Psychiatry* 131 (September 1974), pp. 981-86; Diana E. H. Russell, *The Politics of Rape: The Victim's Perspective* (New York: Stein & Day, 1975); Pauline B. Bart, "Rape Doesn't End With a Kiss," unpublished manuscript, Department of Psychiatry, Abraham Lincoln School of Medicine, University of Illinois, Chicago, 1975, published in abridged version in *Viva*, June 1975; Malkah T. Notman and Carol C. Nadelson, "The Rape Victim: Psychodynamic Considerations," *American Journal of Psychiatry* 133 (April 1976), pp. 408-13; Ann Wolbert Burgess and Lynda Lytle Holmstrom, "Rape: Its Effect on Task Performance at Varying Stages in the Life Cycle," in *Sexual Assault: The Victim and the Rapist*, Marcia J. Walker and Stanley L. Brodsky, eds. (Lexington, Mass.: D. C. Heath, 1976), pp. 23-33; Carroll M. Brodsky, "Rape at Work," *Ibid.*, pp. 35-51.

2. Discussed in Chapter 7. See also Lynda Lytle Holmstrom and Ann Wolbert Burgess, "Rape: The Victim and the Criminal Justice System," *International Journal of Criminology and Penology* 3 (1975), pp. 101-110.

3. "When an individual appears in the presence of others, there will usually be some reason for him to mobilize his activity so that it will convey an impression to others which it is in his interests to convey." Erving Goffman, *The Presentation of Self in Everyday Life* (Garden City, N.Y.: Doubleday Anchor Books, 1959), p. 4. "I assume that when an individual appears before others he will have many motives for trying to control the impression they receive of the situation. This report is concerned with some of the common techniques that persons employ to sustain such impressions and with some of the common contingencies associated with the employment of these techniques." *Ibid.*, p. 15.

4. *Ibid.*, pp. 22-24.

5. Donald W. Ball, "An Abortion Clinic Ethnography," *Social Problems* 14 (Winter 1967) p. 296.

6. *Ibid.* (emphasis in the original).

7. Robert M. Emerson, *Judging Delinquents: Context and Process in Juvenile Court* (Chicago: Aldine, 1969), p. 172.

8. Ibid., pp. 174-83. The discussion here owes much to Emerson's analysis.

9. John N. Hazard, "Furniture Arrangement As a Symbol of Judicial Roles," *ETC.: A Review of General Semantics* 19 (July 1962), p. 181.

10. Robert A. Kessler, "The Psychological Effects of the Judicial Robe," *The American Imago: A Psychoanalytic Journal for the Arts and Sciences* 19 (Spring 1962), p. 59. A well-known dispute over the merits of the robe occurred between Jerome Frank and Walter Kennedy. Jerome Frank, "The Cult of the Robe," *Saturday Review of Literature* 28 (October 13, 1945), pp. 12-13, 80-81; Walter B. Kennedy, "The Cult of the Robe: A Dissent," *Fordham Law Review* 14 (November 1945), pp. 192-97; Jerome Frank, *Courts On Trial: Myth and Reality in American Justice* (Princeton, N.J.: Princeton University Press, 1949), pp. 254-61.

11. For analyses of clothing, culture and social organization see Mary Ellen Roach and Joanne Bubolz Eicher, eds., *Dress, Adornment, and the Social Order* (New York: Wiley, 1965).

12. Goffman, op. cit., pp. 106-140.

13. Not all legal systems are as intent as the American one is on recording the proceedings word for word. Hazard, op. cit., p. 186.

14. *Webster's Third New International Dictionary of the English Language*, unabridged (Springfield, Mass.: G. & C. Merriam Co., 1963, p. 31.

15. This statement is applicable not only to the adult criminal justice system but to the juvenile system as well. The juvenile court rape hearings observed in our study were adversary proceedings complete with defense counsel and either district attorney or police prosecutor. The data suggest that from the *victim's* point of view, the *courtroom experience itself* (as distinct from the disposition of the case) is not very different in juvenile court as opposed to criminal court. Juvenile court is private rather than public. Nevertheless, numerous people are present and the victim must testify in front of them. And, just as if the proceedings were in a criminal courtroom, the victim must face the attacker and must undergo cross-examination. As for the accused, the ideology connected with the founding of juvenile courts was to make them distinct from criminal courts—to treat the accused not as criminals but as children in need of aid and guidance. But the result in practice, as Dunham and Emerson have noted, is that juvenile court personnel are committed to conflicting orientations of a "legal" image (to restrain, control, and punish the accused) and a "social-agency" image (to help and treat the accused). Emerson states that the conflict is resolved ideologically by separating the finding and the disposition. 'The child is given an impartial hearing on the facts of the case against him, and only after a finding of 'delinquent' has been made does the court begin to function as a social agency, now operating with a different set of rules and purposes." H. Warren Dunham, "The Juvenile Court: Contradictory Orientations in Processing Offenders," *Law and Contemporary Problems* 23 (Summer 1958), pp. 508-27; Emerson, op. cit., pp. 3, 14.

16. There was only one exception, a hearing for probable cause in which just one side was argued in the courtroom. Two rape victims from separate incidents testified. At the end of each victim's testimony the defense lawyer said he had no questions. We have no data on why he took that approach. We do not have systematic behind-the-scenes data on how hard each side tried to win each case in the sample, how much they wanted to win, or why they adopted certain strategies. Our data consist of scattered information

on the above issues, plus systematic observational data from watching the hearings and trials themselves.

17. Defendants also have to listen to a version of the story be presented that is opposite from what they maintain in court to be true. We have no data on what these defendants maintained is the truth when they were in other settings; for example, we do not know what they told their defense lawyers or their family and friends.

18. "Kant said that every war in which the belligerents do not impose some restrictions in the use of possible means upon one another, necessarily, if only for psychological reasons, becomes a war of extermination"; if they do not refrain from at least certain acts, they demolish that confidence in the thought of the enemy which alone makes possible the creation of a peace treaty at the conclusion of the war. Georg Simmel, *Conflict*, Kurt H. Wolff, trans. (Glencoe, Ill.: Free Press, 1955), p. 26. (Trans. from Georg Simmel, *Soziologie*, "Der Streit," 3d ed., 1923.) Malinowski, noting that the essence of an institution is that it is built upon fundamental rules, states "This does not mean that people do not quarrel, argue, or dispute. . . . It means. . . . that all such disputes are within the universe of legal or quasilegal discourse." Bronislaw Malinowski, "An Anthropological Analysis of War," *American Journal of Sociology* 46 (January 1941), pp. 530-31. The rules of war are many. See Quincy Wright, *A Study of War*, Vol. II (Chicago: University of Chicago Press, 1942).

19. Simmel, op. cit., p. 35. (Emphasis in the original.) Coser's reformulation of Simmel's proposition reads in part that conflict "usually takes place within a universe of norms prescribing the forms in which it is to be carried out." Lewis A. Coser, *The Functions of Social Conflict* (New York: Free Press, 1964), p. 128. (First published 1956, Free Press.)

20. Simmel, op. cit., p. 37.

21. Thomas C. Schelling, *The Strategy of Conflict* (Cambridge, Mass.: Harvard University Press, 1960), p. 4.

22. Ann Wolbert Burgess and Lynda Lytle Holmstrom, "Coping Behavior of the Rape Victim," *American Journal of Psychiatry* 133 (April 1976), pp. 413-18.

23. Some writers have focused on the public defender; others on "cooperative" defense attorneys, whether they be public defenders or privately retained.

24. Some analysts not only talk of plea bargaining, but go so far as to speak of perfunctory trials.

25. David Sudnow, "Normal Crimes: Sociological Features of the Penal Code in a Public Defender Office," *Social Problems* 12 (Winter 1965), p. 262.

26. Ibid., p. 269.

27. Jerome E. Carlin, Jan Howard, and Sheldon L. Messinger, "Civil Justice and the Poor: Issues for Sociological Research," *Law and Society Review* 1 (November 1966), p. 39.

28. Jerome H. Skolnick, "Social Control in the Adversary System, *Journal of Conflict Resolution* 11 (1967), p. 53.

29. Abraham S. Blumberg, "The Practice of Law As Confidence Game: Organizational Cooptation of a Profession," *Law and Society Review* 1 (June 1967), pp. 20-21.

30. Eighteen victims' cases were settled by 17 trials. The charges of rape by one defendant on two victims in the sample were handled simultaneously.

31. We wish to thank David A. Karp and Seymour Leventman for discussions that helped clarify aspects of the definition of the situation.

32. William I. Thomas and Dorothy Swaine Thomas, *The Child in America*, (New York: Alfred A. Knopf, 1928), p. 572. See also the analyses in William I. Thomas, *The*

Unadjusted Girl, (New York: Harper and Row, 1967), pp. 41-44. (First published 1923, Little, Brown); William James, "The Will to Believe," in *Pragmatism and Other Essays,* (New York: Washington Square Press, 1963), p. 209. (First published June 1896, *The New World.)*

33. Alfred Schutz, "On Multiple Realities," in *Collected Papers, Volume I: The Problem of Social Reality,* Maurice Natanson, ed. (The Hague: Martinus Nijhoff, 1962), p. 230.

34. Maurice Natanson, "Introduction," in Schutz, *Collected Papers,* p. xxxvii. Natanson adds, "As Sartre puts it: for the Romans, Carthage was conquered, but for the Carthagenians, Carthage was enslaved."

35. Hans Peter Dreitzel, ed., "Introduction," in *Recent Sociology No. 2: Patterns of Communicative Behavior,* (New York: Macmillan, 1970), p. xiii.

36. Aaron V. Cicourel, *The Social Organization of Juvenile Justice* (New York: Wiley, 1968), p. 327.

37. Arlene Kaplan Daniels, "The Social Construction of Military Psychiatric Diagnoses," in Dreitzel, op. cit., p. 182.

38. For a history of changing legal definitions of rape and of the meaning of consent, see H. A. Snelling, "What Is Rape?" and "What Is Non-Consent (in Rape)?" *Rape Victimology,* LeRoy G. Schultz, ed., (Springfield, Ill.: Charles C Thomas, 1975), pp. 145-63). (First published, *Australian Journal of Forensic Sciences,* Sidney). For an American article reviewing nonconsent and the consent standard, see "Forcible and Statutory Rape: an Exploration of the Operation and Objectives of the Consent Standard," *Yale Law Journal* 62 (December 1952), pp. 55-83.

39. Com. v. Fogerty (1857) 74 Mass. 489, 8 Gray 489, 69 Am. Dec. 264.

40. Com. v. McCan (1931) 178 N.E. 633, 277 Mass. 199, 78 A.L.R. 1208.

41. The verbatim notes on judges' instructions at the seven trials used for the analysis here were all taken by the same observer (Holmstrom).

42. There have been studies showing how judges categorize rape cases. Bohmer's interview study of 38 Philadelphia judges found that they divided rape cases into three types: genuine victims; consensual intercourse (the victim was "asking for it"—e.g., "meets a man in a bar, agrees to let him drive her home, and then alleges he raped her"); and vindictive female (e.g., "a woman who is tired of her husband or boyfriend, wants to get rid of him, and so convinces her daughter to allege the defendant raped her"). Carol Bohmer, "Judicial Attitudes Toward Rape Victims," *Judicature* 57 (February 1974), pp. 303-07.

43. At district level, a rape case is heard before a judge and no jurors are present. At superior court, there may be a trial by judge or a trial by jury. With one exception, all trials observed were by jury.

44. Susan H. Klemmack and David L. Klemmack, "The Social Definition of Rape," in Walker and Brodsky, op. cit., p. 144.

45. W. Andrew Harrell and June Sagan, "Sex Differences in the Perception of Rape and the Sentencing of Rapists," paper presented at the American Sociological Association annual meeting, Montreal, August 1974, pp. 7-8.

46. Marvin E. Wolfgang and Marc Riedel, "Race, Judicial Discretion, and the Death Penalty," *Annals of the American Academy of Political and Social Science* 407 (May 1973), pp. 119-33. John Hagan, "Extra-legal Attributes and Criminal Sentencing: an Assessment of a Sociological Viewpoint," *Law and Society Review* 8 (Spring 1974), pp. 371-72.

47. Cathaleene Jones and Elliot Aronson, "Attribution of Fault to a Rape Victim As a Function of Respectability of the Victim," *Journal of Personality and Social Psychology* 26 (June 1973), pp. 415-19; S. Hoffman and T. Dodd, "Effects of Various Victim Characteristics on Attribution of Responsibility to an Accused Rapist," paper presented at the Southeastern Psychological Association annual meeting, 1975, cited in Klemmack and Klemmack, op. cit., p. 136.

48. Martha Burt, private communication.

49. Don D. Smith, "Sexual Aggression in American Pornography: The Stereotype of Rape," paper presented at the American Sociological Association annual meeting, New York, August 1976.

50. Harry Kalven, Jr. and Hans Zeisel, *The American Jury* (Boston: Little, Brown 1966), p. 10.

51. Ibid., pp. 253-54.

52. Ibid., p. 254.

53. Bohmer, op. cit.

54. For a how-to-do-it article giving advice to both prosecutor and defense counsel, see Richard A. Hibey, "The Trial of a Rape Case: An Advocate's Analysis of Corroboration, Consent, and Character," *American Criminal Law Review* 11 (Winter 1973), pp. 309-34.

55. Preliminary findings on blame-the-victim themes were reported in Lynda Lytle Holmstrom and Ann Wolbert Burgess, "Rape: The Victim Goes on Trial," paper presented at the American Sociological Association annual meeting, New York, August 1973.

56. Emerson, op. cit., p. 156. Emerson comments that researchers have noted the underlying phenomenon in counterdenunciation in various contexts. McCorkle and Korn have analyzed "rejection of the rejectors" and Sykes and Matza have analyzed "condemnation of the condemners." Lloyd W. McCorkle and Richard Korn, "Resocialization Within Walls," *Annals of the American Academy of Political and Social Science* 293 (May 1954), p. 88. Gresham M. Sykes and David Matza, "Techniques of Neutralization: A Theory of Delinquency," *American Sociological Review* 22 (December 1957), p. 668.

57. Emerson, op, cit., p. 167.

58. Ibid., p. 168.

59. The process of "blaming the victim" is analyzed by William Ryan in his book of that title. He notes critically that "the generic process of Blaming the Victim is applied to almost every American problem." Giving an example in the area of medicine, he describes how "the miserable health care of the poor is explained away on the grounds that the victim has poor motivation and lacks health information." Moving to an example of how blaming-the-victim ideology works in the area of the economy, he notes that "if one comes to believe that the culture of poverty produces persons *fated* to be poor, who can find any fault with our corporation-dominated economy?" William Ryan, *Blaming the Victim* (New York: Random House 1972), pp. 5, 28. (Emphasis in the original.) (First published 1971, Random House.)

60. Question a colleague was asked after presenting a paper on rape to a professional audience.

61. The victim, a young slender girl with no training or practice in self-defense, commented during a court recess, "All I remember is I wanted to get home in one piece and I just concentrated on that."

62. Wood makes a similar point about the difficult predicament of women vis-a-vis the issue of resistance. Pamela Lakes Wood, "The Victim in a Forcible Rape Case: A

Feminist View," *The American Criminal Law Review* 11 (Winter 1973), pp. 345-47.

63. A. Nicholas Groth and Murray L. Cohen, "Aggressive Sexual Offenders: Diagnosis and Treatment," in *Community Mental Health: Target Populations,* Ann Wolbert Burgess and Aaron Lazare (Englewood Cliffs, N.J.: Prentice-Hall, 1976), p. 222.

64. Menachem Amir, "The Interpersonal Relationships Between Victim and Offender," in *Patterns in Forcible Rape* (Chicago: University of Chicago Press, 1971), pp. 229-52; Ann Wolbert Burgess and Lynda Lytle Holmstrom, *Rape: Victims of Crisis* (Bowie, Md.: Robert J. Brady Co., 1974), p. 8; Russell, op. cit., p. 87.

65. Vern L. Bullough, "Formation of Western Attitudes," in *The Subordinate Sex: A History of Attitudes Toward Women,* (Baltimore: Penguin Books, 1974), p. 49. (First published 1973, University of Illinois Press.)

66. Janet Saltzman Chafetz, *Masculine/Feminine or Human? An Overview of the Sociology of Sex Roles* (Itasca, Illinois: F. E. Peacock, 1974), p. 39.

67. A. Kay Clifton, Diane McGrath, and Bonnie Wick, "Stereotypes of Woman: A Single Category?" *Sex Roles: A Journal of Research* 2 (June 1976), p. 135. Respondents were asked to describe housewife, bunny, clubwoman, career woman, and woman athlete. In addition to the distinctive stereotypes of housewife and bunny, there was evidence for a third stereotype combining the nontraditional role alternatives (pp. 145-46).

68. "At trial, evidence of bad reputation or unchastity is generally admissible as substantive evidence bearing on the consent of the prosecutrix." Wood, op. cit., p. 343.

69. The judge instructed the jury that there were three possible verdicts in this case: not guilty; guilty of rape under 16 without consent (forcible rape); and guilty of rape under 16 (statutory rape). Legally in Massachusetts a female under 16 cannot consent to sex. Therefore, for statutory rape, the Commonwealth need only prove that sex occurred, that it was unlawful (it would not be unlawful, for example, if the female were married to the defendant), and that the female was under 16. In this case, one defendant said in court that he had "sexed her." The main disputed point was whether it was against her will. The jury concluded that it was not against her will. The defendants were found guilty of statutory rape. Each received a sentence of between one and five years.

70. Mention of the man's criminal record is allowed for certain limited purposes.

71. The clinical observations suggest that Lauren was telling the truth. One of the most highly intelligent and reflective of the young girls in our sample, she showed great emotional control during the trial, an event that is as stressful as rape itself. As for her ability to remember the telephone number, she commented, "Well, if there is something I want to remember, I remember it." She also demonstrated her ability to remember information even in upsetting circumstances. At one point during the four-day trial she wanted to telephone one of the authors for some moral support. She asked the other author for the telephone number, committed it to memory rather than writing it down, and proceeded to make the call, thereby showing her ability to remember information even when under stress.

72. DAs like the current fresh complaint rule and believe it favors the prosecution. In general, a witness cannot say what the victim said because it is hearsay. But fresh complaint is an exception to the hearsay rule. A parent or police officer, for example, can testify that the woman made a complaint and thus their testimony can be used to corroborate the victim's story.

73. For a discussion of feminine malice and rape trials, see Wood, op. cit., pp. 336-38.

74. Interpersonal aspects of feminine sex role stereotypes include traits such as "petty, flirty, coy, gossipy, catty, sneaky, fickle," Chafetz, op. cit., p. 36.

75. All the clinical evidence and observations of the family in this case suggest that she, rather than he, was telling the truth. For example, the medical record states that "small lacerations of the hymen" were seen, that the "lesions appear to be recent," and that to do the internal examination a "small virginal speculum was inserted." Observations of the family suggest that they never have permitted her to remain out until 6 A.M. Indeed, the night of the incident, they became concerned when she was late getting home and they went and got her. She was seen by the police and then admitted to the hospital by 3:30 A.M.—in other words, long before 6 A.M. The male who was perceived to be her new boyfriend is in fact the boyfriend of the victim's sister and he was with the family at the hospital that night. He was not and never has become the victim's boyfriend.

76. Testimony about what sex occurred was given in all the hearings and trials observed. But the issue of whether sex really occurred became a point of dispute in 6 of the 28 hearings and in 6 of the 12 trials.

77. For the 92 adult rape victims in our study, the gynecological exam showed no sperm present in 45 cases, sperm present in 32, and no data (e.g., no chart, exam done past 48 hours, profuse bleeding) in the remaining 15 cases.

78. Of an offender sample of 133 rapists, almost 40 percent suffered sexual dysfunction at the time of the assault: "23 experienced difficulty in achieving orgasm (retarded ejaculation), 22 experienced difficulty in achieving erection (impotency), and 5 experienced premature ejaculation." A. Nicholas Groth and Ann Wolbert Burgess, "Rape Crisis: Victim and Offender," panel presentation at the American Psychological Association meeting, Washington, D.C., September 5, 1976.

79. The authors found no psychological evidence to suggest any reason to doubt Ivy's story. She was one of the most mentally stable individuals in our study population. Her story was consistent from the beginning. She suffered all the emotional reactions that other victims with more physical evidence of rape suffered. But because the physical evidence of rape was so lacking, almost everyone was openly suspicious of her story or discounted the seriousness of the incident.

80. The case is not a case from the main first-year sample and is not included in Tables 1 and 2.

81. There were three assailants (two male, one female) for the robbery of this victim but two assailants (the males) for the rape.

82. A. Nicholas Groth, Talk given to Central Massachusetts Family Planning Council, Inc., Worcester Chapter, meeting held in Shrewsbury, Mass., June 29, 1973. Also of interest is Groth and Cohen's discussion about two opposing myths: "The rapist is frequently regarded either as a normal, healthy, 'red-blooded' American male who is the victim of a provocative and seductive but punitive woman or as some oversexed, demented, inhuman fiend. . . . Neither image corresponds to reality." Groth and Cohen, op. cit., p. 221.

83. Groth, op. cit. Cohen and colleagues have delineated four patterns of rape: rape—aggressive aim; rape—sexual aim; rape—sex-aggression defusion; and antisocial character disorder. Describing the second type, rape—sexual aim, they note that it is not an impulsive act, but rather first has been lived through many times in fantasy. The fantasy goes as follows: "The woman he attacks first protests and then submits, more resignedly than willingly. During the sexual act, he performs with great skill,

and she receives such intense pleasure that she falls in love with him and pleads with him to return." Murray L. Cohen, Ralph Garofalo, Richard Boucher, and Theoharis Seghorn, "The Psychology of Rapists," *Seminars in Psychiatry* 3 (August 1971), p. 318. Gebhard and colleagues also note that among "aggressors vs. adults" there is frequently a wishful self-delusion that their victims have become desirous of seeing them again. Paul H. Gebhard, John H. Gagnon, Wardell B. Pomeroy, and Cornelia V. Christenson. *Sex Offenders: An Analysis of Types,* (New York: Harper & Row and Paul B. Hoeber, Inc., 1965), p. 199.

84. David Mellinkoff, *The Language of the Law* (Boston: Little, Brown 1963), p. vii.

85. Frederick A. Philbrick, *Language and the Law: The Semantics of Forensic English.* (New York: Macmillan, 1949), p. v.

86. Barbara J. Culliton, "Abortion and Manslaughter: A Boston Doctor Goes on Trial," *Science* 187 (January 31, 1975), pp. 334-35.

87. Thomas J. Scheff, "Negotiating Reality: Notes on Power in the Assessment of Responsibility," *Social Problems,* 16 (Summer 1968), pp. 14-15. Also of interest is Linton's discussion of open-ended, "why" questions versus questions requiring simple yes-no answers. N.K. Linton, "The Witness and Cross-Examination," *Berkeley Journal of Sociology* 10 (1965), p. 9.

88. Hibey, op. cit., pp. 323-24.

89. Barrie Thorne and Nancy Henley, "Difference and Dominance: An Overview of Language, Gender, and Society," in *Language and Sex: Difference and Dominance* (Rowley, Mass.: Newbury House Publishers, 1975), p. 11. Ervin-Tripp says style refers to "the co-occurrent changes at various levels of linguistic structure within one language." Susan Ervin-Tripp, "On Sociolinguistic Rules: Alternation and Co-occurrence," in *Directions in Sociolinguistics: The Ethnography of Communication,* John J. Gumperz and Dell Hymes, eds. (New York: Holt, Rinehart and Winston, 1972), p. 235.

90. Thorne and Henley, op. cit., p. 10.

91. For an account from the defendant's point of view suggesting bias in the opposite direction, see A. Robert Smith and James V. Giles, *An American Rape: A True Account of the Giles-Johnson Case* (Washington, D.C.: New Republic Book Co., 1975).

92. Emerson, op. cit., pp. 168-71.

93. Dorothy Miller and Michael Schwartz, "County Lunacy Commission Hearings: Some Observations of Commitments to a State Mental Hospital," *Social Problems* 14 (1966), p. 29. Quoted in Emerson op. cit., p. 170.

94. Schultz, op. cit., p. ix.

95. Peter L. Berger and Thomas Luckmann, *The Social Construction of Reality: A Treatise in the Sociology of Knowledge* (Garden City, N.Y.: Doubleday Anchor Books, 1967), pp. 108-09. (First published 1966, Doubleday.)

96. Ibid., p. 109.

CHAPTER 7

■

The Rape Victim's Reaction to Court

I feel like we were on trial. I felt like I was a criminal when I was up there [testifying]. Why should we have to defend ourselves?

RAPE VICTIM, AGE 19,
ONE OF A GROUP OF
THREE VICTIMS

The trial is 200 times worse than the rape. . . . This thing is really weighing me down. It just hangs there over my head.

RAPE VICTIM, AGE 18

Prior research on child victims has suggested that the features of court they find most upsetting are the same ones that are thought important for the defendant according to our social definition of a fair trial. Libai has put the matter well:

The well-being of some child victims, according to psychiatric opinions, may best be safeguarded by minimum and short interrogations, restricted cross-examination, avoidance of courtroom confrontation of the victim and accused, and shielding of the child victim from publicity. Yet, these characteristics of legal proceedings, which may contribute to mental trauma, are essential safeguards of fair trial for the accused in our adversary system.[1]

UPSETTING FEATURES OF THE COURTROOM

The courtroom in the present study, already has been described from the observer's vantage point. What does it mean to the rape victims themselves? Do they find it upsetting? And if so, what features are salient? Victims were asked about their reactions. Overwhelmingly, both adult and young victims found court an extremely stressful experience. The features they found most upsetting (judged by the frequency with which they mentioned them) were the cross-examination and the defense lawyer, the confrontation between accused and accuser, and the public setting (see Table 1). They also found it difficult to listen to the defendant's version of what happened and were upset when informed belatedly about the length of the court process. A few mentioned the lack of women on the jury and the formality of the occasion.

Table 1. *Upsetting Features of the Courtroom Experience of 40 Rape Victims**

Cross-examination and the defense lawyer		23**
Blame-the-victim strategy	16	
Linguistic strategy of defense	16	
Confrontation between accused and accuser		18***
Seeing the accused	16	
Being identified as the accuser	4	
Public setting		17
The adversary's story		9
Belated information about the length of the court process		9
The male scene		4
Formality of the courtroom		2

*Table based on the 40 adult and preadult rape victims from the main sample for whom we have data on reactions to court. Tabulated from answers to open-ended questions and informal conversations. Some victims mentioned more than one feature.

**The subcategories total more than 23 because some victims mentioned both items.

***The subcategories total more than 18 because some victims mentioned both items.

These victims—like the prior analyses of child victims—focus especially on items presently thought to be integral features of our legal system.

UPSETTING FEATURES OF THE COURTROOM EXPERIENCE

Cross-Examination: Defense Lawyer as Assailant

Rape victims' comments about their courtroom experience focus most often on the defense lawyer and on cross-examination. They describe the defense lawyer in negative terms: "nasty," "ugly," "mean," "awful," "horrible," and "insulting." In one case, the victim and her family labeled the lawyer "The Creep." A few victims described what they felt like doing to the attorney. One said she would have liked to have "gone over and punched him." Another said, "I always wanted to tell that defense lawyer to lower his voice." Still another said, "I wish I could tell him off." Only rarely did a victim have anything positive to say about the defense attorney. One victim said, "The defense attorney went and shook my friends' hands afterwards and said he was sorry about what had happened to me. . . . He was nice to me."

Blame-the-Victim Strategy. Many victims were upset by the blame-the-victim strategy of the defense. One main problem here for victims is lack of information control. As Goffman notes, it is difficult to give a good presentation of the self if one does not have control over what material is presented—if one's secrets are revealed.[2] The life of a person usually contains at least a few facts that, if brought to light during the performance, would discredit or weaken the claims the person is trying to make.[3] Several writers have noted the difference between rules of interaction in everyday life and those of the courtroom.[4] In everyday face-to-face interaction there are expectations of being tactful, avoiding embarrassing areas, of not publicizing discrediting information. But "normal expectations about the use made of discrediting information do not apply in the courtroom."[5] The rules are transformed; embarrassing, humiliating, and discrediting information *is* introduced. A related problem for victims is lack of control over what the defense lawyer will say whether or not it has any factual basis. Defense lawyers may utilize discrediting facts from the victim's life or they may simply invent discrediting "facts" when none exist.

Rape victims find the blame-the-victim strategy—whether based on revelations from their lives or invented by the defense—to be very painful. Victims in our study said of the defense lawyer, "He made it sound like it was all my fault" (victim crying), "He kept playing up the fact that I was a cocktail waitress. . . . He was trying to make me look like a slut. . . . It was shitty," "I just couldn't go through with the questioning again. They make you feel guilty," "I am being treated like I am on trial," "He was trying to make me out a lush, I'm not going to talk to him [anymore]," and "They tried to say my shorts were too short. . . . They just make the victim look stupid." In one instance, three victims, roommates who were raped and robbed in their apartment by intruders, spoke at length about their feelings of being blamed.[6] Right after the hearing for probable cause, their conversation went as follows:

First victim:	I feel like we were on trial. I felt like I was a criminal when I was up there [testifying]. Why should we have to defend ourselves?
Second victim:	The defendant has more rights than we have. He's assumed to be innocent until proved guilty. We're assumed guilty until proved innocent.
Third victim:	It's all part of the game.

Emotionally these three victims had a hard time understanding the criminal justice system and the rights that exist in it for the defendant. As one of them said, "But we know he did it." She kept saying, "It isn't right that it should be this way."

Some victims realized prior to testifying that certain information probably would be held against them. For some, this realization presented a dilemma. They wondered how they should answer certain questions they thought peripheral if the truth would be held against them. For example, one victim had been walking to her boyfriend's apartment when two strangers grabbed her, forced her into a car, and raped her. Waiting for court to start she was wondering what to say about where she had been going. "If I say I was on my way to my boyfriend's to spend the night it will look bad."

A few victims commented after court was over that honesty did not work. One victim decided, after the judge did not find probable cause, that she had told too much. She said, "I tend to be very honest and perhaps I said things which were too honest . . . [like saying] I was being seen in psychotherapy." Another, after the trial ended in acquittal, had this advice for future rape victims:

You should never mention drugs [when testifying]. That was my biggest mistake. . . . You should punch yourself or cut yourself and take pictures of it. I'm not joking. . . . If it happened again, the first thing I would do is beat myself up [so there would be bruises]. . . . [The DA] was a little too idealistic. He just figured if I told the truth it would be cool. He has a lot to learn.

The message from these two victims is that if one tells the truth on peripheral items, one will not be believed on the central question of whether a rape occurred.

Linguistic Strategy of Defense. Rape victims' comments reveal that they are upset by the defense lawyer's linguistic strategy. Describing the cross-examination, victims say things such as, "He tried to twist my words," "He kept trying to confuse me," and, "They push you so."

Questions the defense lawyer asks the victims are often phrased so as to be controlling (see Chapter 6). Victims react negatively to the controlling nature of the experience. One victim was very upset because when the defense asked "Could you have screamed?" she was unable to put her answer into context. She said afterward:

> I couldn't answer him so he kept asking questions around this and I got so confused. I am not the type that can scream under any conditions and he was trying to say I didn't scream and that it was weird if I didn't scream.

Another victim, when asked by us what was the hardest thing about court, replied: "I couldn't say what I wanted to say. I had to just answer their questions."

Victims find the three delivery styles described in Chapter 6 painful. Regarding rapid-fire attack, for example, one victim said, "I couldn't stand the questions they were firing at me." Needling proved unnerving as well. For example, the victim described in Chapter 6 who received gibes about her appearance left the courtroom in tears. Sobbing, she kept coming back again and again to the question the defense lawyer asked her about her hair style:

> Why did he ask about my new hairdo? Why did he ask about my new hairdo? I don't understand. I tried to do it nicely.

Tedious monotony, although less dramatic, is nevertheless unnerving. For example, one victim, who was on the stand for several hours and who was subjected to incredibly lengthy and tedious questioning, said:

> I don't want to go back to court. I don't think I will go tomorrow. I won't go if I have anything to say about it. I can't remember every little detail, and they expect me to.

In another case where the victim was subjected to repetitive and tedious questioning, she and her husband reacted as follows:

> *Husband:*   That defense lawyer was something else. He just kept asking all these picky, insignificant questions about details—just to make her break down and make the case seem wishy-washy.
>
> *Victim:*   Yes—like he'd ask what time did this happen and what time did that happen. What did he expect, that I kept checking my watch all the time?

Charges in this case were dropped at the victim's request.

As a result of the defense lawyer's linguistic strategy, a few victims simply "tuned out" while on the witness stand. One said, "I stopped listening." Another said, "After a while I didn't care what I said."

Confrontation Between Accused and Accuser

A second major focus of rape victims' complaints was the confrontation between accused and accuser. Most often these victims focused on how upsetting it was to see the accused again. One said:

> Today went OK. The only bad moments were when I had to see the guy. It gave me a bad stomach. . . . He looked a thousand times worse. I got so nervous.

Others said things such as "The boys just kept staring at me and made me feel real nervous," "He looks sickening" (said as defendant was brought into the courtroom), "I watched him and felt sorry for him that he had to be put in a position to lie. . . . I felt uncomfortable for him," and "When they brought the guy in I got all quivery." Some victims reacted visibly to seeing the defendant. One became visibly nervous as the defendant, his family, and friends came in and sat down behind her in the courtroom. Another stiffened and looked down as the assailant walked in.

A few of these victims focused on the problem of being identified as the accuser. They said they did not like giving identifying information—name, address, occupation—in court. Each of the victims who worried about being identified also expressed a fear that the defendant or his friends and family might seek revenge and harm them for having testified.

Public Setting

A third major focus of rape victims' complaints was the public nature of the hearings and trials. One victim, whose case attracted many spectators, spoke as follows:

> Oh, those court bums! They come just to watch the cases. We have the most popular case in the courthouse—more sex and violence than any other. I wish the court could be cleared. I was raped once in private, I don't want to have it done again in public.[7]

Some victims not only talked about the public setting, but reacted visibly to the public presence. In one case, for example, the victim stiffened when 20 fifth graders, notebooks in hand, walked into the courtroom.

Victims who specified what it was about the public presence that bothered them talked of it being embarrassing, making them nervous, or making the scene impersonal. One said:

> One thing I'd suggest is to have a closed court. It was so embarrassing to talk in the big room when your reputation is at stake. To have all those outsiders was terrible. Then the judge would say he couldn't hear and I would try to talk loud but my voice just wouldn't come out. Why do they have open hearings?

Another said, "I'm so nervous—I can't even talk in front of a classroom, let alone in front of a court!" Still another said, "People were walking in and out of the courtroom while I was [testifying] and I just wanted to scream out at them. No one seemed to care about me or what was going on. I could hardly stand it."

Even closed sessions may have a number of people present and hence seem somewhat public. For example, as one victim said regarding such a session, "All those people looking at me—that was [the most] upsetting."

The Adversary's Story: Hearing His Lies

Some victims mentioned how difficult it was to listen to the defendant's version of the story in court. They referred to his version as lies. In one case the victim said, "What makes me mad is that he knows what he did and he lied." In another—Ann's case, which was presented in Chapter 6 to illustrate a spite defense—the victim, her older sister, and the sister's boyfriend were very angry about the defendant's testimony. After the hearing, their conversation in the corridor went as follows:

Victim: (with righteous indignation) How can he lie like that under oath?
All three: Lies, lies!
Sister: Why, I'd never let her stay out until six o'clock in the morning!
               . . . He and his friend sure got together [on the story]. And the
               lawyer, too!

Still another victim, as already mentioned, reported feeling "uncomfortable" for the defendant as he testified. She also said, "He lies. He had to. He lied poorly, though, I think—but maybe that's because I know the truth."

Sometimes victims reacted visibly to hearing the defendant's testimony. Following is a case in point:

> During the testimony of the two boys, the young victim and her girl friend were whispering and giggling together. Then as the testimony progressed, she paid more attention and became increasingly upset. During the boys' testimony about the sexual activity, she cried silently and kept whispering, with much emphasis, "That's not true, that's not true."

Belated Information About the Length of the Court Process

Some victims indicated they were upset when they found out that court would be such a long process. The news that they would have to return was unsettling. They simply had no idea that many court appearances might be required. One victim, after a trip to district court, said, "I thought I'd just have to go down once." Another cried when she found out that grand jury was not the last step. Still another got upset when told she would have to come back to superior court again the next day. Throughout the entire process of going through the criminal justice system, the lack of information and the length of the process both are bothersome to victims.

The Male Scene: A Lack of Sisterhood

The courtroom scene was typically male. All the district attorneys and almost all the defense lawyers and officials were men. Most of the jurors were male. Sometimes the original group of jurors called contained a number of females, but there was attrition of these women during the period of challenges. Attrition also occurs because of the Commonwealth law stating that women jurors must be informed that they may decline to hear a case involving a sexual crime, such as rape.

A few victims commented on how women were missing from the courtroom, and especially from the jury, and that this bothered them. One said, "I would rather have had the women [jurors] stay." Another said what disturbed her about all the women leaving the jury was that she was pressing charges for their sake; that is, for the sake of other women. She said, "I'm doing this for them, I'm not doing this for myself."

Formality of the Courtroom

A few victims focused on the formality of the courtroom. One spoke as follows regarding district court:

> Then, facing the judge, I just couldn't say anything. When I first went in it was so scary. I saw that big long desk with all the papers on it, men whispering to each other, lots of questions being asked. That got me real nervous. The judge seemed scary sitting there.

Another, preparing mentally for her grand jury appearance the next day, said, "The whole legal thing—formal, stiff, and to the point. I've never been exposed to it so of course it makes me nervous."

COURT AS UPSETTING AS THE RAPE

The court experience, for the rape victim, precipitates as much of a psychological crisis as the rape itself. Victims undergo a multitude of intense reactions to specific features of court, as indicated above. They also experience more generalized psychological reactions as well: time suspended, being "on," the rape relived, betrayal, and allaying silent suspicion (see Table 2).[8]

Table 2. Psychological Reactions of 40 Rape Victims to the Courtroom Experience*

Time suspended	26
Being on	13
The rape relived	8
Betrayal	5
Allaying silent suspicion	3

*Tabulated from answers to open-ended questions and informal conversations. Some victims experienced more than one of these reactions.

In addition, victims report and exhibit many signs and symptoms of stress.

Time Suspended: Court As a Millstone

Rape, and the events it leads to, greatly disrupts the victim's life. Her normal routine is shattered, her daily and weekly activities are upset due to the attack. Time becomes suspended. This period in her life when she must deal with the rape and its aftermath is so upsetting and such a departure from her prior existence that it is a time merely to be survived. The victim becomes so preoccupied with what has happened to her that she is not really living. It is like treading water until the ordeal is over.

For rape victims who go through the court process, the time-suspended reaction often is accentuated. Going to court is so upsetting for many that while they are in the process, or at least as each new court date approaches, court dominates their thoughts. Time suspended was by far the most frequent general reaction. One victim spoke as follows:

> The trial is two hundred times worse than the rape. If I had known more fully about all this I never would have prosecuted. . . . This thing is really weighing me down. It just hangs there over my head.

Another said, "I have been so upset with the thought of court. I can't even talk about it. . . . It's on my mind constantly." Still another said, "I can't stand this fucking [court] any longer. What really gets me is I'm the one who is doing all the suffering and nothing will probably happen to him." One victim put the matter very succinctly. She said, "I want to start living again."

Victims look forward to the end of the court process. The conclusion of the process may be seen as a major demarcation. One victim expressed this turning point as follows:

> I'm so relieved it is over. . . . It was the worst five months I've had in my life. . . . It's like taking a big millstone off from around my neck.

Still another said she had spent all her time at work dreading that the phone would ring and that it would be someone calling about the case. She said, "I'm really glad it's over and I can start living a somewhat normal existence again."

Being On: A Concern With Performance

A distinction between times when people feel "on" versus times when they feel "natural" has been proposed by Messinger and colleagues. This conceptualization was suggested to them partly by the remarks of entertainers such as Sammy Davis, Jr. Commenting on the hazards of fame, Davis said, "As soon as I go out the front door of my house in the morning, I'm on, Daddy, I'm on." He further states, "But when I'm with the group I can relax. We trust each other."[9] Davis seems to indicate that there are times when even though he is offstage, he feels onstage. Messinger interprets these comments as suggesting that "under some circumstances in everyday life the actor becomes, is, or is made *aware* of an actual or potential discrepancy between his 'real' and his 'projected' selves, between his 'self' and his 'character.'"[10] Thus there are times when one has a sense of playing a role and others when one feels natural and spontaneous.

Court, the present study suggests, is a setting where people are apt to feel that they are "on." The second most common theme in rape victims' general reactions to court was a concern with performance—a concern how they would do, how they would come across in the courtroom. These victims worried about whether their emotions would show ("I'm worried I'll stutter if the lawyer gets me nervous," "I'm worried about my temper. Sometimes I cry when I'm mad and I don't want to do that at court," and, "I feel sorry for him. . . . How will this look on the stand? Won't this come through when I testify?") They were concerned about whether they would be able to remember the details of the incident for their testimony, sometimes rehearsing it mentally ahead of time ("I never let my testimony out of my mind. Whenever I thought the case was coming up I ran over what did happen to be prepared"). They were conscious of their clothes and grooming, and of the impression that these items might convey to others. In one case the victim discussed the choice of clothes as follows:

Victim:	Do I have to dress up for court?
Boyfriend:	It's all a game of appearances.
Victim:	I think I can borrow something [more conservative] from my mother to wear.

In another case, both the young victim and her father were concerned that she look nice for court. On the day of the trial when the DA arrived, the father showed him the girl's fingernails, indicating how nicely done they were for the occasion. He added, "I told her to look like a lady." Victims seemed pleased if they got positive feedback afterward on how they had done ("[The DA] told me I looked good—that I didn't come across as cheap"). Thus, the courtroom appears as a stage not only to observers, but also is experienced as such by many victims.

The Rape Relived: Going Through It Again

Some victims talked of reliving the rape as they went through the court process. This reliving may occur several times, especially since the victim may testify at various levels—at hearing for probable cause, grand jury, and trial at superior court.

Some victims reported reliving the incident as they rehearsed for court:

> Going to court frightens me. I've been reliving the rape to have it straight. . . .
> I want to be mentally prepared so as not to stammer and to have an answer ready.

Others talked of reactions during or after testifying. One said, "I got upset on the stand. I could just feel myself going through it all over again." Another said, "I went to grand jury this morning. . . . I gave my story—that stirred up a lot of feelings." Still another, who dropped charges partly for this reason, said, "I'd never go through with [court] again. . . . I'd just be upset if I had to tell everything again."

Betrayal: Will They Be on My Side?

People that the rape victim meets on her way through the criminal justice system may end up betraying her cause. Either deliberately or unwittingly, even people she expects to support her—friends she expects to be loyal, police who are to protect the public, professionals who are to help—may end up doing things that diminish the chances of a successful prosecution. Thus, the victim may be plagued by the nagging question, "Will they be on my side?"

A few victims explicitly mentioned betrayal as an issue. A couple were very disturbed by the physician's testimony—as one said, succinctly, "I don't think the doctor helped." In one case, the victim and her family reported feeling betrayed by defense lawyers who visited their home without identifying themselves. The victim later said, "I thought I was supposed to talk with them." Her father said, "I don't know who to talk to now. I thought the men who came to see us were on our side. I thought they were going to represent us." A couple of victims felt betrayed by their girl friends. In one case, the victim's friend, also raped during the same incident, began the court process, but then decided to quit. The victim said, "I'm mad at Erica. She got me into [pressing charges] and then she didn't go through with it. I wouldn't have gone to the police if it hadn't been for her." In another case, the victim's "best friend," who had been with her at the time of the rape, later changed her story; instead of supporting the victim, her allegiance shifted to the assailants.

Allaying Silent Suspicion: Will They Believe Me?

The prevailing attitude toward rape victims in our society is one of suspicion. Rape victims are aware of this bias. People may not tell the victim blatantly that they do not believe her. But she may nevertheless feel an atmosphere of silent suspicion around her. One victim, right after reporting the rape, said, "I feel like I have to prove it happened—to the police, to the doctors, and to you."

The atmosphere of suspicion becomes accentuated in the court setting. Suspicion, previously often covert, now becomes overt. Skepticism is considered appropriate in court. Defense counsel tries openly to prove that the victim is telling falsehoods, or at best that she is mistaken. A few victims explicitly mentioned the problem of not being believed. As one said, "It was very upsetting last time at grand jury. I didn't think they believed me." At superior court she said, "It seems I have to just convince everyone that I was right; no one believes me." Reading between the lines suggests that worrying about not being believed was an issue for many others as well. For example, the concern for performance, already discussed, also implies a concern with trying to make others believe one's testimony. And, as is discussed in the next chapter, verdicts of not guilty sometimes were interpreted by victims to mean that the jurors thought they were lying.

The Emotions: Nervous and Scared

Victims' main emotional reaction at the time of the rape is fear. They report being scared that they would be killed. The rape clearly is experienced by them as a life-threatening event.[11] At the time of court, victims' main expressed reactions are those of being nervous and scared, and, to a lesser degree, angry and embarrassed (see Table 3).

Being nervous was the most common reaction to court. Victims said things like, "Do I have to tell about my problems in court? . . . I can't sleep worrying about it. I'm a nervous wreck," "I was nervous before I went up [to testify], but once I got on the stand I was OK," "I was pretty shaky [after court]. [The guy] gave the story that he was where they found him because he had been out drinking. . . . I got nervous about that."

Being scared was almost as common as nervousness. Sometimes there was a generalized, nonspecific sense of being afraid of court ("I'm scared of the trial"). Sometimes it was linked to specific features of court (e.g., scared of the big courtroom). Most often, fear was linked to the idea of possible retaliation for testifying—a very persistent theme in the career of the victim.

Anger is the third most common response, being reported by about one-fourth of these victims going to court. Targets of victims' anger include the defendant ("The boys were lying. . . . It made me mad"), the defense lawyer and cross-examination ("The questions made me mad"), the system (anger that the court "is so unorganized"), and miscellaneous items such as proposed restitution ("I'm angry that they wanted to make a settlement"). Anger is not something that rape victims in general express with regard to rape

Table 3. Expressed Emotional Reactions of 40 Rape Victims to the Court Experience*

Nervous	23
Scared	20
Angry	11
Embarrassed	5

*Tabulated from answers to open-ended questions and informal conversations. Some victims expressed several emotions.

itself.[12] Thus it is of some interest that as many as one-fourth of these victims did state how angry they were at some aspects of going through the criminal justice system. A few stated (and others implied) that the situation was embarrassing. The victims described above openly expressed their emotions about court. In contrast, a few victims were guarded about expressing their feelings. Their statements—"I couldn't care less," for example, did not reveal what they were really feeling.

Signs and Symptoms of Stress

Victims also exhibited many signs and symptoms of stress during the court experience. Signs may be regarded as overt indicators of stress—crying, fidgeting, sweating—visible to an observer. Most of the rape victims (30 of the 40 for whom we have data) going through court exhibited pronounced signs of stress. They fidgeted with paper or tissues, began to take longer and longer to answer questions, giggled, smiled nervously, ventilated, frequented the water fountain, had sticky hands, wiped their hands repeatedly on their clothes, needed to go to the bathroom repeatedly, or chain-smoked. One 15-year-old victim was trembling, had tears welling in her eyes, and was unable even to talk at the hearing for probable cause. Another victim, age 33, kept running her fingers through her hair, smoking cigarettes down to the very end, and was sweating profusely at district court. Another, age 23, broke down after testifying in superior court.

> Sharleene moved very quickly from the witness stand to a nearby chair, put her hands to her face, and wept loudly. The court officer went over to a group of young women and asked if they were her friends. When they said yes he suggested, "Why don't you help your friend out?" They had been restraining themselves during this time—looking at each other as to what to do because they felt unable to move freely in the courtroom. With his permission, they rushed to comfort Sharleene—one hugged her, one went for Kleenex, another gave her the Kleenex, and another was holding her shoulder. The victim became composed quickly, suppressed her emotions, and made a crack about missing so much work. Relief and laughter followed from the others.

Victims going through court also reported symptoms. These may be regarded as statements that something is wrong—having disturbing thoughts, a "bad stomach," phobias—that are not necessarily visible to the observer. As court dates approached, victims often reported a recurrence of many of the symptoms they experienced right after the rape. Some victims reported new symptoms that they had not experienced before. The most extreme case was that of a 12-year-old girl without any prior psychiatric history who became psychotic due to the stress of the court experience. She stated the evening before court that there was a hand on her bed that was trying to get her. At the courthouse she perceived that the other people at court were crying. Later symptoms were that she stated that things were coming off of her head, that mice were crawling around, and that her mother was turning into a man. Since these statements did not match reality, it appears that she was hallucinating. Unable to deal with the reality of the stress of court, her mind defended itself by becoming psychotic.[13]

VICTIMIZATION BY THE COURT PROCESS

The statements of rape victims reported above clearly indicate that victims of all ages find the courtroom an extremely stressful experience. Court, for many, is as upsetting as the rape itself. One woman, waiting for a court session, summarized the matter:

I'll tell you what it's like to be a victim. The victim gets screwed and the guy goes free. I wouldn't mind [the hassle of going through court] if something came of it, but nothing will. . . . The victim is always the victim.[14]

Like this woman, many see themselves victimized not only by the rape itself, but again by the legal proceedings.

NOTES

1. David Libai, "The Protection of the Child Victim of a Sexual Offense in the Criminal Justice System," *Wayne Law Review* 15 (1969), p. 979.
2. Erving Goffman, *The Presentation of Self in Everyday Life* (Garden City, N.Y.: Doubleday Anchor Books, 1959), p. 141.
3. Ibid., p. 209.
4. N. K. Linton, "The Witness and Cross-Examination," *Berkeley Journal of Sociology* 10 (1965), p. 8; Robert M. Emerson, *Judging Delinquents: Context and Process in Juvenile Court* (Chicago: Aldine, 1969), pp. 204-05.
5. Ibid., p. 205.
6. These three victims are referral cases, not part of the main first-year sample.
7. This quote is not from a victim in the main sample. It is from a victim who was raped by the same man who raped a woman in the main sample. Both victims went to court.
8. Several of these are discussed in Ann Wolbert Burgess and Lynda Lytle Holmstrom, *Rape: Victims of Crisis* (Bowie, Md.: Robert J. Brady Co., 1974), pp. 203-07.
9. *Life Magazine*, December 22, 1958, p. 116, quoted in Sheldon L. Messinger with Harold Sampson and Robert D. Towne, "Life As Theater: Some Notes on the Dramaturgic Approach to Social Reality," *Sociometry* 25 (1962), pp. 98-99.
10. Messinger, op. cit., p. 99 (emphasis in the original). As should be apparent, this article is an examination of the dramaturgic approach, especially of Goffman's work.
11. Ann Wolbert Burgess and Lynda Lytle Holmstrom, "Rape Trauma Syndrome," *American Journal of Psychiatry* 131 (September 1974), p. 983.
12. Elaine Hilberman, *The Rape Victim* (Washington, D.C.: American Psychiatric Association, 1976), p. 47.
13. This case is reported in detail in Burgess and Holmstrom, *Rape: Victims of Crisis*, pp. 252-55.
14. This quote is not from a victim in the main sample. It is from a victim who was raped by the same man who raped a woman in the main sample. Both victims went to court.

CHAPTER 8

■

The Outcome of the Court Process

I feel lousy . . . that they didn't believe me.

> RAPE VICTIM,
> DEFENDANT ACQUITTED

I feel really sorry for him. I feel like I ought to hate him, but I can't.

> RAPE VICTIM,
> DEFENDANT CONVICTED

It was a victory. . . . Now I have the upper hand. . . . The tables were turned.

> RAPE VICTIM,
> DEFENDANT CONVICTED

The decisions arrived at during the court process suggest that females are considered fair game. Rape is committed against them frequently. Furthermore, when they are raped, they have enormous difficulty substantiating this claim in court. Their version of what happened typically is seen as less plausible than that of the defense. They are what Weis and Borges call "legitimate victims"—people whom social conventions define as justifiable to victimize.[1]

Weis and Borges have analyzed the societal creation of such victims. They use the concept of victimization to refer to societal processes that include preparation of the victim for the crime, the victim's experience during

237

the crime, and the responses that will be encountered as the aftermath of the crime. "If these processes of victimization are successful with regard to rape, the raped woman is a 'legitimate' or 'safe' victim who will not be dangerous to the rapist, since she is unable to relate her experience to others or to effectively direct blame and accusation against the person who raped her."[2]

VICTIMS NOT DANGEROUS: LOW CONVICTION RATES

Weis and Borges's idea that rape victims typically are not dangerous to their rapists is borne out by the low conviction rates for this crime. Data from our study and from other studies[3] show that only a minority of rapists are ever convicted of the crime.

In our study, 109 rape cases were reported to the police. As previously stated, only 24 made it sufficiently far through the criminal justice system to be tried or plea bargained. The 18 tried cases resulted in 10 verdicts of not guilty (not guilty of any crime), 1 mistrial (hung jury), 3 convictions on lesser included charges (e.g., indecent assault and battery, assault and battery), and 4 convictions for rape (adult victim) or abuse of a female child (victim under 16)[4] (see Table 1).

Table 1. Verdicts in 18 Tried Rape Cases

Not guilty of any crime	10
Mistrial, hung jury (case eventually dismissed*)	1
Guilty of a lesser included charge	3
Guilty of rape or of abuse of a female child**	4
Total	18

*Authorities were unable to locate victim for second trial.
**Sometimes guilty of other charges as well (e.g., kidnapping, robbery).

One additional case went to trial, not to try the rapist (who was never arrested) but to try one of his accomplices. The charges were armed robbery and breaking and entering. He was found guilty on both counts. He was also tried for assault with intent to murder another victim—a small child—not included in the present sample. Later he was tried for the strangling and stabbing deaths of two (one elderly and one middle-aged) male neighbors.

The seven[5] plea-bargained cases resulted in four convictions for rape, one for abuse of a female child, one for indecent assault and battery (male victim), and one for assault and battery. In one additional case, the grand jury did not return an indictment for rape. By mutual agreement the other charges of kidnapping and unnatural act were simply placed on file. This defendant, however, pleaded guilty to seven crimes (one kidnapping, four rape, two assault and battery with dangerous weapon) committed against other victims—specifically, two teen-aged girls not in the present sample.

The conviction rate is even lower than the above figures indicate when one considers the issue of multiple assailants. The question addressed so far

Table 2. Attrition of Multiple Assailants in Tried and Plea-Bargained Cases Leading to Conviction on Any Charge of at Least One Assailant

Case	Number of Assailants*	Number of Assailants Tried or Plea Bargained	Number of Assailants Convicted on Any Charge	Number of Assailants Never Tried or Plea Bargained
1	2	1	1	1
2	4	1	1	3
3	2	1	1	1
4	2	1	1	1
5	4	2	1	2
6	2	2	2	0
Total	16	8	7	8

*Total number of assailants involved in the incident.

is whether a victim's case led to the conviction of any assailant. But it is important also to look at what happens to potential codefendants. Forty-three of the 115 rape victims seen at the hospital had been attacked by more than one person, and many of these 43 were raped by more than one person.[6] These latter victims were victims of "pair" or "group" rape.[7]

In the multiple-assailant cases, it was rare for more than one assailant to reach the plea-bargaining or trial stage. Attrition in the six multiple-assailant cases where trial or plea led to a conviction (on any charge) of at least one assailant is shown in Table 2. These six cases led to the conviction, on some charge, of seven assailants. For an additional eight assailants a trial or plea bargaining never occurred. These potential codefendants had a variety of fates. Several did not go very far in the system; for example, no identification or no arrest was made. One was convicted for crimes against other victims, examined at a psychiatric diagnostic center, and recommended for an indefinite civil commitment to a security treatment center. His civil commitment hearing is still pending.[8] Another was shot in the head and partially paralyzed with a fugitive in Georgia.

The fate of multiple assailants in cases where at least one person was tried and found not guilty of any crime is also of interest. In these 10 cases, 9 defendants were tried (1 defendant had raped 2 victims) and acquitted. But among these 10 cases, 6 of the victims were attacked by more than 1 assailant. There were 13 additional assailants whose cases were never tried or plea bargained; they suffered attrition long before reaching this stage.

In summary, most rapists can rape with impunity. As the figures presented above clearly show, little if anything will happen to them legally. Only a minority will have to go through the rigors and humiliation of the court process. For them, the process may be extremely stressful, painful, and fateful, as it is for the victims. But even many of these rapists will walk out of the courthouse exempt from further sanction.

It is clear that conviction rates for rape presently are low. But are they lower than for other types of major crimes? Recent research by Williams and by Heiple suggests that they are. Working with data from the superior court of Washington, D.C., Williams computed conviction rates for five types of major crimes. She defined sexual assault as "the forcible sexual assault of an adult of either sex, or the sexual assault of a child without regard to whether it was forcible or not."[9] Conviction rates were computed as guilty pleas or guilty findings divided by arrests (cases that did not result in arrests were not considered). The comparative conviction rates were as follows: murder and manslaughter, 51 percent; burglary, 48 percent; robbery, 36 percent; aggravated assault, 26 percent; and sexual assault, only 21 percent.[10] Heiple used data from California Superior Courts for the years 1966 to 1972. He compared the conviction rates for rape, homicide, assault, and sex offenses other than rape. For each of the seven years examined, rape had the lowest percentage of convictions. Also a greater percentage of defendants were acquitted for rape than for the other crimes studied.[11]

Sentences are also important to look at in analyzing societal reaction to rape. The defendants in our study who were convicted of rape, carnal knowledge and abuse of a female child, or indecent assault and battery (male victim) received a great range of sentences, from life to three years probation (see Table 3). The longest sentence given was by a judge after a jury trial. The shortest sentences given were in plea-bargained cases. However, as Table 3 indicates, there is some overlap in length of sentence between guilty pleas and guilty findings.

The rarity of the life sentence in this sample is of particular interest. Only one defendant received a life sentence. The next longest maximum time was 20 years. Victims frequently are told by police, "You know, he could get life for this." The infrequency of this outcome is in striking contrast to the frequency of the warning given to victims. As for rapists, such statistics pose an interesting risk situation. Most rapists can rape and get away with it. In a small number of cases, a fairly stiff penalty will be imposed. On rare occasions, an extreme penalty will be invoked.

The other striking finding about sentences is the emphasis placed on imprisonment (i.e., punishment) rather than rehabilitation or treatment. For convictions for rape and abuse of a female child, the most common place of confinement is Walpole, a Massachusetts correctional facility typically used for persons convicted of the more dangerous crimes and with longer sentences.

The Commonwealth of Massachusetts has a law providing for the indefinite commitment and *treatment* of "sexually dangerous persons." After criminal conviction, persons so classified *may* be referred to a special center, The Treatment Center at Bridgewater, that was founded to implement this law.[12] The facility has treatment programs aimed specifically at sexual offenders, and the therapeutic work of the staff has been reported in the psychiatric literature.

As our study indicates, however, it is difficult to get convicted offenders into this treatment program. Both authorities and offenders are reluctant to participate in it. To the best of our knowledge, the court exercised its option of considering the treatment program for only two convicted defendants in our sample. In one case, the defendant eventually entered the program after spending three years in prison. It took two years just to get him screened psychiatrically, a prerequisite for transfer to the Center for further evaluation. Authorities passed the buck, each saying that someone else should make the necessary arrangements. Once the defendant was examined and diagnosed, additional delays were encountered; his lawyer fought his transfer. After three years he was committed to the treatment facility and entered into psychiatric care. In the second case, the defendant successfully avoided commitment to the treatment facility through the services of his

Table 3. Sentences for Defendants Convicted of Rape, Carnal Knowledge and Abuse of a Female Child, or Indecent Assault and Battery (on a Male Victim)* by Method of Conviction

Found guilty by jury trial**

Rape	Walpole***	Life (plus two 25-year consecutive sentences for kidnapping and for robbery)
Abuse of female child (age 5)	Walpole	12-15 years (plus concurrent sentences of 8-10 years for kidnapping and 8-10 years for assault and battery)
Rape	Walpole	9-18 years
Abuse of female child (age 15)	Walpole	9-15 years

Defendant pleaded guilty****

Rape	Walpole	12-20 years
Rape	Walpole	7-15 years
Rape	Walpole	6-15 years (plus concurrent sentence on kidnappings and assault and battery with dangerous weapon)
Rape	Walpole	6-10 years (plus concurrent sentence of 3-5 years on assault with dangerous weapon)
Indecent assault and battery (male victim, age 6)	Concord	2 years suspended sentence, 1 year probation (already serving 8 plus 8 year consecutive sentences at Concord for abuse of 2 female children)
Abuse of female child (age 15)	In custody of parents	3 years probation with two conditions: that the boy finish school so long as that was financially feasible for his family and that he be respectful to the victim and her family

*At the time this offense was committed the law against rape applied only to female victims and hence in the case of a male victim a different charge had to be utilized.

**The additional trial of a rapist's accomplice for armed robbery and breaking and entering resulted in a sentence to Concord for 6 years.

***These institutions are known officially as Massachusetts Correctional Institution, Walpole; Massachusetts Correctional Institution, Corcord.

****The additional case plea-bargained over two teenage victims rather than the victim in the present sample resulted in a sentence to Walpole for 8-25 years.

lawyer and thus served a determinate prison sentence instead.

THE IDEAL RAPE CASE

Laws against rape, Reynolds argues, act "primarily to punish those men who do not rape *appropriately.*"[13] She therefore asks what kind of woman can be appropriately raped. She concludes that a plausible thesis is that "rape is viewed as a legitimate punishment for women who give the appearance of violating traditional female role expectations."[14] It is, for example, seen as legitimate punishment for a female who "gives any appearance of not closely adhering to the double standard."[15] Reynolds therefore emphasizes the theme of rape as social control:

> Rape and the threat of rape operates in our society to maintain the dominant position of males. It does this by restricting the mobility and freedom of movement of women, by limiting their casual interaction with the opposite sex, and in particular by maintaining the males' prerogatives in the erotic sphere. When there is evidence that the victim was or gave the appearance of being out of her place, she can be raped and *the rapist will be supported by the cultural values.*[16]

Much has been said in the present study about the way various professional groups define a "real rape" or a "good case." Much has been made of the issues used to blame victims in the courtroom. Everything so far suggests that people have in their minds an image of an ideal rape case and that they judge cases in reference to it.

The question remains, however, whether the stereotypes have any systematic connection with actual decision making. Do characteristics of cases discussed so far—for example, the sexual experience of the victim or prior relationship between victim and offender—actually correlate with the outcomes of the cases? The data suggest that they do. A number of tables are presented below based on all tried and plea-bargained cases that led either to: conviction for rape or for abuse of a female child (hereafter referred to as rape); or acquittal (found not guilty of any crime). The one case with two assailants that led both to a conviction by plea and an acquittal by trial has been excluded. The tables indicate whether there is a correlation between characteristics of the cases and outcome. In addition, with regard to some factors, comparison is made between cases leading to conviction for rape and all cases reported to the police that led to any other outcome.

The number of cases for analysis is small, and hence the statistics should be regarded as sensitizing rather than definitive. The composite picture that emerges from the data is, however, striking. With regard to each variable, the figures go in the direction one would predict by the stereotype. One is significant at the .01 level and four are significant at the .05 level. These results are somewhat impressive given the small sample size and the fact that the x^2 measure of significance level depends on sample size. Five others are not statistically significant, but the figures go in the direction predicted. With none of the variables do the figures go opposite to the expected direction. Thus, those cases that match the stereotype are most apt to result in conviction for rape. The only surprise from the data was the degree to which an eyewitness was important.

Eyewitness to the Crime

The most statistically significant finding was the relationship between an eyewitness to the crime and conviction for rape (see Table 4).

Table 4.   *Eyewitness* * *to the Crime and Outcome*

	Acquittal—Found Not Guilty of Any Crime	Conviction for Rape or Abuse of Female Child	Total
No eyewitness to crime	9	1	10
Eyewitness to crime	0	7	7
Total	9	8	17

*Eyewitness to the crime other than a person in the defendant's social network or another rape victim.

x^2 corrected for continuity $= 10.02$. Significant at the .01 level with direction of relationship predicted.($\phi^2 = .59$).

In almost all of the convictions for rape (seven of eight) in our sample, there was an eyewitness. In these seven cases, a person other than someone in the defendant's social network or another rape victim saw the defendant victimizing the female or saw him trying to run away from the scene. In one case, for example, the rape victim and her boyfriend were out for a walk. He both saw and heard her being attacked, and was attacked himself. In a second case—the case of the five-year-old girl—the police arrived on the scene. As they entered the room they saw the victim, her bloody clothes at her side and the man on top of her in the act of intercourse. A third case is the one in which the defendant paraded the victim around his neighborhood in front of his friends and acquaintances. During this forced walk, the rapist and his badly beaten victim also were observed by an employee in a local business establishment and by the four firemen to whom she eventually ran for help and refuge. In other cases, a roommate witnessed the victim being raped in the foyer of their apartment building; a person heard screams and took down the license number of the car into which the victim was forced; policemen arrived on the scene just as the rapist was trying to run away; or a boyfriend was forced at gunpoint to leave his girl friend and thus became a witness to her kidnapping.

In contrast, among the acquittals, not a single case involved an eyewitness to the incident. In one acquittal case, two victims were raped during the same incident, and each corroborated the other's story. But the statement of a second victim was not sufficiently convincing.

In summary, the data suggest that being an ideal victim on other grounds (discussed below) was not sufficient. To be believed, one also needed an eyewitness to the crime. Needless to say, an eyewitness does not exist often in the crime of rape.

It should be emphasized, however, that an eyewitness to the rape does not guarantee conviction for rape. There were cases with eyewitnesses that led to other outcomes. For example, the case that led to a hung jury and mistrial had a police officer as an eyewitness. He testified in court that he had heard the victim scream for help and seen the defendant on top of her in the act of intercourse. However, the case was less than ideal on other grounds. The victim had, for example, met the man previously and she drank heavily. Despite an eyewitness, the defense lawyer was successfully able to blame her and get his client off.

Social Distance: Victim-Offender Relationship

Social distance between victim and offender is important for conviction. At least two aspects of social distance come into play: whether victim and offender have known each other previously, and whether the rape is interracial or intraracial. Cases involving greater social distance are more apt to lead to conviction.

Prior Victim-Offender Relationship. Whether the victim and offender have known each other previously is important, but it does not differentiate cases at the superior court level. There is no relationship between prior acquaintanceship and outcome of cases at this point in the criminal justice system (see Table 5).

Table 5. Prior Victim-Offender Relationship and Outcome

	Acquittal—Found Not Guilty of Any Crime	Conviction for Rape or Abuse of Female Child	Total
Previously knew each other	2	1	3
Strangers	7	7	14
Total	9	8	17

x^2 corrected for continuity = .01. Not significant at the .05 level with direction of relationship predicted. (ϕ^2 = .0006).

Almost all convictions are cases of rapes committed by strangers; the one exception was conviction in the case of the five-year-old girl brutally raped by an acquaintance in the neighborhood. But most of the acquittals are also rapes by strangers. What these figures mean is that the bias is so strong against cases of rape committed by a person known to the victim that they drop out early in the system, long before they reach either the plea-bargaining or trial stage.

The attrition of cases of rape by offenders known to victims is shown in Table 6. The comparison made here is between cases leading to conviction for rape and cases reported to the police that did not have that outcome. It should be emphasized that in this table the category "known" includes any case in which there was even the slightest prior relationship between offender and victim. It includes some boyfriends, as well as acquaintances, schoolmates, or fellow employees only casually known, and people known "by face" or even just "by name" around the neighborhood.

It is especially difficult to get a conviction for rape when even the slightest prior relationship exists. The conviction rate for cases where victim and of-

Table 6.   Prior Victim-Offender Relationship and Outcome

	All Other Outcomes	Conviction for Rape or Abuse of Female Child	Total
Previously knew each other	39	1	40
Strangers	55	7	62
Total	94	8	102*

*Table is based on the 109 rapes reported to the police minus 1 case leading both to conviction and acquittal, 1 case of no data, and 5 cases in which the victim was unable to ascertain if the assailant was a stranger or known (e.g., the victim was grabbed from behind and choked into unconsciousness without seeing the assailant). x^2 corrected for continuity $= 1.53$. Not significant at the .05 level with direction of relationship predicted. ($\phi^2 = .02$).

fender were known was 1 of 40 (2.5%), whereas that for cases of rape by strangers was 7 of 62 (11.3%).

Race Relationship.   The race relationship between victim and offender is related to conviction (see Table 7).

Most convictions were interracial rapes. (In these six convictions, there were four white victims with black assailants, one white victim with a Spanish-speaking assailant, and one American Indian victim with white assailants.) Most of the acquittals were intraracial rapes. (Among the acquittals, there were four white victims with white assailants, and three black victims with black assailants.) The race of the victim alone did not differentiate cases at this level of the court system. (Most convictions and also most acquittals involved white victims.) The race of the offender alone did not differentiate cases here either. (Most convictions and also the majority of acquittals were of nonwhite assailants.)

Because the racial issue regarding rape has an emotional and controversial history, it is worthwhile to look also at the data on this point from the larger group of cases. Comparison is made below between cases leading to conviction for rape and cases reported to the police that led to any other outcome.

Table 7.   Race Relationship and Outcome*

	Acquittal—Found Not Guilty of Any Crime	Conviction for Rape or Abuse of Female Child	Total
Intraracial	7	2	9
Interracial	2	6	8
Total	9	8	17

*Racial groups appearing among victims or offenders in the sample included white, black, Spanish-speaking (Puerto Rican and Mexican), American Indian, Oriental, and Middle-Eastern.

x^2 corrected for continuity = 2.85. Significant at the .05 level with direction of relationship predicted. (ϕ^2 = .17).

In our study, the data again suggest the importance of the issue of interracial versus intraracial rape. The conviction rate for interracial rape is 6 of 35 (17%), compared to only 2 of 66 (3%) for intraracial rape (see Table 8).

Table 8.   Race Relationship and Outcome

	All Other Outcomes	Conviction for Rape or Abuse of Female Child	Total
Intraracial	64	2	66
Interracial	29	6	35
Total	93	8	101*

*Table based on 109 rapes reported to police minus 1 case that led both to conviction and acquittal and 7 cases with no data.

x^2 corrected for continuity = 4.46. Significant at .05 level with direction of relationship predicted. (ϕ^2 = .04).

Race of the victim makes a great difference. The conviction rate when the victim was white was 6 of 60 (10.0%), compared to only 2 of 48 (4.2%) when the victim was nonwhite. The conviction rate was even lower when one looks at black victims alone rather than all nonwhite victims. Among black female victims, only 1 of 43 cases (2.3%) led to a conviction for rape. The one case was that of the five-year-old girl. Thus not one black adolescent or adult woman was able to take her case to the criminal justice system and have her definition of the situation sustained.

Why black victims' cases do not lead to conviction is not clear. A possible explanation is prejudice against black females. Another possible explanation is that—at least in this sample of reported rapes—they were almost all victims of intraracial rapes. Overwhelmingly, these black victims were raped by black assailants, and intraracial rapes have lower conviction rates. In contrast, the white victims were raped by whites and by blacks and by other nonwhites, and interracial rapes have higher conviction rates.

Race of offender alone shows less difference in conviction rates. Conviction rates for nonwhite rapists were 6 of 72 (8.3%), and for white rapists 2 of 30 (6.7%). What seems to matter more regarding conviction is choice of victim. For example, black males can rape black females with impunity. But when they rape white females, especially in front of a witness, the conviction rate is increased. White males can rape white females with impunity. Whether they can rape black females with impunity cannot be determined from our data; the numbers (two cases) are too small for meaningful statistical analysis.

The *dynamics* of the rape, not just the ascribed racial characteristics, seem to be important. The interracial rapes leading to conviction (rather than acquittal) have a striking quality. They were especially daring. These rapists almost always took enormous risks. They raped in ways that were especially likely to result in an eyewitness. White assailants raped an American Indian victim in front of her boyfriend, a black assailant paraded a white victim around his neighborhood, a Spanish-speaking assailant raped a white victim in front of her girl friend. It is as if the rape was part of a direct statement that these offenders were making against a class or group of people they consider as adversaries.[17]

Sexual Experience and General Character

The sexual experience of the rape victim is a factor in conviction. Here the relationship seems to hold only one way. A "good reputation" seems to be necessary for, but does not guarantee, conviction (see Table 9).

Table 9.   Sexual Experience of Victim and Outcome

	Acquittal—Found Not Guilty of Any Crime	Conviction for Rape or Abuse of Female Child	Total
Sexually exper- ienced; not involved with one particular partner at time of rape	5	0	5
Virgin or sex- ually involved with just one partner at time of rape	4	8	12
Total	9	8	17

x^2 corrected for continuity = 3.9. Significant at the .05 level with direction of the relationship predicted. (ϕ^2 = .23).

In all cases of conviction for rape, the victim was either a virgin or sexually involved with just one partner at the time of the rape. In other words, she was either not sexually experienced or was "claimed" by a particular male. In cases of acquittal, about half of the victims were of similar "good reputation"; the other half were sexually experienced and either had sex with a variety of partners or were of dating age and thus had the *image* of being available.

A victim of good "general reputation" also is useful for conviction, but this factor does not seem as salient as sexual experience. The figures for general reputation are in the predicted direction. In the majority of convictions, the victim was of "respectable character." In most acquittals, the victim's character was discredited in some way (through family problems, welfare, alcohol or drug use, prison record, or psychiatric history). But the figures for general reputation were less pronounced than for sexual experience. (For "general reputation," x^2 corrected = 1.42.)

Prompt Reporting

Prompt reporting of the rape is important for conviction. Here again the relationship seems to hold only one way. Reporting promptly seems to be necessary for, but does not guarantee, conviction (see Table 10).

Table 10. *Promptness of Report and Outcome*

	Acquittal—Found Not Guilty of Any Crime	Conviction for Rape or Abuse of a Female Child	Total
Delayed report	5*	0	5
Prompt report	4	8	12
Total	9	8	17

*Includes one case in which the victim reported the rape promptly but delayed in revealing the assailants' names.

x^2 corrected for continuity $= 3.9$. Significant at the .05 level with direction of the relationship predicted. $(\phi^2 = .23)$.

In all cases of conviction for rape, the police were quickly notified. In cases of acquittal, about half were prompt reports and half were delayed.

Injuries

Injuries are related to conviction (see Table 11). In the majority of convictions, the victims sustained moderate to severe general physical damage.[18] One is the victim with the badly beaten face—multiple bruises, lacerations, and damage to the orbital bone. Another is the five-year-old girl with multiple bruises and lacerations, especially on her forehead and mouth. Still another is the case where the girl and her boyfriend were both attacked and he was badly cut. After losing considerable blood, he collapsed and was taken to the hospital and put on the danger list. In contrast, in almost all the acquittals there were minimal or no general physical injuries.

Table 11.   General Physical Injury[a] and Outcome

	Acquittal—Found Not Guilty of Any Crime	Conviction for Rape or Abuse of Female Child	Total
None to minimal[b] injuries	8	3	11
Moderate[c] to severe[d] injuries	1	5[e]	6
Total	9	8	17

[a]Excludes gynecological damage.
[b]Bruise but no laceration or bleeding.
[c]Laceration(s); treatment necessary.
[d]Bruises and lacerations; consults required; consideration of hospitalization or actual hospitalization.
[e]Includes one case where the boyfriend rather than the rape victim herself was severely injured by the assailants.

x^2 corrected for continuity = 2.91. Significant at .05 level with direction of relationship predicted. (ϕ^2 = .17).

As previously discussed, injuries are often used as indicators of the amount of force used, and sometimes also as evidence of whether the victim struggled sufficiently. What the figures just presented mean is that threat of force is seldom enough to lead to conviction. The use of force is typically required.

Other Factors

Consent to being in the situation, the victim's emotionality, and clinical evidence of sexual intercourse are three additional factors thought to be associated with conviction. The data were in the direction predicted, but were not statistically significant. (The x^2s corrected were .51, .51, and .29 respectively.)

In the majority of convictions, the victim unwillingly accompanied the assailant. In contrast in most of the acquittals, the victim willingly accompanied the assailant.

In the majority of convictions, the victim was visibly upset by the rape. In most of the acquittals, the victim was controlled emotionally and her feelings were masked.

In most of the convictions, there was clinical evidence of sexual intercourse. The test for sperm was positive and/or there was moderate to severe gynecological injury. In the majority of acquittals, there was no clinical evidence of sexual intercourse. The sperm test was negative and there was minimal to no gynecological injury.

Approaching the Ideal: A Clustering of Factors

One can also ask how many factors favorable to conviction are present in a given rape case, and if this number has any relationship to outcome. The data suggest that it does.

The ideal rape case for conviction would be characterized by: eyewitness to the crime, stranger for assailant, interracial, victim white, victim a virgin or sexually involved with just one partner, victim with respectable character, prompt report, victim physically injured, victim unwillingly accompanied assailant, victim visibly upset after rape, and presence of clinical evidence of sexual intercourse.

Conviction cases had an average of 8.25 favorable factors present. In contrast, acquittal cases had an average of 3.89 favorable factors present. The relationship between number of factors present and outcome in shown in Table 12.

In the entire sample, there was one "perfect case": all 11 of these factors favorable to conviction were present. In addition, the defendant committed the crime of robbery upon the victim, and had a prison record. Just prior to the rape he had been paroled on a sexual crime (indecent assault and battery). This perfect case led not only to conviction, but to the one life sentence given in our sample.

It is clear, as Reynolds suggests, that the rape laws punish only those men who rape inappropriately. Victims who violate traditional sex role expectations have difficulty having their cases well received in court. However, to understand the dynamics leading to different legal outcomes one must look at a range of factors: the victim, the defendant, their relationship, the nature of the criminal act itself, the evidence obtained, and the response of others to these items.

Table 12.   Number of Factors Favorable to Conviction and Outcome

	Acquittal—Found Not Guilty of Any Crime	Conviction for Rape or Abuse of Female Child	Total
2 to 5 factors present	8	1	9
7 to 11 factors present	1	7	8
Total	9	8	17

x^2 corrected for continuity $= 7.09$. Significant at .01 level with direction of relationship predicted. ($\phi^2 = .42$).

VICTIMS LOSE WHATEVER THE OUTCOME

Blumberg has suggested that in a criminal case, the accused always "loses," even when the result is an acquittal, discharge, or dismissal of the case. There is hostility of the accused even so, due to such aspects as arrest, incarceration, effects on the person's job, expenses, and other traumas.[19] Our study, while not disputing Blumberg's contention, suggests that in a rape case, the victim often loses, no matter what the legal outcome.

When the Defendant Is Not Found Guilty

One would predict that victims would be upset when the defendant is not found guilty of rape, and the data bear this out. Looking at acquittals and at cases that ended at the hearing level, almost all victims expressed negative reactions at the outcome. Rotten, aghast, upset, lousy, disgusted, shitty, disappointed—these were the words they used to describe their feelings about the result.

Several themes emerged in these negative comments. Two themes were similar to reasons victims gave for wanting to press charges in the first place: the desire to protect other people ("The boys shouldn't do it to others"), and the belief the defendant should be punished ("I thought he was wrong. I was a victim, and he should have served time"). Another theme dealt with the courtroom experience itself and the fact that the jury did not accept their version of the story ("I feel lousy . . . that they didn't believe me"). Still another theme was the recurrent one of fear ("He might try to do something"). Another was the difficulty of believing that the guy got off ("I am just shocked. . . . I never thought the guy would get off not guilty"). A final theme was the hope that the defendant would be found guilty for what he did to another of his victims; even if he got off this time, maybe he would not always be able to ("He's going to have to get something for that other girl").

Only one victim in this group was satisfied at the outcome. It was the case in which, after district court hearing, the charge was lowered to assault and battery and the defendant received a two-year suspended sentence. The victim said she was "pretty happy" with that decision. "It was ridiculous to think of the man in jail for 20 years." She said she was satisfied with the outcome.

Family members also were upset at the lack of conviction for rape. Several mothers had strong reactions.[20] One mother of an adult victim said, "We had three strikes against us from the start—who he was, a woman saying it was rape, and being black." "Who he was" refers to the defendant appearing so respectable. He was a well-educated black man with a professional job and a family image. Another mother, very emotionally involved during the trial, spoke at length:

He's not guilty. I called Sergeant Foy last night and that's what he told me. . . . This is a whopper. I know she didn't lie to us. . . . My mind is all confused. How can they say he is not guilty? . . . I don't think they believed her.

Later she called us to talk:

(Sobbing, weak voice) I am very upset. I called you. I had to talk to someone. . . . When they walked in that first night and she told me she was raped and then to find out he is not guilty, I just can't stand it. [What is the most painful part?] That he touched her and why he is not guilty for that? I just keep thinking about it. . . . [Can you get angry?] I tried getting angry at them all. But I still feel bad. . . . I just feel like screaming. . . . I feel so terrible. . . . No one is out there to help her. I wonder what they would do if it was their daughter. . . . (crying) How could they believe that man and how could they think my daughter was lying?

Still another mother said, "I don't feel there was any justice."

When the Defendant Is Convicted of Rape

One might expect a positive reaction by victims when the defendant is convicted of rape—possibly a sense of victory or at least a sense that justice was carried out. Yet a conviction was not a cause for celebration on the part of most victims. On the contrary, the majority of victims whose cases led to conviction for rape expressed dissatisfaction, or at best ambivalence at the outcome. Two themes emerged. One was that the victim felt sorry or badly about what had happened. For example:

> He was convicted on all three counts. . . . It's really strange. All sorts of things are going through my mind. It's really bad about what happened. I feel really sorry for him. I feel like I ought to hate him, but I can't. I feel guilty for walking down the street [that day]. It's all really unfortunate. The whole thing was unfortunate. Things *had* to be done, [he had to be prosecuted], I recognize that, but still it's unfortunate.

A second theme was that the defendant really needed help, not the prison sentence that he received.

> I told the judge I didn't think either should go to prison—they should get treatment. But both went to prison. They had long histories of kidnapping and rape, but no convictions on the [earlier] charges.

The following victim combined both themes:

> I don't think he deserved what he got. . . . He needs help and he sure won't get it at Walpole. . . . I felt sorry for him. He looked so pathetic. What he did was wrong. They said he was on drugs. Having the gun and all was wrong. But I don't think jail will help him. . . . I hope it isn't too tough on the guy, I hate to see people punished.

Another victim expressed her ambivalence when she said, "I'm glad they got *something*. But they'll be back on the street and will be hardened criminals, from being in jail."

Conviction does not necessarily cause the victim's fear to disappear. One victim, after sentencing, spoke as follows:

> I have fear that when he does get out of prison he might try and get back at me. There were friends of his at the trial and I still wonder if they will try to do something—get revenge in some way.

A minority of victims reacted very positively to the news of conviction. As one said:

> They were guilty. One said he did it. They deserved it. I felt good [about the outcome].

The victim who was most enthusiastic about conviction spoke as follows:

> It was a victory. [How do you feel about his going to prison?] Good—the best place for him. Wish it was for longer. He's just an animal. Nothing could help him. But he's off the street now. [How did you feel about seeing the offender?] I knew my position. Now *I* have the upper hand. . . . He felt like I did [before]. The tables were turned.

People in the victim's network seemed to react positively to conviction, sometimes more positively than victims themselves did. One victim compared her father's reaction with her own:

> My father wanted to know what the sentence for the guy was. . . . I didn't care what the guy got. Whatever he got, whether one year or a lifetime, it is time he has to spend in jail.

Her father even telephoned long-distance to get information from the district attorney on the outcome. In another case, the boyfriend's main reaction was that it was too bad that only one assailant was arrested and convicted. He said, "We got one, didn't get the other." In another case, the mother said, "I'm glad he got what he did." Relatives and friends did not seem to share the ambivalence over conviction that some victims expressed. This difference between victims and their networks is similar to discrepancies discussed earlier; for example, the cases in which the family and friends were more enthusiastic about reporting the rape than were the victims themselves.

In summary, when the defendant was not found guilty of rape, almost all the victims had negative reactions to the outcome. When the defendant was found guilty of rape, the majority of victims still expressed negative or ambivalent reactions at the result. Whatever the outcome, emotionally the victim still may lose.

NOTES

1. As discussed in Chapter 4, one sometimes hears emergency ward personnel use the term "legitimate victim" to mean the exact opposite; namely a victim who in their view was "really raped" and who, therefore, according to social conventions, has a legitimate complaint to make.

2. Kurt Weis and Sandra S. Borges, "Victimology and Rape: The Case of the Legitimate Victim," *Issues in Criminology* 8 (Fall 1973), p. 72.

3. Kristen M. Williams, "Sexual Assaults and the Law: The Problem of Prosecution," Revised version of paper presented at the American Sociological Association annual meeting, New York, September 1976. In Ventura County, California, 108 reported rapes in 1971 led to only nine convictions for rape. Ventura Region Criminal Justice Planning Board, "Rape in Ventura," (Mimeographed report, 1974), p. 8. Data from Seattle (1974) and Kansas City, Missouri (1975) show that 635 rape complaints reported led to only 10 convictions for rape or attempted rape. Camille E. LeGrand, Jay A. Reich, and Duncan Chappell, *Forcible Rape: An Analysis of Legal Issues* (Seattle: Battelle Law and Justice Study Center, 1977), p. 4.

4. Sometimes referred to as carnal knowledge and abuse of a child under 16.

5. A total of 24 victims had cases that led either to trials or plea bargains. One case with multiple assailants led to both a trial and a plea. Thus 18 cases were settled by trial and 7 by plea.

6. There may be a discrepancy between the total number of assailants involved in the incident and total number who themselves commit forced sexual acts. For example, in one case there were three assailants. Two of them raped and the third watched them rape. In another case, there were two assailants. Both robbed and one also raped.

7. Amir uses the terms *pair* and *group* rape. Pair rape refers to two offenders assaulting one victim. Group rape refers to three or more offenders raping one victim. Menachem Amir, *Patterns in Forcible Rape* (Chicago: University of Chicago Press, 1971), p. 38.

8. The law defining the civil commitment process for sexually dangerous persons is discussed later in this chapter.

9. Williams, op. cit., p. 1.

10. Ibid., p. 9.

11. Phil Heiple, "Legal, Judicial, and Social Aspects of California Rape Law," (unpublished master's research paper, Department of Sociology, University of California at Santa Barbara, 1975), pp. 22-34.

12. For descriptions of the law and/or the facility, see Harry L. Kozol, Murray L. Cohen, and Ralph F. Garofalo, "The Criminally Dangerous Sex Offender," *New England Journal of Medicine* 275 (July 14, 1966) pp. 79-84; A. Louis McGarry and Raymond D. Cotton, "A Study in Civil Commitment: The Massachusetts Sexually Dangerous Persons Act," *Harvard Journal on Legislation* 6 (1969) pp. 263-303; Harry L. Kozol, Richard J. Boucher, and Ralph F. Garofalo, "The Diagnosis and Treatment of Dangerousness," *Crime and Delinquency* (October 1972), pp. 371-392; and A. Nicholas Groth and Murray L. Cohen, "Aggressive Sexual Offenders: Diagnosis and Treatment," in *Community Mental Health: Target Populations*, Ann Wolbert Burgess and Aaron Lazare (Englewood Cliffs, N.J.: Prentice-Hall, 1976), pp. 212-38.

13. Janice M. Reynolds, "Rape As Social Control," *Catalyst* 8 (Winter 1974), p. 63. (Emphasis in the original.)

14. Ibid., p. 65.

15. Ibid.

16. Ibid., pp. 66-67. (Emphasis added.)

17. We would like to thank Jeanne Guillemin for discussions that helped clarify various issues in analyzing interracial rapes.

18. Gynecological injuries are considered later in connection with clinical evidence of sexual intercourse.

19. Abraham S. Blumberg, "The Practice of Law As Confidence Game: Organizational Cooptation of a Profession," *Law and Society Review* 1 (June 1967), pp. 26-27.

20. We have no data on the fathers' reactions in these cases.

CHAPTER 9

■

Policy Recommendations for the Institutional Response to Rape Victims

*The wonder of all this female
activity, decentralized grassroots organizations and [rape]
programs. . . is that none of it
had been predicted, encouraged, or faintly suggested by men
. . . in more than five thousand
years of written history. That
women should organize to
combat rape was a women's
movement invention.*

BROWNMILLER, 1975

We have examined the career of the rape victim through the criminal justice system. We have seen what happened to a sample of victims in their encounters with the police, the hospital, and the court. Looking at them and the trauma they suffered gives us clues as to how these institutions respond to rape victims in general. These institutions may help victims. But in many ways these institutions further harm the very people they are supposed to help.

To think through the policy implications of this study requires a thinking through of values. Various value judgments could be made about the findings presented in this book. One could blame victims and see any subsequent unsympathetic response to them as justified. One could see victims as doubly victimized—by the crime and by the subsequent societal reaction—and thus deserving of a more sympathetic response. The latter is our position.

The recommendations made in this chapter reflect the value position we made explicit in the preface to the book. We are interested in promoting a more humanistic response to victims. We see it as desirable to promote victim rights, to have a balance between defendants' and victims' rights. We accept—as a short-term goal—efforts to increase the conviction of rapists. We are in favor of the victim having a more well-defined and important role in the criminal justice system. And we think it worthwhile also to speculate about alternative models of the criminal justice system. The victims in our study would share the first goal—promoting a humanistic response to victims. Whether they would accept the others is a more open question. People in the course of their daily lives do not necessarily have well-formulated views on the overall criminal justice system. The issue may not have been a salient one for them, especially if much of their lives has been relatively untouched by crime. Even if salient for them, they might or might not agree with us. Nevertheless, it seems important to raise these issues for public discussion. Our recommendations fall into three main categories: delegitimizing rape, professional and bureaucratic changes, and changes in the criminal justice system.

DELEGITIMIZING RAPE

Rape in many ways is seen as a legitimate act. True, there are laws on the books prohibiting it, and there is public outrage in certain cases—for example, the brutal rape of a child by a stranger. But as Weis and Borges make clear, in general the rape victim is a legitimate victim—one who is not dangerous to the rapist, one who cannot relate the experience to others and have it confirmed by them. And as Reynolds argues, rape laws in fact punish mainly those offenders who do not rape appropriately. These views are substantiated by various studies on the social definition of rape. The data show that what clearly is a rape to one person is not seen as a rape by another. Our study further confirms this theme. Professionals who come into contact with victims often ask, "Is it a real rape?" Convictions for rape are few. Those rape cases that approximate the "ideal case" are more likely to lead to conviction, but departures from the ideal case create problems. It is difficult, for example, to get a conviction for rape when the slightest prior relationship exists between victim and offender. The sexual experience of the rape victim is also a factor. A "good reputation" seems to be necessary for, but does not guarantee, conviction.

The first and most important task, therefore, is to *delegitimize rape*—to make it be seen as unacceptable behavior. This means changing the social definition of rape. It means seeing rape as an act of aggression and violence, motivated primarily by power or anger, rather than by sexuality.[1] And it means seeing that rape—forced sexual acts without the victim's consent—can occur in many circumstances where people now will not acknowledge it. It means seeing, for example, that rape can occur when the victim initially accompanies the offender willingly, between people who are not strangers, when the victim is not a virgin, when there are no bruises because the victim did not dare to fight, and when both offender and victim are of the same race.[2]

Progress already is being made. Major credit must be given to the women's movement for bringing this issue to public attention. There were "speak outs" on rape where women began saying publicly what they dared not say before.[3] Numerous movement people worked on the rape issue, holding conferences, pressuring legislatures, drafting model laws, and working in countless other ways.[4] The importance and innovativeness of this group activity should be emphasized. As Brownmiller notes, the amazing aspect of the growth of these grassroots women's groups is that such an approach to the problem of rape had never been suggested by men. "That women should *organize* to combat rape was a women's movement invention."[5] This collective response may well serve as a model for other victim groups.[6] This movement work has been paralleled by the work of many professionals who also have been attempting to redefine rape. It is important that these movement and professional efforts continue so that further progress in redefining and delegitimizing rape can be made.

The problem of rape cannot be solved in isolation. What happens in rape and subsequently in the criminal justice system is not unique, but reflects male and female roles in the broader society.[7] The data in our study show that police, hospital staff, juries, lawyers, and judges have clear ideas of how a woman ought to act, and base their judgments on such considerations.

In these images, women are at a disadvantage vis-à-vis men. The cultural categories pertaining to "the way women ought to behave" systematically operate to place women in a structurally disadvantageous power position. Spradley and Mann nicely document this disadvantage in their work on the cocktail waitress. Analyzing male-female interaction in a college bar, they note that much of it is governed by a "handicap rule."[8] In some games in our society, there is an "equal application rule" stating that each person must play by the same rules. In baseball, each player must tag each base when going around the baseball diamond. But in other games, including the relations between the sexes, there is an arbitrary "handicap rule" placing some players at a disadvantage. For example, in "Brady's Bar," male employees have the right to drink in the bar before work, but female employees do not. The arbitrary rules imposed on females are often justified by reference to "instinctual traits"—for example, "women are too emotional" or "women can't hold their liquor." Spradley and Mann state:

> As in the wider culture, females are repeatedly required to play with an arbitrarily imposed handicap. It is as if all the players in the game made a tacit agreement that women must play by different rules than men. . . . Handicap rules for women in our culture . . . function to insure that males stay at the center of social significance, and that women remain "in their place" at the periphery.[9]

What happens in the medical and criminal justice systems mirrors what happens in society generally. Definitions of reality are produced, sustained, or dismissed in the same way as they are in everyday life. In the courtroom or not, for example, people rely on the same kinds of information, the same categories, the same typifications, the same cognitive sets that typically produce the same result: less credibility to female versions of reality and, conversely, greater credibility to male definitions of reality.

Because the medical and criminal justice systems rely on these same cultural stereotypes (it cannot be otherwise) in "producing" and "uncovering" motives, most victims' cases are lost long before they enter these systems. Most actors in these institutions have assumptions about male and female roles prior to hearing evidence and they evaluate the evidence in terms of these assumptions. In other words, they accept the "handicap rule" before information about a case comes in, and they evaluate the information they get in terms of that rule. Thus, the process of delegitimizing rape needs to be linked to the process of altering the handicap rule for male-female interactions in general.[10] In addition to this very broad goal, there are specific changes that need to be made in the institutional response to victims.

PROFESSIONAL AND BUREAUCRATIC CHANGES

When suggesting changes in the institutional response to rape victims, it is useful to separate short-term and long-term goals. This section deals with the former. It deals with changes that could be instituted immediately, changes that do not necessitate sweeping revisions of fundamental principles. It is based on themes that emerged from the victims. These themes are applicable to the police, medical personnel, and court personnel. These recommendations should be of interest to professionals who want to provide a more humanistic response to rape victims. They include the creation of victim programs; systematic evaluation of organizational procedures; rethinking roles; sensitizing and emotionally supporting professionals; providing information, explanation, and advice; privacy; careful collection and recording of information about the incident; continuity of services; interprofessional cooperation; and reducing delays in the institutional response.

The Need for Victim Programs

Many institutions deal with rape victims. But frequently these institutions have no one who, as part of their role, is assigned the responsibility of seeing what happens to victims over time and of protecting their rights. At present there often is no one to follow victims through the system and no one to systematically pressure for long-term change. Thus, one main policy recommendation is that special programs for victims of crime be instituted and that specially trained people be assigned to work with victims. Fortunately, the trend in the United States is already in this direction. Special victim programs have sprung up in many places, in large measure as an outgrowth of the women's movement. Existing institutions such as hospitals and police departments have begun to set up special programs within their institutions to assist rape victims. Examples are the programs sponsored by the Public Health and Metropolitan Police Departments in Washington, D.C.,[11] the police department in New York City,[12] Philadelphia General Hospital,[13] Boston City Hospital,[14] Jackson Memorial Hospital in Miami,[15] Beth Israel Hospital in Boston,[16] Harborview Medical Center in Seattle,[17] and the District Attorney's office in Dorchester, Mass.[18] In addition, independent rape crisis centers and hot lines have been set up to work with victims. Examples are the Rape Crisis Center (Washington, D.C.), the North Side Rape Crisis Line (Chicago), and Bay Area Women Against Rape (Berkeley).[19] Often these independent and largely volunteer centers have been in the vanguard, helping rape victims before established institutions came to recognize their pressing needs. Furthermore, various task forces have been set up to recommend and work for policy changes. Groups with extensive reports include, for example, the District of Columbia Task Force on Rape,[20] Citizens' Advisory Council on Rape, Cook County, Ill.,[21] and the Task Force to Study the Treatment of Victims of Sexual Assault, Prince George's County, Md.[22] Feminist groups also have set up task forces on rape, a well-known example being that of the National Organization for Women.[23]

Victim programs such as those described above differ in their goals. They also differ in where they are located vis-à-vis the decision-making structure—some are outside and others inside established institutions. Overall, however, victim programs can do three main things. The first is an immediate task: to help victims as they deal with the current system. Individuals from these programs can be in contact with victims as they wend their way through the present medical and criminal-justice labyrinth. (In some cases, they may help victims who choose not to deal with authorities at all.) They can explain things to them, give them emotional and psychological support, and try to make them feel somewhat less dehumanized. The second is a more far-reaching task. These groups can act as pressure groups to help bring about middle-range and long-range changes that will restructure the medical and criminal justice systems so that in the future the lot of the victim will be less painful. As such, these groups can help provide pressure to bring about some of the changes proposed below. Third, these groups can act as watchdog groups. They can pressure for professional accountability and try to ensure that victims' rights as defined at a particular point in time are indeed honored. One may get official guidelines and protocol as described in professional training manuals changed so as to benefit victims, but such statements do no good unless they are honored in practice.

Systematic Evaluation of Organizational Procedures

To accommodate victims' needs, one has to know what those needs are. Organizations that deal with victims should institute systematic reviews of their organizational procedures, with an eye to how they affect victims. One cannot expect the same people to be responsible for both short-term delivery of services and for long-range evaluation and planning. The day-to-day burden of patients to be treated and cases to be investigated and prosecuted almost always ensures that the immediate task at hand takes precedence over long-range evaluation and planning. Review and planning must be structured into the system, either by assigning this duty to a particular position or by assigning a specific time for doing it. Such a review could document the problems victims face and be used as a basis for recommending changes. Some changes will be hard to implement. But many times, small, easily made changes in the organization's routine would greatly benefit victims. For example, a hospital may have a rule that victims, if they wait, must wait alone. A review might suggest that rape victims find such isolation upsetting. It might be that there would be little inconvenience to the organization if victims were permitted to have friends or family stay with them. In the criminal justice system, a review might suggest that victims greatly prefer to be interviewed in offices rather than in the hallway, and such a protocol could then be recommended.

The main difficulty in conducting such a review is to ensure that one truly taps the client's concerns. As Kelman, speaking of consumers' evaluation of medical care, has emphasized, surveys often are done from the point of view of the *providers* and the questions asked reflect *their* concerns rather than the concerns of patients.[24] One should be aware of this potential bias when designing a review.

Rethinking Roles

There are aspects of various roles in the institutions that deal with rape victims that cause difficulty for the victim. More thinking needs to be done regarding the rights and obligations of persons in official positions as they deal with rape cases.

As our study shows, for example, in the emergency ward there is tension between the therapeutic and the legal duties of the staff. The legal aspects of the work receive a lower priority. Nevertheless—even though it may be a source of tension—these latter duties must be performed if a case is to be prosecuted. Only physicians (and possibly, in the future, nurses) have the credentials to perform these duties. Thus greater attention should be given to the clinician's forensic duties. They should be seen as an important and legitimate part of the clinician's role.

In the criminal justice system, the district attorneys in our study covered a great range in how they fashioned their role vis-à-vis rape victims. A minority adopted the role of legal counselor; that is, one who provides legal advice to the victim. It is recommended that further attention be given to this aspect of the district attorney's work. If the system truly is to be an adversary one, not only the defendant but also the victim should have the right to legal counsel. The DA is a likely candidate for providing this service.

We also found that no one has, as part of their role, the responsibility of watching out for the victim. In some quarters, a new role is being promoted in an attempt to remedy this lack—the role of victim advocate. The Hospital Subcommittee of the Citizens' Advisory Committee On Rape, Cook County, Ill., has gone to some length to try to define the role of such an advocate. It states:

> The role of the advocate is to see that the victim receives appropriate attention at all levels by hospital personnel and police alike. . . . The advocate will be a trained, female volunteer and function in the capacity of a lay

person. . . . The advocate will monitor the performance of the medical staff and police interrogation to ensure that the victim is treated with dignity, understanding, and compassion without sacrificing prompt and efficient care.[25]

In other quarters, victim specialists are being employed by institutions dealing with victims.[26]

The victim's role has been ill-defined up to now, especially in relation to the court system. However, as is discussed in detail later, this issue has become a matter of great concern to victimologists and legal scholars, and many suggestions are being made for change.

Sensitizing and Supporting the Professionals

Without being constantly resensitized to the suffering of victims, it is easy for police, hospital, and court staff to react with bureaucratic impersonality and professional neutrality. While such detachment has its merits, all too easily it slips into an attitude of indifference toward human needs. Without some kind of emotional support given to professionals to help them deal with suffering, it is easier for them to deny their own feelings. What emotional response there is centers on "the case." It becomes one of noninvolvement with the victim. As several staff people in our study mentioned, "I've gotten hardened," or "You'd go soft if you really thought about the cases." It is our belief that if staff are to deal with victims in a more humanistic way in the future, they must be resensitized to the needs of victims. If they are to move beyond a defensive stance of emotional noninvolvement, they in turn must have some kind of emotional support built into the institutional system to help them deal with the client's suffering and with their own feelings about this suffering.

The review of organizational procedures described previously can alert professionals to the sufferings of victims. So can talking to victims about their feelings. Such awareness, however, often may be emotionally upsetting to staff. Our research on training crisis counselors shows that counseling rape victims often triggers strong emotional reactions in staff. Furthermore, a study by Zonderman of volunteer counselors found that some developed several of the symptoms that rape victims usually develop. A small minority of the volunteers developed five to seven such symptoms. Zonderman calls this phenomenon the "rape counselor syndrome."[27]

What then needs to be done is to provide the professionals with some support so that they can cope with their own feelings. A landmark model in this regard is the work of psychiatrist Kübler-Ross, who pioneered an interdisciplinary seminar to deal with death and dying. Patients were eager to talk but it took the staff a longer time to openly discuss their own feelings about death.[28]

An approach similar to Kübler-Ross's is to schedule periodic "feelings" sessions where professionals who are members of the team—for example, of the rape team—can discuss items that become emotional issues for them. This kind of session was incorporated into the Boston City Hospital Victim Counseling Program that was instituted following our study. At BCH, weekly meetings were held for the discussion of rape cases. Occasionally, rather than present a case the time was used to discuss the feelings of the counselors. One session, for example, was given over to counselors discussing the symptoms that they developed after starting this work—nightmares, phobias, fears for their own safety or that of their children, angry feelings toward men. Another session was used to share with one another how they felt when they accompanied a rape victim to court and how they felt when they themselves were put in the stressful situation of being put on the witness stand. Our research on training counselors supports Kübler-Ross's observation regarding nurses; namely, that "they were quickly able to express their real concerns, conflicts, and coping mechanisms when their statements were used to *understand* a given conflictual situation rather than to *judge* them."[29]

Information, Explanation, and Advice

Police, hospital staff, and DAs tend to keep the victim in ignorance. Rape victims complain again and again that they are never told anything. They say they have difficulty finding out from police what is happening on the case. They complain that the hospital staff does not give them sufficient information. Some even say that after their case was tried they had difficulty finding out the result.

The general tendency still is for police, hospital staff, and DAs to follow the older professional model—to decide *for* the client what needs to be done.[30] They do not provide the client with sufficient information so that he or she may participate in the decision-making process. Observations of interaction between professionals and rape victims confirm this state of affairs. Physicians tend not to explain the more controversial aspects of the medication they routinely give rape victims. DAs tend not to give much information or advice on how to prepare for court, nor do they tell victims what options are open to them. What information *is* given is offered on an *individual* basis, rather than as part of a role; for example, a particular police officer may go out of his or her way to explain to a victim what is happening, but it is not considered a norm that policemen in general should inform the victim.

Victims want more information than they now are getting. In the long run, the professional-client model[31] may change so as to involve more sharing of information and greater participation on the part of the client.[32] In the short run, the use of victim specialists may be an alternate way of providing information. In rape crisis centers, volunteers often serve this function. In the hospital setting, a nurse-counselor or social-work-counselor may do so. In the court setting, pilot projects have utilized victim specialists. A good example is the Victim/Witness Assistance Project in the Assistant District Attorney's office in the Dorchester district of Boston. Among other duties, the victim specialist in this program explains to the victim-witness the role he or she has in the criminal justice system, gives advice on documenting any financial loses, explains provisions of the Victim of Violent Crime Compensation Act and the Federal Crime Insurance Act, gives notification of the trial date, explains what has happened in the court sessions, and makes sure the victim-witness is informed of the outcome of the court action and the disposition of the case.[33]

Privacy

Victims of crime often have little privacy. One of the victim's main concerns may be whether people will find out what has happened, especially in crimes such as rape that cause the victim great embarrassment. Yet often, as our study shows, the police, medical, and court personnel as they do their work make the victim's situation known to the community. Victims may ask police to refrain from making noise so as to not alert the neighbors. But as one such victim reported with dismay, "Before we could drive away, another [police car] arrived with its siren blaring." At the hospital, many people in the victim's network may press for information. One victim's brother asked insistently, "But wouldn't there be tightness there [if nothing had happened]?" At the court, victims may be interviewed in the corridor, as well as having to testify in public trial.

Organizational protocol needs to be reevaluated with regard to the criterion of maintaining victim's privacy. For example, police need to give more thought to how they may respond to and contact victims without calling attention to their plight. Hospital staff need to think through such issues as who has the right, morally and legally, to know the results of the medical examination. And court staff need to think of ways to shield the victim from indiscriminate public view. Given our society's commitment to public trials, the legal area is the most difficult to change regarding privacy. However, as is discussed later, various legal thinkers have given consideration to ways in which the privacy of certain victims could be increased.

Obtaining and Recording Information[34]

The rhetoric used by lawyers during a trial places great emphasis on the importance of bringing out the "facts of the case." That is supposed to be one of the main purposes for having the trial. The irony is that so little is done in the system prior to the trial to obtain or to preserve the facts of the case.

Style of Interviewing. Victims are interviewed by authorities—police, hospital personnel, and the district attorneys—prior to a court hearing or trial. One of the difficulties is that the interviewing may be either intimidating or suggestive in style, thus encouraging the victim to provide an account that is less than accurate. Intimidating interviewing, especially in embarrassing crimes such as rape, may encourage the victim to remain silent and withhold information. In one case, for example, despite several interviews, the victim never told anyone the full range of sexual acts that had been forced upon her until after the court session was over. Had this information been elicited earlier, the state would have had the option of bringing additional charges against the assailant. Interviews may also be suggestive in style. In one case, the DA kept pressuring the victim to make a stronger statement about the knife—to say that she had seen something, perhaps a flashing blade. Thus, attention should be given to developing and utilizing interviewing techniques that are less intimidating and less suggestive.

Recording of Information.   Rape victims may give many statements to officials, but these statements often are not recorded in the victim's own words. Sometimes they are not recorded at all. First, the victim's statements are often translated into the official's language.[35] The rape victim may say, regarding her attempt to stop the assailant, "I told him I was a married woman." The DA writes down, "You remonstrated him." Second, the accounts given are greatly collapsed in the written version. Police reports and hospital records often are very brief—a short paragraph, maybe a page. They tend to be very selective in focus. Much of the great detail that the victim can provide at the time is not written down; later, however, the defense will cross-examine the witness about these seemingly irrelevant details. Third, sometimes the victim's statements are not recorded at all. In the district courts that we observed, the testimony is not taken down by a court stenographer. The defense lawyer, however, often tape-records the victim's testimony or prepares his or her own written summary of what the testimony was. The prosecution does not keep comparable records of the testimony that was given. Thus the defense, but not the victim, has access to the victim's prior testimony.

Statements that victims do give should be more accurately recorded to facilitate prosecution. Special attention should be given to recording statements verbatim and also to recording all the relevant information, such as bruises, that the professional independently observes. Once a case is in court, it does not seem to occur to anyone that a record might have been carelessly written. Any discrepancy between what the victim says in court and what the record says is held against the victim.

It is notoriously difficult to get institutions to keep good records. Nevertheless, one useful practice instituted in the Victim Counseling Program at Boston City Hospital is to have someone—in this case the nurse-counselors—act as a watchdog group in rape cases. The counselors try to make sure that all relevant information, such as bruises that the staff observes, gets recorded on the medical record. Another useful practice is to create a category system for collecting information that makes sense to the person responsible for gathering the information. One form that has proved useful in the BCH program uses the categories of "signs and symptoms of rape"—observable signs of physical trauma, reported symptoms of physical trauma, observable signs of emotional trauma, and reported symptoms of emotional trauma.[36] Better court records also would help protect the rights of both victim and defendant. District courts should have court stenographers. Prosecution as well as defense should have access to an official transcript of prior testimony if and when the case goes on to a higher court.

Victims should be encouraged to write down for their own use a detailed account of the incident. They could use this account to refresh their memories prior to testifying. Victim-counselors could help victims make such a record. At the time of trial, defense lawyers typically ask numerous questions about minute details, and victims become uncomfortable when questioned about details that they can no longer remember. One victim in our sample, after trial, asked that we provide other victims with the following advice:

> Tell the girl to write down [the facts] immediately—everything from the time she sees him until she doesn't—what she was wearing, what he was wearing. That's the most important thing—to write it down. All the conversation too. [My boyfriend and I] wrote *part* of it down—not as much as we should have. [The defense] picks on every little thing—even the little most minute detail— where he walked, where she walked . . . how long each thing took, if she locked the door or didn't. Write down everything. . . . If she writes it all down, then when she's on the stand she'll be sure of herself.

A written account to refer to could increase victims' self-confidence when they testify. If the victim felt uncomfortable about having a written account in the home—perhaps, for fear that a family member might come upon it—it could be kept in the counselor's files. The victim could have access to it when needed.

Continuity of Services

Lack of continuity of services is a problem for rape victims. One factor that contributes to victims feeling neglected, as our study shows, is that victims typically are not seen by the same person on their return visits to various institutions. In our study, the police were the one group that by and large had solved this problem; the same officer or officers followed a case from start to finish. In the hospital, however, if rape victims came back for a later check-up or for further treatment, they often got sent to the outpatient department rather than returning to the emergency ward where they were seen initially. A change of department and/or personnel meant that someone new would inquire why they were there. To be seen they would have to explain again that they had been raped. This need to explain all over again was one of the things that victims complained about. Likewise in the criminal justice system there is little continuity in who prosecutes the case. A victim, especially if there are several postponements in the case, may have a series of district attorneys. There is another change in DAs as the victim goes from district court to superior court. Victims thus must keep telling their story anew to each DA.

Continuity of professional services for rape victims should be instituted. Policy should be to have victims return at least to the same medical department for their follow-up, preferably to the same practitioner. And the same DA should handle the case from start to finish. Rape counselors also may be useful for increasing a sense of continuity. They can keep in contact with victims as they move between institutions, going from police to hospital to court. Rape crisis center members sometimes provide such a link. Another example is the follow-up provided by counselors in the BCH program; the nurses and other counselors keep in touch with victims and may even accompany them to court.

Interprofessional Cooperation

The main groups of professionals who work with rape victims are police, health personnel (physicians, nurses, social workers), and lawyers. The most striking thing about these groups is their specialization and professional isolation. There is a lack of communication between them. As our study shows, each group tends to stick to its own limited field. It neither learns from others nor teaches others any of its specialized knowledge even though this knowledge could be applied to the duties at hand. For example, physicians who gather evidence and lawyers (both prosecutors and defense lawyers) who use this evidence in court seldom talk to one another about the general issues involved. Emergency ward physicians are largely uninformed about legal procedures. Thus the medical evidence that will be used in court either to acquit a defendant or to prove him guilty is being collected by physicians who often do not know the definitions of various crimes or what types of evidence are considered necessary to make such a judgment. The collection of evidence in criminal cases is not given much emphasis in medical school. And as new physicians begin their work on the emergency ward often the only orientation they receive on criminal cases is informal and is handed down from senior resident to new resident. A person trained in law or in police procedure does not instruct them, even though these physicians will be called upon in their work in the emergency ward to examine alleged victims of many types of violent crimes. Emergency ward personnel in general are trained only very selectively in the techniques that could be used to gather evidence. The medical records they write may exclude information useful for prosecution and include information both irrelevant and harmful for prosecution. Lawyers and judges, for their part, often do not know the meaning of medical terms, even though they make judgments based on their reading of medical records.

Effort should be put into increasing cooperation between the professional groups that deal with rape victims—especially the police, health personnel, and district attorneys. As with long-range planning, it is often hard for people enmeshed in the day-to-day task of providing services to break out of their daily routine and seek the cooperation of other groups. As with long-range planning or other victim-oriented proposals, a catalyst may be needed to initiate change. A rape counselor or a crisis center might be able to invite these diverse groups to talk to one another. The agenda would be to discuss ways in which their work might be better integrated so as to better protect the rights of both victim and defendant.

One obvious project for such an interdisciplinary group would be to discuss the most up-to-date evidence collection techniques. The physicians might be willing to obtain and share information on the latest research (for example, advances in sperm typing or in tests for seminal fluid).[37] Police officers might be willing to discuss some of the evidence collection techniques for rape cases that are advocated by police training manuals—that the victim's clothing should be collected and folded properly to prevent dried stains from brushing off, that victims can be given a comb and envelope to gather hair samples that might have been left by the assailant, and that the victim's fingernails may be clipped to provide skin scrapings of the assailant.[38] Such procedures could become part of the emergency ward protocol if greater interdisciplinary effort was made and if greater communication existed between physicians, police, and district attorneys.

A second project for such a group would be the creation of a more appropriate medical record sheet—forms that would be useful both to medical personnel and the criminal justice system, forms that would protect both the victim's rights and the defendant's rights. District attorneys could inform physicians of the types of medical evidence considered appropriate for use in court. Physicians could inform district attorneys of the types of information they must gather to do an acceptable medical work-up—information including such things as gynecological history and vaginal infections that many people would argue have nothing to do with whether the alleged rape occurred. After such an exchange of information, record forms could be devised that would protect the victim's rights, but also would provide the criminal justice system with the evidence defined as relevant to the alleged crime.

Speeding Up the Institutional Response

Rape victims suffer when there are delays in the institutional response to their dilemma. In our study, for example, an issue of considerable importance to victims was whether they had to wait at the hospital. Of those adult rape victims who mentioned the issue, the majority criticized the length of time they had to wait before being seen by a physician. The court system, however, was by far the most striking in the delays it imposed upon the victim. Victims often waited hours at the courthouse just for a case to be called. Furthermore, victims often found their cases postponed several times, rescheduled for a new date weeks or months later. Victims responded very negatively to court delays. The costs to them, in psychic energy, money and time, and memory loss, were enormous.

Professional groups dealing with rape victims should institute procedures that will reduce the delays and speed up the institutional response. Hospitals, for example, should reexamine the triage system at their emergency wards and review the current priority ratings that are given to different types of cases. It is true that by the time rape victims arrive at the hospital their lives usually are no longer in danger. Nevertheless, the psychic difficulties of waiting after such an assault are great. It is recommended that rape victims be given a high priority ranking in triage systems.

Criminal justice personnel also should institute changes to reduce court delays.[39] Such delays, are, Haynes suggests, somewhat like other "cosmic subjects," such as love and the weather, that have been talked about and grumbled about throughout the ages.[40] The theme appears not only in legal writings, but in the works of Goethe, Dickens, Chekhov, and Molière.

There is much conversation and many reports but little action for improvement.[41] Nevertheless, it seems worthwhile to present, as a stimulus for thinking about the problem, some of the recommendations that have been made by others for reducing delays in the criminal justice system. Recommendations made by Ash, Foschio, Haynes, Nayar, Bleuel, and Reed, for example, fall into several categories. They focus on witnesses, continuances, entry of cases, the overall system, and research. Some of their suggestions are presented below.

Recommendations focusing on witnesses

1. *Witness's appearance control projects.* Establish projects that would "develop, implement, and test devices for (1) reducing the number of unnecessary trips to court required of both police and civilian witnesses, and (2) assuring their timely production at court when their presence is in fact required."[42]

2. *Witness liaison and support squads.* Institute squads to "represent the interests of the court system to the witnesses and, more importantly, the interests of the witnesses to the court system. Its members would keep witnesses informed about changes in court dates, court procedures, reasons for postponements and delay, and in general, about what is going on in courtroom and courthouse."[43]

3. *"Witness interest" as a criterion in management studies.* Have court management studies "sharply focus on the ways in which court operations affect witnesses, and . . . expressly employ 'witness interest' as one yardstick of success."[44]

4. *Rethinking laws, practices, and customs* in terms of their impact on witnesses.[45].

Recommendations focusing on continuances

1. *Requiring adequate reasons for the request.* Have "stricter insistence to show adequate grounds for continuances."[46]

2. *Requiring advance notice of the request.* Require advance notice (for example, two days) for requesting a continuance and if such notice is not given, the continuance should not be granted.[47]

Recommendations focusing on entry of cases

1. *Early screening.* Have an experienced prosecutor "carefully and critically examine each case at the outset of proceedings, determine whether it is likely to be 'successful,' and not permit 'bad' cases to enter the system at all."[48]

2. *Diversionary devices.* Use diversionary devices to "'divert' certain types of offenders, especially first offenders, from the criminal courts to more appropriate agencies."[49]

3. *Enter rape cases at higher court level.* For rape cases, eliminate the hearing for probable cause in district court and go directly to the grand jury, and, if indicted, on to trial.[50]

Recommendations focusing on the overall system

1. *Improved coordination in the now-fragmented system.* Use various techniques to coordinate; for example, "monitor the entire system by the use of computer and human resources" and have "organizational development meetings" that would be attended by "representatives from all parts of the system."[51]

2. *Improved communications.* Use techniques such as eliminating unnecessary forms.[52]

3. *Improved physical facilities.* Improve the physical plant since "courts . . . are housed in inadequate and aged buildings, which, if used for industrial purposes, would have been condemned long ago."[53]

Recommendations focusing on research

1. *Simulation research.* Obtain information on the usefulness of alternatives by doing simulation research. "If a model is built to simulate the case flow in the criminal court system, one may experiment with the model instead of the actual system."[54]

2. *Operations research.* Apply concepts and techniques of operations research to judicial administration problems such as delay.[55]

An additional and more controversial way to reduce delay specifically for victims—the videotaping of testimony prior to trial—is discussed later.

THE CRIMINAL JUSTICE SYSTEM OF THE FUTURE

The criminal justice system and its components have come under attack from many quarters. Glaser, for example, suggests that the courts may be one of our least successful institutions:

> One finds that courts: (1) do not select wisely or equitably those offenders for whom state action is appropriate; (2) do not reach decisions efficiently; (3) do not conduct criminal procedure fairly; (4) do not maintain public support for themselves. From these standpoints courts may well be the most unsuccessful major institutions in our society.[56]

The evidence is overwhelming that from many points of view—for example, that of defendants, deterrence, efficiency—the criminal justice system, including the courts, is not working well.

Our study documents that the criminal justice system is not working well for victims. Rape victims have little success in bringing their claim of rape to court and having their definitions of the situation accepted. Going to court may be as much of a crisis for them as the original rape itself. Rape victims' reactions to the court experience are overwhelmingly negative. They are upset by the cross-examination, confrontation between accused and accuser, the public setting, the adversary's story, and the length of the court process. The conviction rate for rapists is low. Victims tend to be dissatisfied with the verdicts. Almost all victims felt this way when the verdict was not guilty. The majority of victims were dissatisfied, or at best ambivalent, when the verdict was guilty of rape. The few persons in our study who were convicted of rape tended to be dealt with by punishment—imprisonment. Almost none entered into the security treatment programs that exist for such offenders.[57] Presumably the deterrence effect of these convictions is minimal. Although those in prison are kept from raping persons in the outside community for the duration of their imprisonment,[58] any long-range deterrence effects of imprisonment on these particular assailants is at best questionable. The symbolic[59] importance of their conviction presumably is minimal. Convictions occur in such a small percentage of cases that the main message they convey is that rape is acceptable rather than unacceptable behavior.

In summary, our study makes it clear that the courts and various other sectors of the criminal justice system are not working well for victims. These data do not give us firm clues on how to proceed in the future. Nevertheless, it seems worthwhile to spend some time on proposals for change that are more speculative, long-term, and less firmly grounded in data than the previously discussed bureaucratic and professsional recommendations. This more speculative venture takes us into legal and especially victimological literature. Various themes from this literature are presented below as a stimulus for thought. The recommendations cited fall into two main categories: tinkering with parts of the system, and changing the overall model of the criminal justice system.

Tinkering With the Criminal Justice System

Numerous suggestions have been made for changing parts of the criminal justice system to improve the lot of the victim. Some focus on procedures during court sessions: confrontation, public access to hearings and trials, and cross-examination. Others focus on compensation. Still others focus on the rape laws.[60]

Confrontation, Public Access, and Cross-Examination. Our study and others[61] have shown that seeing the accused face to face, the public setting of court sessions, and cross-examination are three especially upsetting features of the current court system. Can anything be done about these aspects that will help diminish the psychic trauma of victims but at the same time not deprive defendants of their socially defined rights?[62]

Libai has done considerable thinking on this problem regarding *child* victims of sexual assault. He has come up with several proposals for "protecting child victims without abridging the rights of the accused."[63] One wonders why—if they really are effective and if they do not abridge the rights of the accused—Libai's proposals could not be extended to apply to adult victims. One also would hope that some of Libai's suggestions—such as testifying before a one-way glass—would be optional, since some victims might find this setting more disturbing than a standard courtroom.

Libai's proposals regarding court deal especially with the issues of confrontation, public access, and shortening the court process for victims. His first proposal is for a trial in a "Child-Courtroom." This courtroom would be specially designed to obtain the child victim's testimony in an informal and relaxed way. The arrangement would be such that the child would only be able to see four persons: the judge, prosecutor, defense lawyer, and the child examiner.[64] The defendant, jury, and audience would sit behind a one-way glass that would separate them but still enable them to observe the proceedings. Microphones and earphones can be used so the defendant and his lawyer can communicate with each other. When identification is at issue, the accused can be asked to enter the judge's room for a few moments for identification. These special arrangements would be used as long as the child was giving evidence. Upon conclusion of the child's testimony, the proceedings could be resumed in a standard courtroom. Regarding public access, Libai states that the child-courtroom might do away with the need to exclude the public. However, he also notes that "the right to a public trial does not require that a large number of seats be provided for the audience in the Child-Courtroom. . . . The minimum necessary to satisfy the public trial requirement has been stated by Mr. Justice Black, to be that the accused is allowed to have his counsel, family, relatives and friends present."[65] And, as Libai notes, "child victims 'of tender years' are protected in some jurisdictions by limited exclusion of the public."[66]

Libai's second proposal deals with creating a "procedure whereby the child victims would be allowed to testify *before* the trial without violating the accused's right to confrontation."[67] This practice would prevent having the long waiting period, so psychologically difficult for victims, between time of apprehending the defendant and time of giving testimony. The testimony would be over and done with. To accomplish this, Libai proposes a *special hearing for the child victim*. Note that his prior suggestion dealt with taking child victim's evidence *during* a trial. This suggestion deals with taking the child victim's evidence *prior* to the trial—again while still protecting the accused's rights to confrontation. Cross-examination would occur. The testimony would be recorded on videotape. The child's recorded testimony legally could be defined as similar to a dying declaration. The tape would be admitted as evidence at the subsequent trial. The two goals of confrontation—namely, cross-examination in front of the jury and observation of the witness' demeanor by the jury—are accomplished by the videotape rather than by live testimony from the child.[68]

Cross-examination is another crucial issue and the present study suggests that more thinking needs to be done about the types of cross-examination that are permitted.[69] Two issues come to mind: questions on the victim's background, especially sexual background; and "declarative and accusatory questioning."

Current thinking seems to be more and more that in rape cases the victim's sexual background should be regarded as irrelevant when considering the issue of whether the rape occurred. Moves are being made to make such information inadmissible as evidence. This change would seem appropriate, especially given the changes in sexual behavior that have occurred in our society. Changing the rules of evidence in this way is a step in the right direction. However, as our study shows, this change alone will not solve the problem, since often a defense attorney can get a witness to give such information in response to indirect questions.

A more fundamental and general problem is the present practice of allowing attorneys to use accusatory and declarative phrasing in cross-examination. In such instances, attorneys often are presenting their definition of the situation by use of inadmissible evidence or sometimes even by painting a picture for which they may not have any basis in fact. For example, defense lawyers in our study often made declarative statements before the jury during cross-examination that they knew probably would be thrown out—"You have been under regular treatment at the hospital for alcoholism," "So you changed your testimony." These "declarative questions" may be excluded by the judge, but by then the jury already has heard them. It is thus recommended that there be controls placed on the use of accusatory and declarative sentence structure in cross-examination questions.

Compensation for Victims.   Many proposals focus on compensation. Our study documents that rape victims may suffer considerable financial loss as a result of the crime inflicted upon them. The rape may lead to medical bills. It may cause physical and psychic trauma that turn into lost worktime. Victims who go to court find it costly to do so. The monetary sacrifices of being a witness—in lost work- or schooltime, interrupted days, transportation expenses—are high.[70] Victims in our sample who testified did receive a small witness fee and sometimes money to reimburse them for travel expenses. However, the money they received did not cover their total expenses and they did not get money for time lost from work because of their testifying.

Compensation, either by the state or by the offender,[71] for victims of violent crime such as rape should be provided.[72] Although there are some beginning steps in this direction, the amount of money in existing government programs is insufficient, the programs are not well publicized and hence victims do not know their rights, and the amount of red tape a victim must go through can be discouraging. At a bare minimum, provision should be made to pay for the medical services that the victim requires as a result of the rape. Furthermore, it would seem reasonable that the state should reimburse the victim for the costs, including the costs of lost worktime, entailed in being a witness for the prosecution.

Whether one wishes to go beyond this narrow focus on compensation is a deeper question and one that has implications for alternative models of the criminal justice system. Eglash has written on "creative restitution"— something that goes beyond mere financial compensation.It is a more constructive act aimed at opening up real concern for the victim.[73] Schafer has talked of "correctional restitution":

> Correctional restitution is something the offender must perform himself and not something done for or to him. In this respect it goes a significant step further than compensation, for it requires him to maintain a relationship with the victim until the victim's preinjury condition has been restored to the fullest extent possible. Correctional restitution . . . makes a contribution to the reformative and corrective goals of criminal law and finds its proper place in the criminal justice system.[74]

The rape victims we observed were not keen on maintaining any further relationship with the offender. Thus, if "creative restitution" or "correctional restitution" is to be incorporated into the criminal justice system, new support systems[75] will have to be devised to help victims with this innovation, just as new support systems are being developed to help them deal with conventional criminal trials.

Alternative Models of the Criminal Justice System

Proposals for victim compensation and for alleviating victims' suffering during the court process, although important, constitute only minor tinkering with the criminal justice system. Victimological research has led thinkers to suggest more sweeping proposals, ones that make fundamental challenges. One hears it said that in the not-too-distant future the criminal justice system as we now know it will become obsolete. There is much

discussion of what might take its place. Important victimological contribu-
tions in this regard have been made recently by Sebba and by Sheleff.

One important theme in both Sebba and Sheleff is the desirability of
bringing the victim into the criminal justice process. Sebba states that since
"notionally, at least, the failure of the victim to play an active role in the
penal process is an illogical deviation from the principles of justice on which
the American criminal trial is based, the reinstitution of the victim to his
erstwhile role would remove that deviation."[76] He notes that present approaches to the problem have been piecemeal. What is needed is "an overall
and comprehensive approach to the problems of the role of the victim in the
criminal procedure."[77] On a practical level, for example, an integrated approach would need to deal with the *victim's role* not just at one point but at
a *series* of decision points in the process: making a complaint, making an arrest, pursuing an investigation, receiving aid, pretrial detention of suspect
and defendant, pursuing prosecution, being a civil party to a criminal prosecution, procedures during court hearings, sentencing, and postsentencing
correctional decisions.[78] Sheleff, in his paper, states that "if victimology is
to have any practical impact, then it is necessary to examine a form of ad-
judication where the victim's interests are paramount."[79] He further argues
that "the sense of injustice can only be exacerbated when the victim is by-
passed and the state itself—in all the power of its police capacity, in all the
glory of its duly-constituted judicial agents—seeks revenge, redress, or
reform."[80]

A second theme in Sebba and Sheleff is the difficulty of clearly
distinguishing between criminal and civil law, and the fact that this ambiguity has implications for future models of the criminal justice system.
Sebba notes that various people have discussed the "evolution of the civil-
criminal dichotomy, whereby the state is seen as the injured party in
criminal cases, while the victim fulfills this role only in civil cases."[81] The
important point Sebba makes, regarding this dichotomy is how difficult it is
to find any criterion that successfully differentiates civil from criminal matters; the same behavior often constitutes both a tort and a crime. Sebba suggests that persons interested in victim-oriented reforms have not paid sufficient attention to the writings of procedural lawyers "dealing with the
respective roles of civil and criminal actions, and the possibilities of their
combination."[82] The difficulty of distinguishing between criminal law and
civil law is important in Sheleff's argument as well:

> The line of distinction between criminal law, based primarily on the imposition
> of punitive sanctions on the wrongdoer, and civil law, based primarily on
> restitution to the aggrieved party, is not, and never has been, clear. . . .

[Furthermore] there is nothing inherent in the average criminal act—of harm
to property or persons—to make state intervention with punitive consequences
preferable to a direct confrontation between the parties with the possibility
of a resolution of the conflict through restitution in its various forms.[83]

He argues that once one challenges traditional thinking about criminal law,
there arises in crimes *with* victims the "possibility of by-passing the criminal
law and using instead the traditional civil law remedies of restitution and
compensation."[84]

A third theme in both Sebba and Sheleff is the desirability of concep-
tualizing alternative models of the criminal justice system. Sebba suggests
three possible models: Adversary-Retributive Model, Social Defense-
Welfare Model, and Reconciliation Model. The Adversary-Retributive
Model would retain confrontation between aggriever and aggrieved, and
the injury to the victim would be a major factor in sentencing. The Social
Defense-Welfare Model essentially would eliminate confrontation between
victim and offender, and instead the state would play a mediating role vis-à-
vis each party.[85] The Reconciliation Model, which in some respects com-
bines the best of the other two models, would apply arbitration and dispute-
settlement techniques to the criminal law.[86] Sheleff, discussing alternatives,
delineates a Conflict Resolution Model. He states:

> We have become too hide-bound by the weight of tradition and inertia in
> using penal processes and punitive measures, where reparations and recon-
> ciliation may be more meaningful and effective. . . . There are distinct
> possibilities of a new approach to crime as jurists question some of the basic
> concepts of the law. Instead of a criminal law based on accusation, guilt and
> punishment, in an atmosphere aimed at degradation, as described by Gar-
> finkel, it is possible to conceive of a process aimed at resolution of the conflict
> between wrongdoer and victim, whereby the rehabilitation of the former may
> be best guaranteed through enforcing restitution to the latter.[87]

Sheleff notes that in other areas, conflicts have been going "from an all-or-
nothing approach to resolution of conflicts as no-lose or all-win."[88] He concludes that it may be possible to move toward "a concept of the trial, not as
an arena for pure conflict, but as a framework for conflict resolution."[89]

SUMMARY

We have seen how difficult the lot of rape victims may be as they wend their
way through the medical and criminal justice systems. The policy question
is how the institutional response to rape victims can be made more

humanistic. Three types of recommendations have been made after viewing the situation of the victims in our study. The first recommendation is to delegitimize rape. Efforts need to be directed at redefining rape—to make it be seen as unacceptable rather than acceptable behavior. The second recommendation is that the groups that work with victims—police, medical personnel, and court personnel—institute various professional and bureaucratic changes. These changes can be implemented right now. They include such things as establishing victim programs, providing information and explanations to victims, and reducing delays in the institutional response. The third recommendation is that more thought be given to what the criminal justice system of the future might look like. The suggestions here are of two types: tinkering with parts of the system and changing the overall model of the criminal justice system.

NOTES

1. Alan J. Davis, "Sexual Assaults in the Philadelphia Prison System and Sheriff's Vans," *Trans-Action* (December 1968), pp. 8-16; Murray L. Cohen, Ralph Garofalo, Richard Boucher, and Theoharis Seghorn, "The Psychology of Rapists," *Seminars in Psychiatry* 3 (August 1971), pp. 307-27; Ann Wolbert Burgess and Lynda Lytle Holmstrom, *Rape: Victims of Crisis* (Bowie, Md.: Robert J. Brady, 1974), p. 4; Julia R. Schwendinger and Herman Schwendinger, "Rape Myths: In Legal, Theoretical, and Everyday Practice," *Crime and Social Justice: A Journal of Radical Criminology* 1 (Spring-Summer 1974), p. 20; Pauline B. Bart, "Rape Doesn't End With A Kiss," (Unpublished manuscript, Department of Psychiatry, Abraham Lincoln School of Medicine, University of Illinois, Chicago, 1975), p. 2. Published in abridged version in *Viva* (June 1975); Deena Metzger, "It Is Always the Woman Who Is Raped," *American Journal of Psychiatry* 133 (April 1976), p. 405; Elaine Hilberman, *The Rape Victim*, (Washington, D.C.: American Psychiatric Association, 1976), p. ix; A. Nicholas Groth, Ann Wolbert Burgess, and Lynda Lytle Holmstrom, "Rape: Power, Anger, and Sexuality," *American Journal of Psychiatry* 134 (November 1977), pp. 1239-43.

2. An important additional issue, not raised by the victim sample in the present study, is that of redefining rape to include marital rape. See especially the work of Russell and of Gelles in this regard. Diana E. H. Russell, *The Politics of Rape: The Victim's Perspective* (New York: Stein & Day, 1975), pp. 71-81; Richard J. Gelles, "Power, Sex, and Violence: The Case of Marital Rape," *The Family Coordinator* 26 (October 1977), pp. 339-47. Redefining rape also means broadening it to include forced oral and anal intercourse, not just forced vaginal intercourse.

3. Judith Hole and Ellen Levine, *Rebirth of Feminism* (New York: Quadrangle Books, 1971), pp. 157, 424.

4. Maren Lockwood Carden, *The New Feminist Movement* (New York: Russell Sage Foundation, 1974), p. 68; Mary Ann Largen, "History of Women's Movement in Changing Attitudes, Laws, and Treatment Toward Rape Victims," *Sexual Assault: The Victim and the Rapist*, Marcia J. Walker and Stanley L. Brodsky, eds. (Lexington, Mass.: D. C. Heath, 1976), pp. 69-73. For references to a number of movement publications

on rape, see Barbara Fagan, Diana E. H. Russell, and Margaret Stone, "Bibliography," in Russell, op. cit., pp. 305-11. Two of the most widely cited writings in the popular literature are Susan Griffin, "Rape: The All-American Crime," *Ramparts* 10 (September 1971), pp. 26-35, and Germaine Greer, "Seduction Is a Four-Letter Word," *Rape Victimology*, LeRoy G. Schultz, ed., (Springfield, Ill.: Charles C Thomas, 1975), pp. 374-95. (First published, *Playboy*).

5. Susan Brownmiller, *Against Our Will: Men, Women and Rape* (New York: Simon & Schuster, 1975), p. 397 (emphasis in the original).

6. There are some other crime victims who have organized; for example, victims of guns.

7. Williams's study shows low conviction rates for sexual assault when the victim is female *or* male. Kristen M. Williams, "Sexual Assaults and the Law: The Problem of Prosecution," Revised version of paper presented at the American Sociological Association annual meeting, New York, September 1976, p. 19. One possible interpretation of such a finding is that the sex of the victim is irrelevant. Another possible interpretation is that when a male is used like a female, he has the same difficulties that a female has in sustaining his definition of reality.

8. James P. Spradley and Brenda J. Mann, *The Cocktail Waitress: Woman's Work in a Man's World* (New York: Wiley, 1975), pp. 36-38.

9. Ibid., pp. 37-38.

10. We are indebted to David Karp for discussions that helped clarify the connections between definitions of reality in the criminal justice system and in the broader society.

11. Charles R. Hayman, Frances R. Lewis, William F. Stewart, and Murray Grant, "A Public Health Program for Sexually Assaulted Females," *Public Health Reports* 82 (June 1967), pp. 497-504; Charles R. Hayman, Charlene Lanza, Roberto Fuentes, and Kathe Algor, "Rape in the District of Columbia," *American Journal of Obstetrics and Gynecology* 113 (May 1, 1972), pp. 91-97.

12. Mary L. Keefe and Henry T. O'Reilly, "Changing Perspectives in Sex Crimes Investigations," Walker and Brodsky, op. cit., pp. 161-68; Mary L. Keefe and Henry T. O'Reilly, "The Plight of the Rape Victim in New York City," *Victims and Society*, Emilio C. Viano, ed. (Washington, D.C.: Visage Press), pp. 391-402.

13. Joseph J. Peters, "The Philadelphia Rape Victim Study," *Victimology: A New Focus, Vol. III. Crimes, Victims, and Justice,* Israel Drapkin and Emilio Viano, eds. (Lexington, Mass.: D.C. Heath, 1975). pp. 181-99.

14. Ann Wolbert Burgess and Lynda Lytle Holmstrom, "The Rape Victim in the Emergency Ward," *American Journal of Nursing* 73 (October 1973), pp. 1740-45; Ann Wolbert Burgess and Lynda Lytle Holmstrom, *Rape: Victims of Crisis* (Bowie, Md.: Robert J. Brady Co., 1974).

15. Dorothy J. Hicks and Charlotte R. Platt, "Medical Treatment for the Victim: The Development of a Rape Treatment Center," in Walker and Brodsky, op. cit., pp. 53-59.

16. Sharon L. McCombie, Ellen Bassuk, Roberta Savitz, and Susan Pell, "Development of a Medical Center Rape Crisis Intervention Program," *American Journal of Psychiatry* 133 (April 1976), pp. 418-21.

17. Lucy Berliner and Doris Stevens, "Harborview Social Workers Advocate Special Techniques for Child Witness," *Response* 1 (December 1976), p. 1. (Washington, D.C.: Center for Women Policy Studies.)

18. Anna T. Laszlo, "Intake Screening As a Concept in Victim Assistance: A Prosecutorial Model," paper presented at the Second International Symposium on Victimology, Boston, September 1976. (This program deals with victims of rape as well as of other crimes.)

19. The Csidas describe a number of such groups. June Bundy Csida and Joseph Csida, *Rape: How to Avoid It and What to Do About It If You Can't* (Chatsworth, Calif.: Books for Better Living, 1974), pp. 133-62. Mills surveyed 54 rape crisis centers and information on their operation is included in his manual of practical information for rape crisis interveners. Patrick Mills, *Rape Intervention Resource Manual* (Springfield, Ill.: Charles C. Thomas, 1977).

20. Report of District of Columbia Task Force on Rape," in Schultz, op. cit., pp. 339-73.

21. *Recommendations and Report of the Citizens' Advisory Council on Rape,* Cook County, Ill., March 10, 1975. An excerpt is reprinted in Elaine Hilberman, op. cit., pp. 93-98.

22. *Report of the Task Force to Study the Treatment of the Victims of Sexual Assault,* Prince George's County, Md., March 1973.

23. Largen, op. cit., p. 70; Csida and Csida, op. cit., pp. 163-66.

24. Howard Kelman, "Consumers As Evaluators of Medical Care," paper presented at the Multidisciplinary Seminar in Health Services Research and Policy, Boston University, December 14, 1976.

25. Pauline B. Bart, et al., *Report of the Hospital Subcommittee of the Citizens Advisory Committee on Rape,* Cook County, Ill., 1975, pp. 4-6 (mimeographed).

26. Laszlo, op. cit., p. 2.

27. Susan Rae Zonderman, "Rape Crisis Counselors—Stress Factors and Coping Strategies," unpublished manuscript based on Master's Thesis, School for Social Work, Smith College, 1975.

28. Elisabeth Kübler-Ross, "Reactions to the Seminar on Death and Dying," in *On Death and Dying,* (New York: Macmillan, 1969), pp. 218-39.

29. Ibid., p. 224 (emphasis added).

30. Hughes has noted that professionals profess "to know better than their clients what ails them. . . . This is the essence of . . . the professional claim." Everett C. Hughes, "Professions," *Daedalus* 92 (Fall 1963), p. 656.

31. Szasz and Hollender describe three models appropriate for different medical situations. Thomas S. Szasz and Marc H. Hollender, "A Contribution to the Philosophy of Medicine: The Basic Models of the Doctor-Patient Relationship," *A.M.A. Archives of Internal Medicine* 97 (May 1956), pp. 585-92.

32. Marie R. Haug and Marvin B. Sussman, "Professional Autonomy and the Revolt of the Client," *Social Problems* 17 (Fall 1969), pp. 153-61; Marie R. Haug, "The Erosion of Professional Authority: A Cross-Cultural Inquiry in the Case of the Physician," *Health and Society* 54 (Winter 1976), pp. 83-106; and Bernard Barber, "Compassion in Medicine: Towards New Definitions and New Institutions," Lecture presented at Beth Israel Hospital, Boston, 1976.

33. Laszlo, op. cit., pp. 2-3.

34. This section discusses mainly the collection and recording of verbal information, especially from the victim. Collection and preservation of physical evidence is discussed in the section on interprofessional cooperation.

35. And official language varies from city to city. See, for example, the analysis by Chappell et al. of how Boston police reports of rape differ from those of Los Angeles in vocabulary and style. Duncan Chappell, Gilbert Geis, Stephen Schafer, and Larry Siegel, "Forcible Rape: A Comparative Study of Offenses Known to the Police in Boston and Los Angeles," in *Studies in the Sociology of Sex,* James M. Henslin, ed. (New York: Appleton-Century-Crofts, 1971), pp. 182-83.

36. Ann Wolbert Burgess and Lynda Lytle Holmstrom, "Sexual Assault: Signs and Symptoms," *Journal of Emergency Nursing* (March-April 1975), pp. 12-15.

37. Arthur Frederick Schiff, "Sperm Identification—Acid Phosphatase Test," *Medical Trial Technique Quarterly* 21 (Spring 1975), pp. 467-74; Rolando R. Gomez, Christian D. Wunsch, Joseph H. Davis, and Dorothy J. Hicks, "Qualitative and Quantitative Determinations of Acid Phosphatase Activity in Vaginal Washings," *American Journal of Clinical Pathology* 64 (1975), pp. 423-32.

38. A good source in this regard is the evidence protocol for sex crimes cases recommended by Lt. Mary Keefe and Sgt. Harry O'Reilly, Sex Crimes Analysis Unit, New York Police Department. Their recommendations are included in Lisa Brodyaga et al., *Rape and Its Victims: A Report for Citizens, Health Facilities, and Criminal Justice Agencies* (Project Report, U. S. Department of Justice, Law Enforcement Assistance Administration, National Institute of Law Enforcement and Criminal Justice).

39. Reducing delays would lessen the victim's trauma. Whether it would have an impact on the legal outcome of cases is another question. In our study some cases were dropped because the victim finally could not wait any longer or because by time of trial the victim and/or the defendant could not be located. Varying statements however, have been made regarding whether there is a connection between delays and the outcome of cases. Ash says, "The likelihood of successful prosecution seems to decrease, generally, with (1) the length of time between apprehension and disposition, (2) the number of appearances in court by the defendant, and (3) the number of witness appearances. At least, this is the suggestion of Banfield and Anderson (1968)." Michael Ash, "Court Delay, Crime Control, and Neglect of the Interests of Witnesses," in *Reducing Court Delay,* p. 33. In contrast, Foschio reports that postarraignment delay did not correlate with dismissals or acquittals: "In other words, based on the data in this study, the idea that postarraignment delay benefits the accused may not be founded in fact." Leslie G. Foschio, "Empirical Research and the Problem of Court Delay," in *Reducing Court Delay* (Criminal Justice Monograph, U.S. Department of Justice, Law Enforcement Assistance Administration, National Institute of Law Enforcement and Criminal Justice; Washington, D.C.: U.S. Government Printing Office, June 1973), p. 43.

40. Haynes, discussing against whom delay should be assessed, notes that in many instances the proper term is not *court delay* but *criminal justice system delay.* H. Paul Haynes, "Reducing Court Delay," in *Reducing Court Delay,* p. 55.

41. Ibid., pp. 45-46, 55-57.

42. Ash, op. cit., p. 18.

43. Ibid., p. 20.

44. Ibid., p. 26.

45. Ibid., p. 27.

46. Foschio, op. cit., p. 41

47. Practice reported by a police officer from Western Massachusetts attending a workshop at Boston College on rape.

48. Ash, op. cit., p. 23.

49. Ibid., p. 24.

50. This is permissible, for example, under the law of the Commonwealth of Massachusetts and it was done in a few of the cases in our study. It also is being done by the newly founded Major Violators Unit in the district attorney's office in Boston. It is, however, controversial in that some believe that the defendant should have the right to a full hearing in district court.

51. Haynes, op. cit., pp. 59-61.

52. Ibid., p. 62.

53. Ibid.

54. Ravindran Nayar and William H. Bleuel, "Simulation of a Criminal Court Case Processing System," in *Reducing Court Delay,* p. 66.

55. John H. Reed, *The Application of Operations Research to Court Delay,* (New York: Praeger, 1973).

56. Daniel Glaser, *Adult Crime and Social Policy* (Englewood Cliffs, N.J.: Prentice-Hall, 1972), p. 98.

57. One should not assume that treatment-oriented progams will be more effective in terms of deterrence than punitive measures. Glaser, reviewing various studies, notes that "research in a variety of correctional institutions has indicated that programs emphasizing intensive counseling or psychotherapy and a permissive social climate have opposite effects on different types of prisoners. . . . Prisoners with little prior involvement in crime who expressed a desire for counseling and were in these therapeutically oriented programs had lower recidivism rates than similar prisoners in traditional prison programs. Conversely, those prisoners with more prior criminal experience and strong ties to other criminals who were in these therapeutic programs had markedly higher recidivism rates than similar offenders in traditional 'firm but fair' prison regimes." Ibid., p. 105.

58. Sexual violation is common *within* prison walls. Israel Drapkin, "The Prison Inmate as Victim," *Victimology* 1 (Spring 1976), p. 103. Some of the rapes of prisoners undoubtedly are committed by persons convicted for rape. Davis, studying sexual assaults of prisoners, compared 164 sexual aggressors and 103 victims; 14 aggressors and 3 victims had been charged with rape. Davis, op. cit., p. 14.

59. Emile Durkheim, *The Rules of Sociological Method,* George E. G. Catlin, ed., Sarah A. Solovay and John H. Mueller, trans., (Glencoe, Ill. Free Press, 1938), pp. 47-75. (First published 1895.)

60. For analyses of laws pertaining to rape, see Pamela Lakes Wood, "The Victim in a Forcible Rape Case: A Feminist View," *American Criminal Law Review* 11 (Winter 1973), pp. 335-54; Leigh Bienen, "Rape I," *Women's Rights Law Reporter* 3 (December 1976) pp. 45-57; Leigh Bienen, "Rape II," *Women's Rights Law Reporter* 3 (Spring-Summer 1977), pp. 90-137; Camille E. LeGrand, Jay A. Reich, and Duncan Chappell, *Forcible Rape: An Analysis of Legal Issues* (Seattle: Battelle Law and Justice Study Center, 1977).

61. Libai reviews some of these studies. David Libai, "The Protection of the Child Victim of a Sexual Offense in the Criminal Justice System" *Wayne Law Review* 15 (1969), pp. 979-86.

62. Such a search is obviously quite culture-bound. "The Scandinavian states, observing few rules of evidence, no prohibition against hearsay evidence, and only the rudiments of cross-examination, are relatively free to accommodate their rules of criminal procedure to the welfare of child victims without offending their concept of a fair trial. In fact, Scandinavian jurists regard their informal conduct of criminal trials as 'a rational and reasonable way of finding out the truth and evaluating the conduct of the accused.'" Ibid., pp. 1004-05, and Libai citing Andenaes, "The Legal Framework," *Scandinavian Studies in Criminology* 2 (1968), 11.

63. Libai, op. cit., p. 979.

64. Earlier in the article Libai discusses pretrial interrogation of child victims, including special approaches that have been used in Chicago, Denmark, Sweden, and Israel. He

recommends that child victims be investigated by special child examiners similar to Israeli youth interrogators, rather than by regular policemen. Ibid., pp. 1001-02.

65. Ibid., p. 1021. The United States Court of Appeals for the Seventh Circuit upheld a lower court ruling that permitted the exclusion of spectators from court during testimony of a rape victim if they had only a casual interest in the case. The majority opinion held that this practice "'did not create any potential for secret abuse'. . . because persons with more than a casual interest in the case, including news reporters, were allowed to hear the testimony." "Ruling Excluding Court Spectators During Rape Testimony Is Upheld," *New York Times,* August 31, 1977, p. A14.

66. Libai, op. cit., p. 1023.

67. Ibid., p. 1026 (emphasis added).

68. Ibid., p. 1031. Experiments and discussion regarding similar issues for victims (including adult victims) are going on various places. Esther Stanton is conducting research on the videotaping of testimony in the United States. (Esther Stanton, personal communication.)

69. A landmark example of limitations placed on cross-examination is the 1955 Israeli law passed to protect child victims of sexual offenses from the trauma of police questioning and court appearance. The law provides that "1. Youth Interrogators be appointed to interrogate children on the commission of a sexual offence; 2. those children be exempted from appearing in court to give evidence, save with the permission of the youth interrogator." David Reifen, "Court Procedures in Israel to Protect Child-Victims of Sexual Assaults," in Drapkin and Viano, op. cit., p. 67.

70. A recent study sponsored by the Law Enforcement Assistance Administration found that time lost from work was one important factor making crime victims and witnesses uncooperative regarding testifying. A mugging victim, for example, might lose $75 in the crime, but by cooperating with the police and testifying might lose another $49 because of time lost from the job. "Victims Found Fearful of Time Lost at Trials," *New York Times,* December 20, 1976, p. A21.

71. Strictly speaking, compensation comes from the society and restitution from the offender. See Schafer's careful delineation of these two concepts. Stephen Schafer, *Compensation and Restitution to Victims of Crime* (2d ed.; Montclair, N.J.: Patterson Smith, 1970), p. x.

72. For proposals and/or analyses of compensation programs see Margery Fry, "Justice for Victims," *Journal of Public Law* 8 (Spring 1959), pp. 191-94. (First published 1957, *The Observer* [London]); Herbert Edelhertz and Gilbert Geis, *Public Compensation to Victims of Crime* (New York: Praeger, 1974); and LeRoy L. Lamborn, "Compensation for the Child Conceived in Rape," *Victimology* 1 (Spring 1976), pp. 84-97.

73. Albert Eglash, "Creative Restitution," *Journal of Criminal Law, Criminology and Police Science* 48 (March-April 1958), pp. 619-22.

74. Stephen Schafer, "The Proper Role of a Victim-Compensation System," *Crime and Delinquency* 21 (January 1975), p. 49.

75. There currently are some programs in which rapists and rape victims—not from the same rape incident—meet with each other. The sex offender program of Alternatives, Inc., Albuquerque, New Mexico has had a rape victim talk to a group of convicted rapists about what effect the rape had. This practice is worthwhile for breaking through the offender's denial. The emotional reaction of the victim is something they have never had to deal with before. Margot Berger, private communication.

76. Leslie Sebba, "The Victim's Role in the Penal Process—The Need for a Theoretical Orientation," paper presented at the Second International Symposium on Victimology, Boston, September 1976, pp. 17-18.

77. Ibid., p. 24.
78. Ibid., pp. 3-12.
79. Leon S. Sheleff, "Victimology, Criminal Law, and Conflict Resolution," paper presented at the Second International Symposium on Victimology, Boston, September 1976, p. 12.
80. Ibid., p. 15.
81. Sebba, op. cit., p. 13.
82. Ibid., p. 2.
83. Sheleff, op. cit., p. 4.
84. Ibid., p. 11.
85. Sebba, op. cit., pp. 20-21.
86. Ibid., pp. 25-26.
87. Sheleff, op. cit., p. 24. The Garfinkel work referred to is Harold Garfinkel, "Conditions of Successful Degradation Ceremonies," *American Journal of Sociology* 61 (March 1956), pp. 420-24.
88. Sheleff, op. cit., p. 26.
89. Ibid., p. 27.

Index